you first I have to

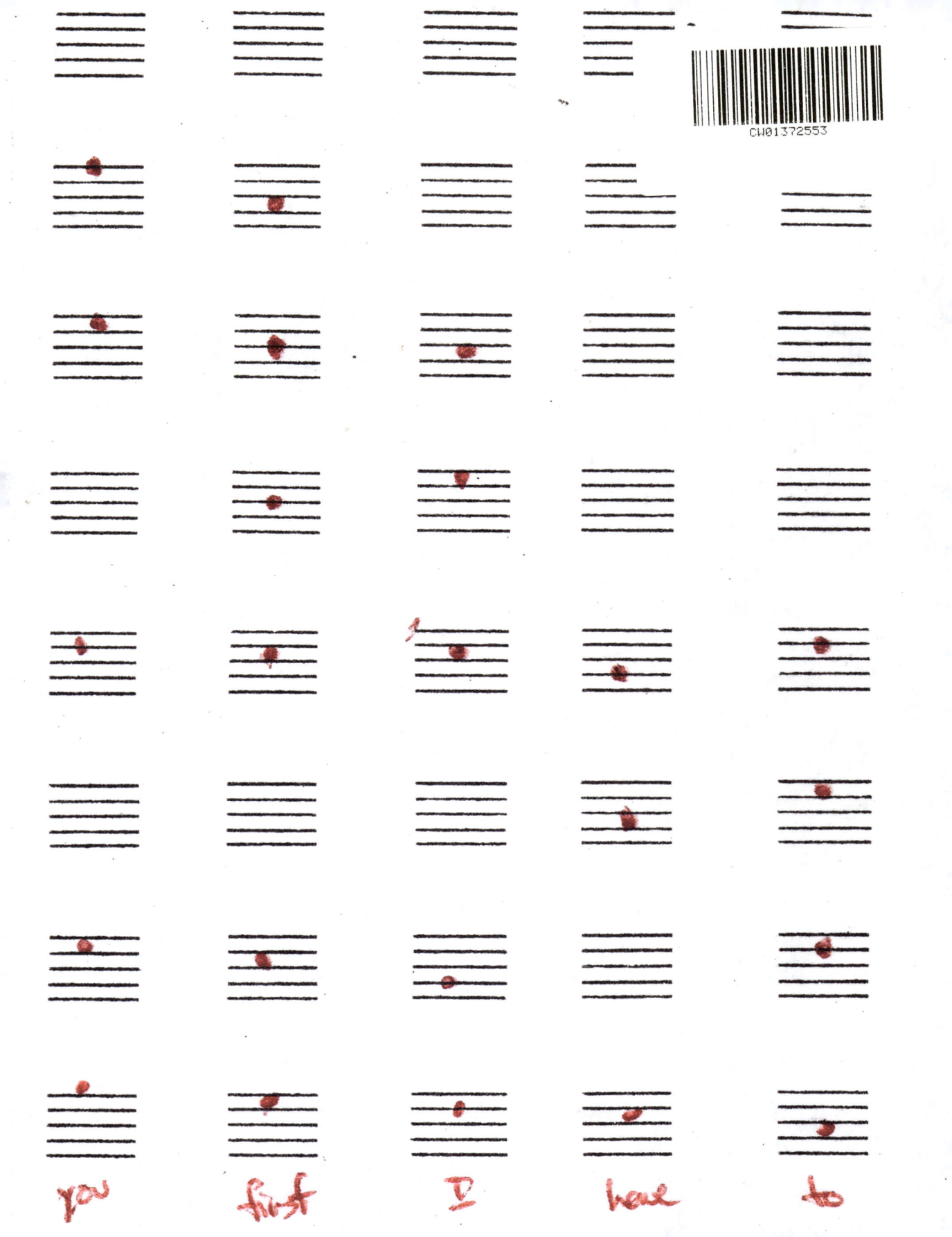

TRAVELS OVER FEELING

By the same author

How Soon Is Now?
Original Rockers
The Lark Ascending
Brittle with Relics

Travels Over Feeling

Arthur Russell A Life

Richard King

faber

First published in 2024
by Faber & Faber Limited
The Bindery, 51 Hatton Garden
London EC1N 8HN

Designed and typeset by Stuart Bertolotti-Bailey
Printed and bound in India

All rights reserved
© Richard King, 2024

The right of Richard King to be identified as
author of this work has been asserted in
accordance with Section 77 of the Copyright,
Designs and Patents Act 1988

A CIP record for this book is available from the
British Library

ISBN 978–0–571–37966–8

10 9 8 7 6 5 4 3 2 1

Contents

	Voices	vii
	Introduction	1
Part I	1951–73	7
Part II	1973–80	47
Part III	1980–86	119
Part IV	1986–92	223
	Acknowledgements	294
	Image credits	295

It's a talk in the dark,
It's a walk in the morning.

'That's Us / Wild Combination'

VOICES

In order of appearance:

Kate Russell – Arthur's sister

Muriel Fujii – Arthur's girlfriend during his time in San Francisco

Tom Lee – Arthur's partner from 1978 until the end of his life

Peter Gordon – composer, leader of the Love of Life Orchestra and frequent collaborator

Bill Ruyle – percussionist, collaborator

Ernie Brooks – former member of The Modern Lovers and musical collaborator in The Flying Hearts, The Necessaries and other projects

Peter Zummo – composer, trombonist, frequent collaborator

Jill Kroesen – musician, collaborator

Lucy Sante – author, historian, former resident of 437 East Twelfth Street

Philip Glass – composer, associate and patron

Steven Hall – musician and collaborator

Jeb Loy Nichols – musician, Lower East Side resident, neighbour

Phill Niblock – composer, founder of Experimental Intermedia Foundation

Will Socolov – co-founder of Sleeping Bag Records

Rome Neal – actor, collaborator

Joyce Bowden – musician, collaborator

Alison Salzinger – choreographer and collaborator

Mustafa Khaliq Ahmed – percussionist and collaborator

Geoff Travis – founder of Rough Trade Records

Stephanie McGuire – photographer

Ed Friedman – poet, neighbour

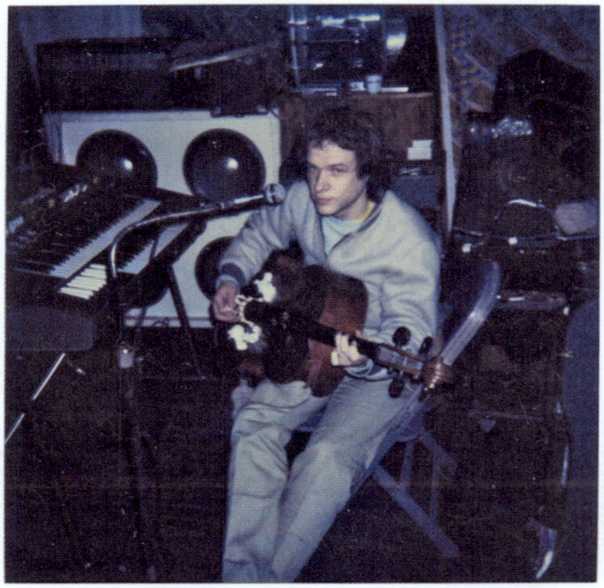

INTRODUCTION

Arthur Russell was born on 21 May 1951 in Oskaloosa, Iowa. He died in New York City on 4 April 1992, aged forty, of complications arising from AIDS. Russell's life ended neither in obscurity nor failure. As a composer, cellist, songwriter and a producer with a sixth sense for the alchemy of the dancefloor, Arthur enjoyed relative commercial and critical success. His more significant achievement was the realisation of a substantial body of work that functioned entirely on its own terms. The orthodox American formula for prosperity, that of resolutely focusing on one particular discipline or genre until the market responds – a formula especially prevalent during the 1980s, when Arthur was at his most active – was an approach he eschewed. Rather than concentrating on a single musical idiom, Arthur's recorded output defies easy categorisation. In one year alone (1980) he wrote and performed a set of folk-pop songs, composed an opera score and released two dancefloor-orientated twelve-inch singles. This activity took place at the exact moment club music was gaining momentum as part of the street-level, grey market social economy of Lower Manhattan. Although he drew inspiration equally from his Midwestern home state and his love of the ocean, like a true New Yorker, Arthur lived to work, and his work reflected his environment.

The uptown world of rigorous composition, sanctioned by conservatories and other public institutions, was more rarefied an atmosphere than the downtown discos and sidewalk boom boxes where Russell heard his dance tracks played. Arthur was distinctive in being sufficiently talented to be comfortable in these separate musical spaces. In addition, he was equally adept at singing his yearning songs on guitar in offbeat, fly-by-night venues, or playing his amplified cello and effects in the arts and performance spaces scattered across the city in the late 1970s and early 1980s. Arthur was resident in the Lower East Side during a period when New York was a city reaching and achieving its dynamic, creative and unrestrained peak.

Arthur Russell was also a curator – one of the few jobs he ever held down was as musical director of the video, arts and music venue the Kitchen. In retrospect, his interdisciplinary resumé reads like the exemplary working life of a twenty-first-century producer–composer. During his own lifetime, however, and prior to his rediscovery in the first half of the 2000s, Arthur's fearless attitude towards his music evoked less a sense of an extraordinary commitment to the muse than missed opportunities and a lack of professional ruthlessness. His tragic death during the height of the AIDS crisis also added to the mystery that attached itself to his life and his work.

It was as an elusive figure from a much-mythologised era in cultural history that Arthur Russell re-emerged during the early years of the twentieth century, a decade or so after his death, when his catalogue was re-evaluated using the new digital technologies and opportunities of the iPod and of file-sharing sites. For the generation born between his most creatively active years and his death, the music of Arthur Russell held the seductive appeal of being relatively little known by their forebears. The means by which the work of this hitherto occluded figure arrived in the listener's awareness only added to the allure of these startlingly original recordings, as did a further discovery: not only had Arthur Russell made music for the heart of the dancefloor during the early hours of the weekend, but he had also written the perfect songs to listen to during the recovery period that frequently followed. The divergent styles Arthur recorded in confirmed him to be an under-appreciated genius of rare integrity. Over a quarter of a century after his untimely death, the world had begun to understand the world of Arthur Russell. An international listenership found itself transfixed by the inscrutable gaze that radiated gently from his record sleeves. As his cross-pollinating influence took hold, 'Arthur Russell' developed into a mysterious and totemic presence in music collections.

Arthur is an artist whose reputation has grown with each passing year since his death and attained a level of recognition that eluded him during his time on earth.

*

At the turn of this century, an obscure white label of a Danny Krivit remix of 'In the Light of the Miracle' and bootleg twelve-inch copies of 'Go Bang!' grew in influence and popularity as the rediscovery of the era in which they were originally released gathered pace. So too the name of Arthur Russell grew in familiarity – particularly thanks to his dancefloor productions. With tracks such as 'Kiss Me Again' by Dinosaur and 'Tell You (Today)' by Loose Joints being featured on compilations including DISCO NOT DISCO, his music once again came to be heard regularly through powerful club sound systems.

This first phase of rediscovery reached its apotheosis in the 2004 Soul Jazz Records compilation THE WORLD OF ARTHUR RUSSELL. The release was quickly followed the same year by CALLING OUT OF CONTEXT, the debut collection of Arthur's previously unreleased material issued by Steve Knutson of Audika Records in consultation and partnership with the Arthur Russell estate.

More of Arthur's music has been released since his death than was available during his lifetime. He left a catalogue of music that includes over a thousand reels of twenty-four-track tape, DATs, cassettes, vinyl acetates and both Betamax and VHS videotapes. In addition, the Arthur Russell archive at the New York Public Library for the Performing Arts contains innumerable notebooks, drawings, flyers, papers, correspondence, musical manuscripts, photographs, scraps and faxes. Arthur, the archive reveals, kept most of his life's paperwork. If laid out in a room the combined papers would extend to 166 linear feet. There are a considerable number of musical manuscript books each filled with scores, drafts of compositional ideas and other notated experiments, which represent a sizable majority of the papers.

The notebooks also contain poems, song titles and chord charts, and sit alongside stand-alone items such as grant applications, record company rejection letters, education certificates, unsent correspondence and taxicab receipts. In many of the photographs of Arthur a notebook and pen are visible in his left shirt breast pocket (painstakingly sewn on to Arthur's shirts and jackets by his sister Julie, at the exact size to house his manuscripts). The papers bear out this sense of a continuous practice of writing and jotting. Many of his notes are decorated and interrupted with the scrawl of everyday life: hastily written phone numbers, addresses, appointments, directions, daydream erotica and examples of Russell's absurdist and playful sense of humour. There is also a smattering of references to many of his short-lived projects such as The Sailboats, Bright & Early, Turbo Sporty and his membership of the new wave band The Necessaries. While Arthur was capable of coining a band name or project idea on a whim, his notebooks demonstrate that the craft and rigour of composition are the dominant focus of his work. The lyrics and chord charts to Arthur's songs that have been compiled on posthumous releases all feature, as do, in granular detail, the thought processes, reflections and technical expertise that led to the creation of WORLD OF ECHO.

I first visited the Music Division of the New York Public Library for the Performing Arts, housed on the third floor of the Dorothy and Lewis B. Cullman Center at 40 Lincoln Center Plaza, New York, in November 2021, the week after pandemic travel restrictions to the United States from the United Kingdom were rescinded.

To gain access to the Arthur Russell papers, the researcher registers with the institution and books a prior appointment. The collection is then delivered in numerous boxes to a reading room with no natural daylight, generous desk space and attended to by extremely courteous and helpful staff. The library's protocols of instruction for conservation of materials, the use of blue rubber gloves and limiting the visitor to view one archive box at a time, will be familiar to anyone who has carried out archival research. They would doubtless also recognise the giddy sense of discovery I encountered as I sifted through the contents of each box and the feelings of intimacy precipitated by immersion in the material they contained: the visible indentations on notebooks made by Arthur's hand; the pale primary colours of a Kodachrome slide made suddenly vivid when illuminated by a light box; the acute experience of pathos at holding a handwritten letter never sent.

Over the following eighteen months I made three subsequent visits to the collection. My immersion in its artefacts led both to inquiries after similar items in the possession of Arthur's family and confidantes and a series of interviews with the same close circle of people from my subject's singular life. This book is an attempt to trace a journey through the archives of that singular life. Given its complexities and nuances it is likely, even inevitable, that another person undertaking similar research would choose differing methods and routes to create a biography of Arthur Russell.

Like any archive of this scale, the papers reveal the contradictions and complexities of its owner's character. They also allow their reader a degree of intimacy with a subject that in the case of Arthur, a person whose historical biography has to date portrayed him as reclusive and enigmatic, has hitherto been unavailable. On the pages of his notebooks, he is lyrical, distracted, wistful and hyper-articulate, frequently in the same paragraph. Once he had established a working method that could function within his budgets for his recording processes, Arthur rarely recorded over existing material, preferring instead to work with new tapes. The notebooks display a similar reluctance towards erasure; crossings-out are rare. Phrases instead are re-ordered or followed by non-sequiturs. The vigour and intensity of Arthur's creative process are visible on the page, as is a palpable sense of industriousness and, more occasionally, frustration. Rather than make sense of the creative decisions Arthur made, the papers demonstrate that a definitive portrait of Arthur Russell is an unrealistic proposition. He was an artist capable of writing folkish, reflective songs of Blakean childlike wonder, who could also write about sex with the same purposefulness, candour and authority as Prince or Betty Davis.

*

I first heard the music of Arthur Russell in 1994, when I was working at Revolver Records, Bristol. Like many independent record stores, Revolver defined itself by its willingness to promote and sell music from outside the mainstream. One of the three members of staff had presumably ordered a copy of ANOTHER THOUGHT on the strength of it being released on Philip Glass's Point label. I would like to take credit for such an act of far-sightedness, but this would be an exercise in self-flattery. Decisions about what stock to order were more often than not informed by an institutional love of obscurity, or the curious listlessness that is a consequence of days spent half-absorbed in music. However it was that the CD had arrived in the shop, my memory of hearing the music on ANOTHER THOUGHT is robust. Before removing the disc to insert it into the CD player I glanced at the back sleeve and noted that the enigmatic portrait of its creator wearing a paper hat had been taken by Janette Beckman, a name I recognised from hip-hop albums such as EPMD's STRICTLY BUSINESS. This information – together with the Philip Glass connection – suggested I was about to hear a very New York-sounding record.

On the album's opening track, the lugubrious voice singing the phrase, 'I'm on another thought now,' had an arresting directness and confidence. The words also suggested the singer was familiar with some form of meditative practice, a feeling that was echoed in the accompanying music, a cello played in a manner that highlighted its bottom-end frequencies, a solitary-sounding chamber music for the soul.

The instrument was played with obvious accomplishment but also with the same single-mindedness I had heard on Pablo Casals' recordings of Bach's six cello suites made during the Spanish Civil War. This comparison may have had something to do with the fact that this was the only piece of music for cello with which I was familiar.

Still in my mid-twenties, carrying the full weight of attitude required to have strong opinions about music in an independent record shop, in truth I had no context in which to place this strange recording. It sounded both ethereal and earthy, the voice and the tone of the cello were in perfect balance and the sense of space surrounding them felt tangible. Out of habit, I reached for musical comparisons and thought I could vaguely detect John Martyn's subaqueous vocal phrasing in some of Arthur Russell's singing. Other than that, this was music of a kind I had never previously encountered.

The sound design of the record also felt curiously dated; it belonged to a previous age, a mythical bohemian downtown New York that no longer existed. I had visited New York in the early nineties and recognised the atmosphere of the city as portrayed in Larry Clark's film KIDS, released the year after ANOTHER THOUGHT. This was the New York of skateboarders and rollerbladers in every park, their activities soundtracked to the same hip-hop albums playing in the Prince Street boutiques of a rapidly gentrifying SoHo. With its refences to lucky clouds and walking on the moon, the snatches of lyrics I caught on ANOTHER THOUGHT seemed of a separate world entirely. I was startled by the proficiency of the musicianship but also uncertain about it. Any sense of the pace and overstimulation of what I understood to be contemporary New York was absent.

I then heard 'In the Light of the Miracle' and its agogô line for the first time and was struck by the realisation that not only was this music I had not heard before, but it was also music I must have hoped had always existed. Nodding my head and rocking my shoulders to the circular rhythms and overlapping vocals all animated by the hypnotic agogô was a process of sharing a secret; a crack of light had appeared in my musical consciousness. It also acted as an invitation to embrace this indescribable sound world, to welcome the fact that this music had been made for everyone. I have come to recognise that this is a common reaction to the music of Arthur Russell, that to become familiar with his work is a form of awakening. I have no recollection of the ANOTHER THOUGHT CD ever being sold.

Four years later, in another record shop, Intoxica on Portobello Road, close to where I was then living off Ladbroke Grove in London, I scanned a top ten of new stock favoured by the staff. Occupying the number one spot on the list was 'Go Bang!' by Dinosaur L (the track's official title was 'Go Bang #5'), next to which was written a brief description of the track, which referred to New York in the early 1980s, and its reputation as a club classic.

A friend and I DJed together sporadically, mainly at birthday parties and weddings. An original 99 Records pressing of 'Moody (Spaced Out)' by ESG had come into my possession while I was working at Revolver and was a staple of our sets. One evening, my friend, who was more of a B-boy than myself, followed 'Moody' with 'Go Bang!' Hearing its bassline descend, ascend and then descend again as it reverberated across the dancefloor provided my second Arthur Russell epiphany. Next to the ultraconfident streetwise minimalism of 'Moody', this was a more urgent, even more funky, borderline hysterical track, which was impossible not to dance to. I was hearing a wilfully out-of-control piece of music that seemed to celebrate its own delirium, and which increased its energy levels as it progressed. The sound was thick with instruments colliding into one another and insistent vocals making the case for Going Bang. I had rarely heard a song so evocative of the near-mythical downtown Manhattan at play as night became morning.

It took several days and the usual forensic examination of writer and production credits before I was able to make the connection between 'Go Bang!' and 'In the Light of the Miracle'. I recognised a similar energy in both pieces: an invitation to share this space with its creator, music that called for a physical response rather than a definition from the listener, whom Arthur Russell appeared to have the gift of placing under a kinetic spell.

To be human is complex. Arthur Russell was a lifelong practitioner of Buddhism who was well connected across a series of musical vectors, but also frequently a recluse who revealed his character and his reportedly excellent sense of humour to only a handful of people, most notably his partner from 1978 to the end of his life, Tom Lee. The choices Russell made in his work are equally unorthodox; an artist resistant to the idea of genre, his talent allowed him to excel in any number of styles and dialogues. The gift Arthur bequeathed in his archive was to demonstrate that such a working practice was not only possible but vital to his musical consciousness. It teaches us that an open mind is the most formidable creative tool. There are several, at times many, Arthurs present in the archive; each of them offers an invitation to share the confidences of one of the most influential figures of late-twentieth-century music.

As noted, the restoration of Russell's music has been overseen with loving care and attention by Steve Knutson of Audika Records in partnership with the Arthur Russell estate, including Arthur's partner Tom Lee.

This book is dedicated to Steve and Tom.

Part I

1951-73

Charles Arthur Russell, Jr was born in Oskaloosa, Iowa, on 21 May 1951, youngest child and only son of Charles and Emily and brother to two sisters, Kate and Julie.

At the time of his birth, Arthur's family was enjoying the material success of the Eisenhower Age. The family home was an architect-designed house partly constructed out of redwood, and they had access to a vacation property at Gull Lake, Minnesota. Arthur's childhood was spent in the prosperous, post-war, middle-class life of the Great Society: his father, known familiarly as Chuck, served two terms as mayor of Oskaloosa and ran a highly successful insurance business; his mother Emily's interests included playing the cello.

OSKALOOSA PUBLIC SCHOOLS

KINDERGARTEN PROGRESS RECORD

Days Present 45
Days Absent   0
Times Tardy   4

Dear Parents:

For several weeks the children have been using their workbooks. These workbooks are designed to help the children get ready for reading in first grade.

While making their names, the children are encouraged to name the letters used. The class discusses all the letters by name when the need arises. Some children like to practice printing at home. A copy of the letter formations used in First Grade can be found in the handbook given you last spring. Capitals are used only for the beginning letters of the names in order that the transition to printed type be easier. It is helpful when the children print at home if they proceed in the same manner as at school.

Oral language is very important in the Kindergarten. The ability to read is very closely connected with the ability to speak. The child needs to hear and pronounce words correctly as a beginning stage in phonics.

The child should understand the meaning of left to right, not only in handedness, but as it applies to manuscript writing, numbers, the using of all books, playing games, reading labels, and going up and down stairs.

The experiences with numbers are so enjoyable they hardly seem like work. Numbers are used in many ways--in games, stories, poems, and songs. Most of the children can easily count to ten, and they know many numbers when they see them.

Although enjoyment is one of our main objectives in Kindergarten music, rhythm, matching tones, and carrying melodies are being stressed more and more. We listen to tones and try to distinguish between high and low notes. Then, too, we listen for changes in volume and tempo. A guessing game we find both enjoyable and instructive is trying to recognize familiar melodies.

Your Kindergarten teacher,

Lucille Barnes

Brief comments on Kindergarten music.

Charley does very satisfactory work in all areas of music- rhythms, hearing the difference in tones, listening, and singing.

Report of Third Quarter, ending 3-22-57

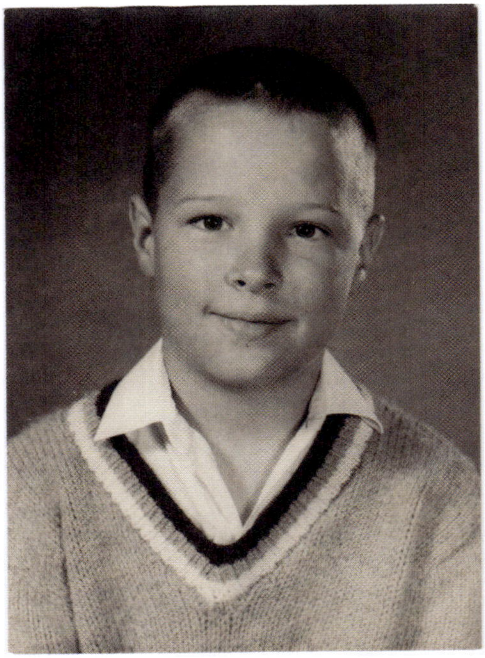

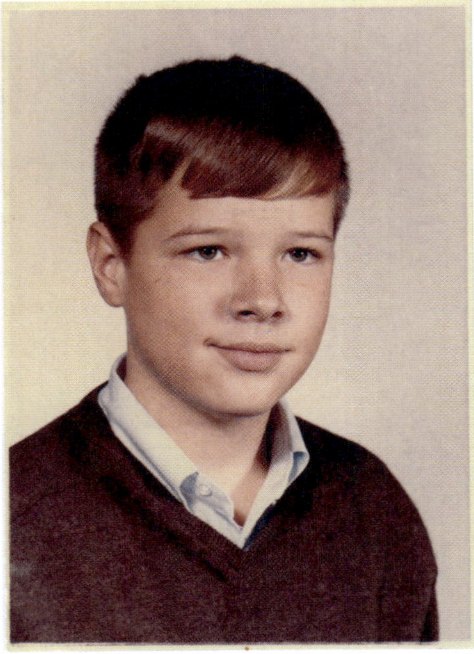

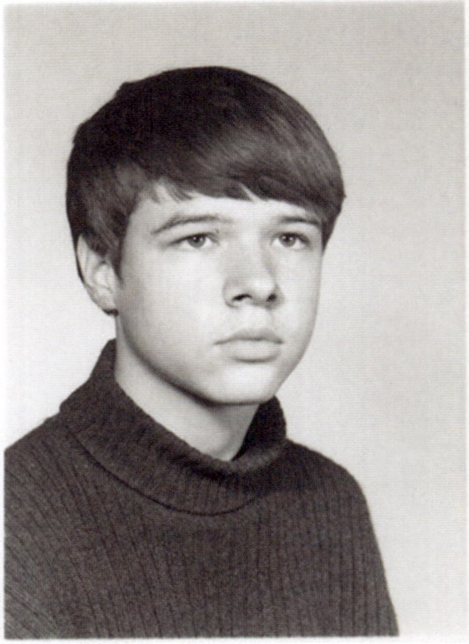

Kate, Arthur and Julie Russell, early 1960s.

Kate Russell: 'Arthur, I have always felt, was off the charts intellectually. He was ahead of his age in the things that he cared about and that led to all kinds of trouble academically and emotionally in the house. I wasn't the best of sisters in that I tried to convince him to be like the rest of the world, too: as his friend, I tried to convince him to go out for sports and all of that kind of crap, which I regret.'

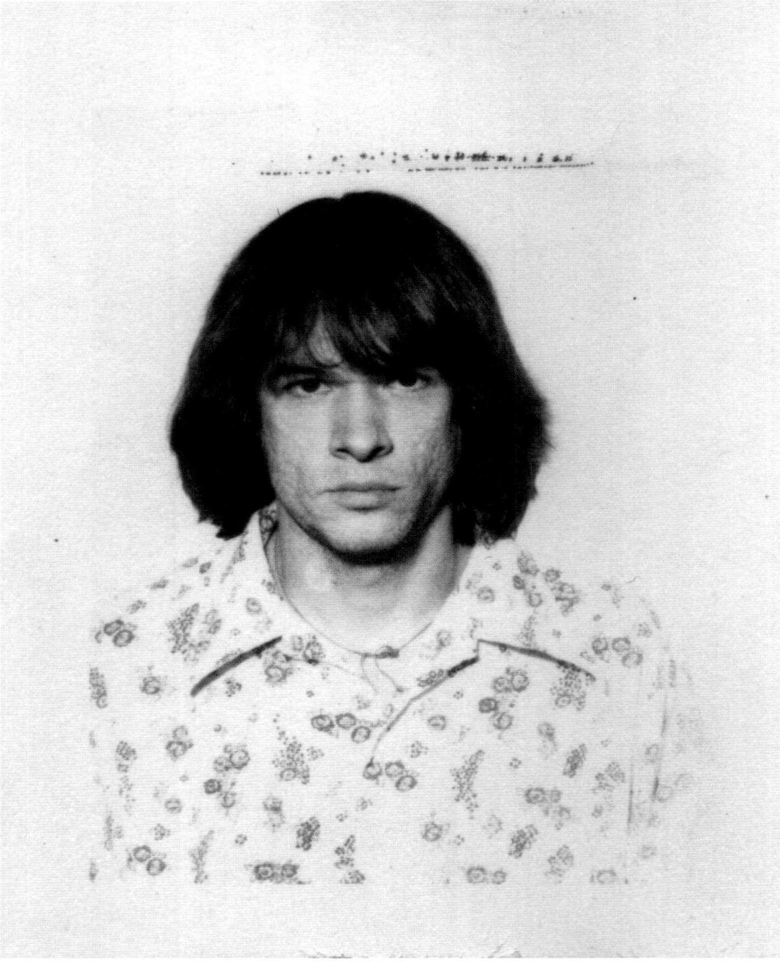

Dear Pat,
I've finally something to say. I hate to burden you with letters (!;;') but I have decided to revelate. The basic difference between you and myself is that I feel it's necessary to open oneself to all criticism and scrutiny and to be frank and unelusive about it. You don't (I'm not criticizing you for it), and I can't tell anything about you; which very frankly bothers me. I imagine I'll get over this when I come to respect and/or disrespect myself more. I'm very self-conscious around people I respect that I don't know. They're always laughing (on a Dear Abby note) at me. Even Kate is, it seems.

I got a book at the Penn College Library called 'Concentration and Meditation' published and written by the Buddhist Lodge, London. It looks very interesting because it's so obscure. I'm using it as a companion volume to the textbook by Alan Watts.

3 weeks later

After reading part of Concentration and Meditation, I've decided that I'm not ready for an effort in Buddhism.

I'll probably try Lsd sometime this year. First peyote, then Lsd. I know what you mean when you spoke of the right attitude toward psychedelics. The same goes for Buddhism; except Buddhism is such a long term investment. I asked a person I know whether an effort in Buddhism requires the same attitude as psychedelics.

My attitude toward psychedelics, I imagine you'll be glad to hear, I think has boiled down to the real

'Conditions here are terrible. I can't stand it.'
A letter written in 1966 to Arthur Russell's school friend Pat, of whom little is known, which makes reference to Walt Whitman, John Cage and Allen Ginsberg.

need. I'm no longer pre-occupied with them. I think this is a great leap forward.

I'm glad you saw Ornette Coleman. He's absolutely fantastic, good training for anybody. He gave way to the present new-thingers in jazz such as Archie Shepp, Albert Ayler, and John Coltrane. Whatever anyone ever tells you about the new jazz, remember Ornette Coleman. The new jazz is part of my life, as are John Cage and Whitman-Ginsberg. Listening to it takes me inside the black culture and, on some wonderful nights, completely inverts me. It's the most intensive cultural ecstacy I can experience. Dylan Thomas did it to me in Under Milk Wood, Allen Ginsberg in Howl, and William Shakespeare in his plays. But most intensive of all — the new jazz. I don't know what John Cage does to me with his lectures, but it certainly has influenced me.

I don't read as much as I should. I don't know anyone in Oskaloosa who does. Conditions here are terrible. I can't stand it.

Oskaloosa three dollars and 27 cents
October 19, 1966

I'm trying to persuade my parents into allowing me to go to a high school run by the University of Iowa, but they don't want me to leave home. I've tried the Carl Sandburg method, but I'm just not as non-sentient as I'd like to be. Everybody in the whole town either hates me or ignores me. This is the lonliest period in my life so far. All of my former friends (they're still friends) think I'm naive and unperceptive.

I KNOW I'M NOT!

If they would only see themselves! Carl Sandburg has taught me so much! I feel there's a distiction between philosophical thought and individual action. Everyone here is still smoking pot and worrying about their hair.

I'm sending you a drawing of Kate's, your tambourine, and a record of the new black jazz. The record is a fairly well distributed disc, and in the Down Beat yearbook it was given ten different reviews. It got anywhere from five stars to one star, so there is a difference in opinion. I would give it five. As far as I know, the only white musician on the record is the cellist with Ayler, and ironically I didn't think he was very good. I know he's not a good musician. I won't give my favorite track. They're all good.

Sorry such a delay in writing the letter, but I am terrible about writing letters. This one has been in progress for 2 months. (2½ month)

As usual, I couldn't read all of your writing, so I don't know what you meant

God knows you need more grade school.

about Tangier.

Yes, I would very much like to come and visit you but my mother says no. I can't go to Cleveland either to see Kate. I would like you to come up here some time even though it sounds presumptuous. Kate isn't coming home till Christmas and I doubt that you would want to come to see just me.

Kate, I think, will come of age in Cleveland. She's doing a lot of wild (!) things, like smoking pot and riding motorcycles, but she's also working very hard. I think she'll learn how to live. Post war babies do have a hard time.

There is so much more to say than I have said. I wish I could see you instead (rhyme, rhyme)

I apologize again for not writing you sooner, but I'm not the dilligent letter writer as I said.

Charley Russell

PS Anytime you want to come up here you're welcome to, but I doubt it would be very rewarding for you. I wish you would come. Also, one bright Saturday you might find me sauntering (I can't stand that word) into Willis Woods dormitories. I've found a prospective ride down there.

PROGRAM NOTES

The idea of an Oskaloosa Children's Theatre has developed quite recently as the result of a group of Jr.-Sr. High School and grade school children studying creative dramatics with Mrs. Cauldwell under the sponsorship of the YWCA. Several college students joined in the project and helped design and construct scenery, assist with directing and ticket selling as well as acting in the play.

The group enthusiasm has encouraged the Director to hope that this will be the beginning of a community effort to bring children's plays to the young people and interested adults in Oskaloosa.

The cast in the play has helped with every aspect of the project—programs, costumes, properties, sets, make up, lighting, music, and stage crew. It has been an educational experience in every sense of the word. It is hoped that this fall, more college students and adults will join the group and make the Oskaloosa Children's Theatre a unique and successful community theatre project.

We wish to thank all the friends who have loaned us their time, talents and possessions to put on the play. A special thank you goes to the Knights of Pythias Lodge for loaning us so many beautiful costumes.

THE EMPEROR'S NEW CLOTHES

A Comedy in Three Acts

To be played by or for children

by

Charlotte Chorpenning

April 16th, 1966   Junior High School

SETTING

Time: Long Ago
Place: A country much like China
Act I: The Street of the Royal Weavers. The middle of the morning.
Act II: A room in Han's quarters in the palace. Noon the next day.
Act III: Same as Act I. Afternoon of the same day.

MUSIC

Composed and Directed by: Charles Russell

Quartet: David Patterson
Nancy Jones
Coleen Grace
Ruth Rouw

DIRECTOR

Caroline Cauldwell

Assistant Director: Leon Van Welden
Stage Crew: Phillip Jones
Joseph Casey
And all male members of the cast
Tickets: Tom Valdivia
Mary Lamberson
Malcolm Cauldwell

CAST
(in order of their appearance)

ZAR	OHS Senior	Charles Johnson
ZAN	OHS Junior	Alan Cauldwell
GONG BOY	Whittier, 5th grade	Mark Kelderman
HAN	OHS Sophomore	Bruce Everhart
TSEIN	OHS Sophomore	Barbara Sunstrum
MONG	OHS Sophomore	Carol Kelderman
L ING	OHS Sophomore	Carrie Walker
FAH	9th grade	Joan Lamberson
OLD WOMAN	OHS Sophomore	Joy Fitch
CHILD	Prine School 6th grade	Marcia Pierson
THE EMPEROR	9th grade	Charles Russell
THE EMPRESS	9th grade	Anne Marie Alsop
THE GENERAL	9th grade	Jerry Van Der Wal
CITIZENS	OHS Junior	Julie Russell
	OHS Junior	Barbara Spayde
	Prine School 5th grade	Libby Pierson
	Whittier 5th grade	Denise Hayes
	Whittier 5th grade	Rozanne Hower
	9th grade	Kent Goshorn
	9th grade	Allen Van Welden
	9th grade	Scot Campbell
	Central College Sophomore	Leon Van Welden

20

At the age of sixteen, the year before the tumults of 1968 that cracked open many of the racial and generational fault lines evident in American society, Russell participated in the mass exodus of teenagers from the overbearing security of school and home. The reasons for Russell's departure are manifold and complex. Even by the standards of a late-1960s teenager, Arthur could appear diffident and remote. A school friend with whom he shared an interest in music and poetry had left Oskaloosa, amplifying his sense of isolation; he fought with his parents, his father in particular.

> Kate Russell: 'He had to leave and run away, but it really didn't have anything to do with my parents. He was reading Lawrence Ferlinghetti and Allen Ginsberg and a whole mess of stuff that urged him to be doing what he did.'

Russell's first intended destination was Iowa City. By the spring of 1968 he had arrived in Haight-Ashbury, San Francisco, where he initially stayed in crash pads and communes and experienced the area's dissolute runaway street life documented by Joan Didion in SLOUCHING TOWARDS BETHLEHEM. Like many of his contemporaries attempting to make sense of their new circumstances, Russell was reduced to selling underground newspapers and was finally arrested for possession of marijuana in 1969. Rather than return to Oskaloosa or reside in a detention centre until he turned eighteen, he entered a Buddhist commune, Kailas Shugendo.

While living as a member of the commune, which was housed in various addresses across San Francisco, he met the Japanese Shingon priest Yuko Nonomura, with whom he formed a close bond and who would prove to be a strong influence on him. Russell's Buddhist faith would endure with varying degrees of commitment throughout his life; his time in San Francisco also resulted in two changes of name. Initially, Chuck, or Charley, became Arthur; as a commune member Arthur was then given the name Jigme.

Kate Russell: 'There was a giant rupture between kids and families in the United States at that time, period. And it was very common, I think, in rural areas, where there was no place to go but gone, particularly if you might be struggling with your identity. In Iowa, it was oppressive. And so it wasn't necessarily about my parents: it was about the school, it was about the community, he had a friend, a very close friend, that moved away in the middle of his junior high career, and that's when that separation sort of started with him, his need to go. Probably the best thing that my parents did was that they didn't disown him; they ran after him and they tracked him down. All three of us, the kids of the family, were escaping in some form at that time. That was happening then: the Vietnam War, feminism, just everything was going on, and my parents were struggling to try to understand it. And they were very liberal people. Wonderful, liberal people.'

While a member of the Kailas Shugendo commune Russell also attended the Ali Akbar College of Music in Marin County and was as devoted to his musical training as to his Buddhist practice. It was as a member of the Kailas Shugendo Mantric Sun Band that Allen Ginsberg first encountered Russell in 1971. The poet invited Russell to join him as an accompanist and band member on his performances and recordings, the start of a friendship that would endure, through various fluctuations, throughout the rest of his life.

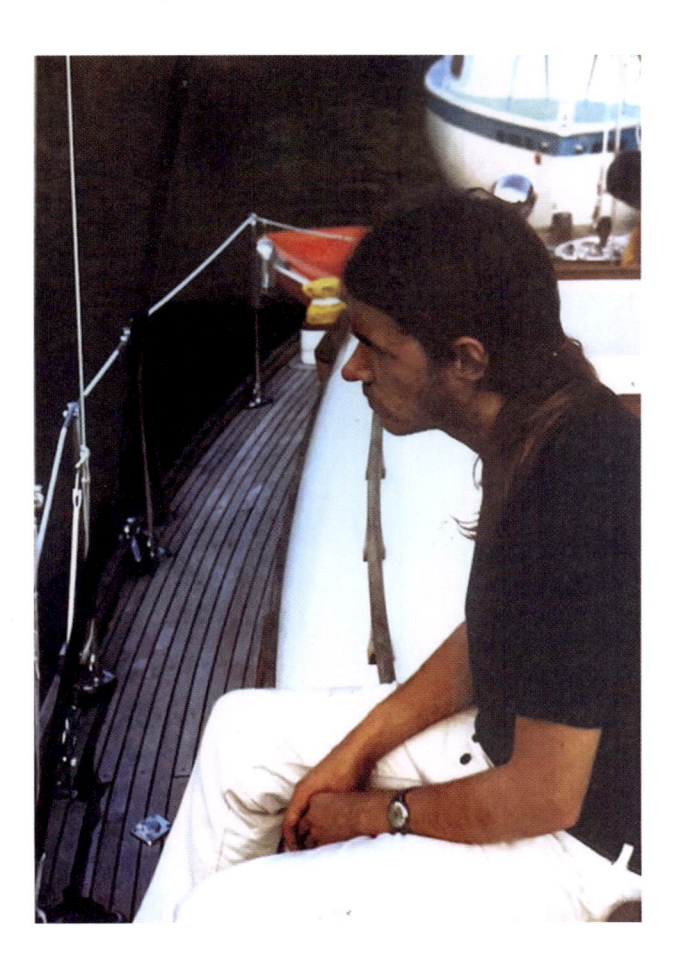

Muriel Fujii: 'My roommate Patty and I were at a poetry reading with Allen Ginsberg, Lawrence Ferlinghetti, Robert Bly, and for that night, Allen Ginsberg wasn't really reading his poetry, but he was doing this kind of chanting with Hindu music, and Arthur was playing a string bass. We were supposed to be watching the door, handing out programmes and Arthur came over and was talking to Patty. He showed up at our apartment in San Francisco the next day. I had come back from classes and Patty opened the door and said, "Oh, it's Arthur, the guy from last night." When we were leaving, he had approached her and asked her for our phone number or address or whatever. He wasn't even speaking to me, and then it turns out he shows up to see me. I didn't know what he wanted and after a while, we both had nothing to say to each other, but he was still there. Around eight o'clock or so, I pretended I had a test to study for the next day, so I went to the kitchen, because he was in the living room, and just pretended to study, but I just couldn't focus on anything. He stayed the whole night, and then the next morning, I get up, and he's still there. I go to classes, I come back, and he's still there. Then we ended up spending mainly weekends together, although he would come during the week at certain times, because he lived out of the city, and on Friday nights, we always went to these Buddhist talks by his friend Yuko Nonomura. At that time, he was living in a Sufi commune, so he was also going to the Ali Akbar Khan School of Music, and a lot of his friends were students at the school who all followed different types of religion. Buddhism was, for him, important.'

ALI AKBAR COLLEGE OF MUSIC -- SCHEDULE OF CLASSES, SPRING 1973

	Monday	Tuesday	Wednesday	Thursday	Friday
Khansahib	4 Teachers' Meeting 5 Beginning Vocal 7 SA Instrumental	Every other week: 5 Bow & Flute 7 Orchestra Alternate weeks: Improvisational Workshop -- 5 Workshop A 7 Workshop B	5 Intermed. Vocal 7 MA Instrumental	10 RE/GA Sitar 12 RE/GA Sarod	10 Advanced Vocal
Sachdev	4 Teachers' Meeting 5 GA Flute 7 SA Flute	5 RE Flute		5 RE Flute 7 SA Flute	
Zakir	4 Teachers' Meeting 5 RE Tabla 7 SA Tabla	4 Folk Drums 5 RE Tabla	Hours Arranged	5 RE Tabla 7 SA Tabla	
Chitresh	12 Advanced Dance 2 Beginning Dance	12 Advanced Dance 2 Beginning Dance	12 Advanced 2 Beginning	12 Advanced 2 Beginning	10 Dance
Teaching Assistants	4 Teachers' Meeting 7 GA Instrumental 10 a.m. New Maihar Band	10 Flute Workshop 10 RE Instrumental 12 Intermediate Vocal	3 Vocal Workshop	10 Sarod Workshop 12 Sitar Workshop 4 Tala 5 SA Vocal 7 SA Instrumental	

Spring class schedule, Ali Akbar School of Music, Marin County, 1973.

Tom Lee: 'Arthur had exposure to Buddhist thinking for the first time at exactly the right age, when he was disillusioned and unhappy and ready to leave his home. He embraced the Buddhist readings and teachings he learned beginning in Iowa and more so in San Francisco and ultimately in New York where he continued to attend talks offered by certain Buddhist teachers. I believe that this guidance greatly helped him spiritually on his journey and specifically as he confronted his own mortality.'

Arthur Russell's Buddhist artefacts: malas (Tibetan prayer beads) and dorje.

Muriel Fujii: 'He was just driven. He was unlike any other guys I knew. All of us, we were away from home for the first time. I'm from Hawaii – Hawaii at that time was just ten years out of statehood and it was really like a small, backwards town, and Arthur, too, came from this really little place, Oskaloosa, Iowa, stuck in the middle of cornfields. He was definitely a runaway, escaping that, and I think at the heart of everything was his music. He was just driven by it.'

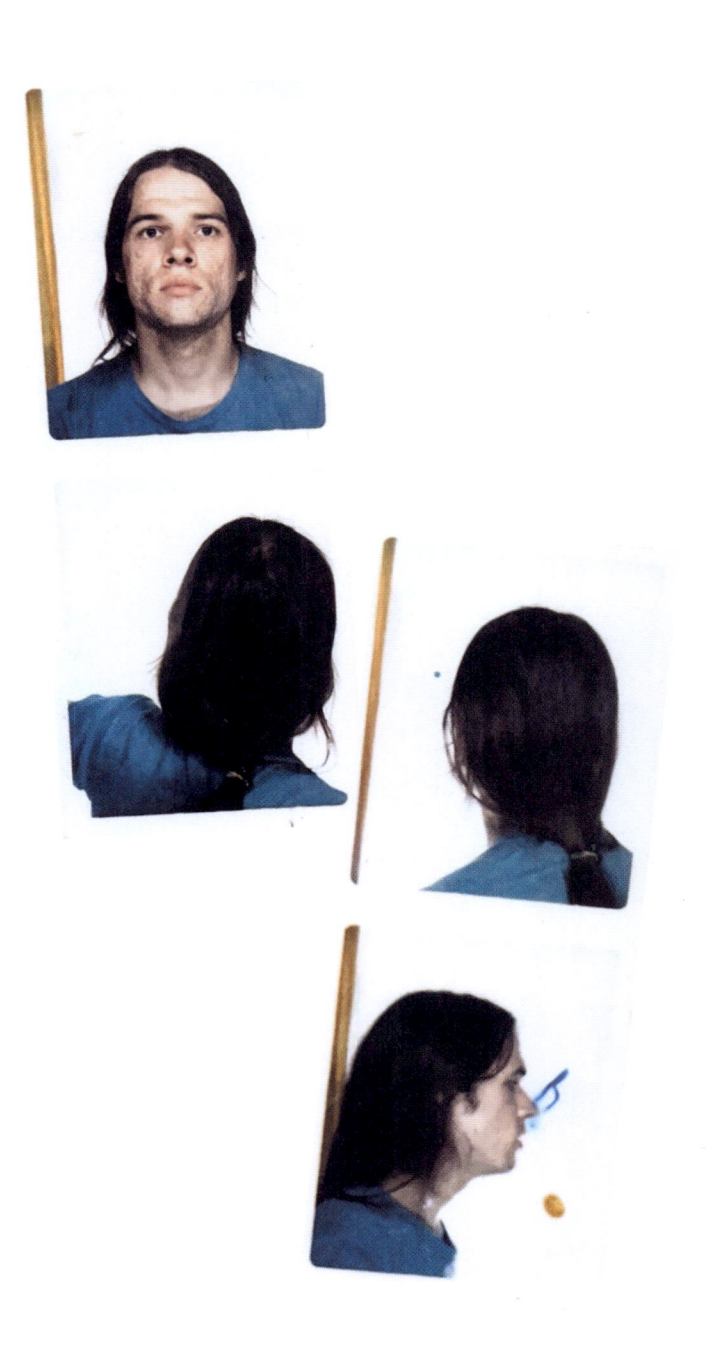

Kate Russell: 'There was a time that my parents tried desperately to bring him back to the Midwest and to continue his schooling there. They felt that the danger at that time was San Francisco, and the Haight-Ashbury hippy world there. When they realised that bringing him back to Iowa was not the best thing, and that he was not coming back to Iowa, ever, they let him go to safe hands, and that was the Buddhist commune. And at the same time, as he was pursuing his music career, they then became comfortable with Arthur pursuing his life at that early age, and he got his GED (General Educational Development certificate).'

Arthur Russell's scholarship record at John Adams Community College Education Center, San Francisco, 1973.

Muriel Fujii: 'Arthur and I were both really late bloomers. He was born two days before me. So we were close, very close. And even though I think we were both twenty at the time, it was more like we were sixteen. I think I was his first real relationship, and the same with me, and we didn't know what we were doing – it was just really kind of odd. I knew he had run away, and I could see he was definitely an oddball and how he wouldn't fit in a small town. Emotionally he was very immature, and I remember he called his father Daddy. I had never called my father Daddy since I was eight years old or something. When we went to his home, he would say something about "Daddy", and I was like, "Oh, my God!"

'Most people, when you're seeing each other, you'd ask each other, "How was your day?" or you'd maybe go on a date somewhere, go to a restaurant – there was none of that with Arthur. All of it, from the very, very beginning, was just talking about his music and what he was doing, and he was always with a musical manuscript notebook, always notating. Sometimes he was transcribing music for people – that's actually how I thought he made his living, because he was doing that for a lot of people – but then a lot of times, it was just him making up stuff, and that was a constant. Sometimes we'd talk about Yuko [Nonomura] or something, but the whole other world just didn't exist. This was toward the end of all that political activity, the demonstrations against the Vietnam War and all that was going on in San Francisco: it was dying out but it was still going on, and all of that just didn't exist for Arthur.

'In those days, it was a kind of narrow view of music he had, because when I was with him, popular culture didn't even exist. There was all that great music in San Francisco going on at the time and he was not at all interested in any of it. He listened to John Cage and Morton Feldman. He never spent money on anything frivolous. His clothes were all from thrift stores, he never seemed to have enough money; he was always behind on the rent, and his housemates were always mad at him because he kept eating all their food and he never contributed. Because all his money was spent on the manuscript books, gas, instruments and equipment.

'At one point we drove to Iowa, and I was really, really surprised when I met his family. I was speechless. They seemed so middle-class, normal. I came from a middle-class family, too, but I didn't think Arthur did: his mother was a cellist – that wasn't her job, but she played the cello, she had a job I think with the school board – and his father was an insurance salesman: how did they produce Arthur?

'The family home was this incredible house that Arthur's uncle had built, and he was a student of Frank Lloyd Wright. It could have been in California, but here it was in small-town Oskaloosa, where on a Friday night, all that was happening was an animal auction or something, that kind of stuff going on, so we went to that.'

Arthur Russell and cello at Gull Lake, Minnesota, where the Russell family had a vacation property, early 1970s. The Russells would also spend time together in Maine, where they would eventually purchase a property, which became the locus for family celebrations and anniversaries, as well as summer holidays.

Kate Russell: 'When he came home, he always had his sheaf of papers in his pocket and he was always writing. When he had something in his mind like a group of words, he would do that when he was with us, he would be kind of quiet to the side, and if we said something he would then just disappear into his work and write. Then he would get up and walk away and go back in his room, and play music, and we would have to draw him back out and say, "Oh, it's time for dessert," or, "We're going to open presents now."

Arthur Russell and sunset at Gull Lake, Minnesota, early 1970s.

'At times, he would be contrary. He would be not fun, and it's things that my sister and I would accept, but it would be hard for my parents. But that's family drama. In Maine, he would go down to a slipway there and I'm sure that that was a place of meditation for him: the water was a theme in his music, in his lyrics, and that was not something that I shared with him, that was a personal, individual thing that he had. I was happy that he could have that here.'

Arthur Russell and cello at Renaissance Fair, San Rafael, California, October 1972.

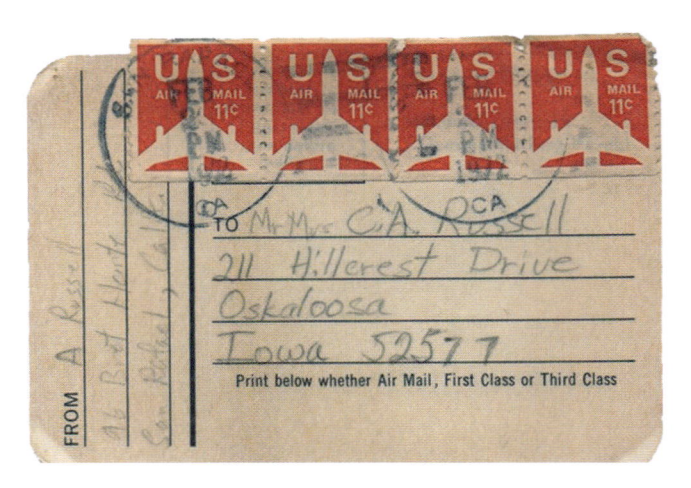

Correspondence from Arthur Russell to his parents, San Rafael, California, 1972.

Muriel Fujii: 'It was a fair, I don't know why they picked the word "Renaissance" for it. It was held every year, and they would hire all these people to do various things, and they all had to be in costume. They hired musicians, actors, who walked around, posing as different types of the people who would be living at that time, like a silversmith or jugglers and all that. Arthur had got hired to play Renaissance music, just to provide atmosphere with the music.

'And of course, he needed the money, but he kept getting cut, because he really wasn't familiar with Renaissance music, he would end up playing Bach and every time, this woman would come and then she would catch him and she would yell at him: "We didn't hire you to play that!"'

> 1750 Arch Street
>
> march 16, 17 / 1973   8 pm
>
> Ernst Bacon:
> Sonata for cello and piano with homage to Walt Whitman
> I, II, III, IV
>
> (intermission)
>
> Arthur Russell:
> archdive for vibraharp, cello and darbukka
> I, II, III
>
> and ... until
>
> experimental music   (for Ezra Pound)
>
> John Bergamo — vibraharp, percussion
> Vince Delgado — darbukka
> Brian Goddin — guitar
> Charles Amir Lewis — hands and mouth
> Karen Nelson — piano
> Arthur Russell — cello

Programme of performances for 16/17 March 1973, at 1750 Arch Street, Berkeley, California. 1750 Arch St was a performance space run by Tom Buckner, a long-time advocate of New Music and the grandson of Thomas J Watson, founder of IBM. The concert is considered to be the first occasion at which Russell performed one of his own compositions in public.

'The whole time we were together, I never saw him take drugs and he didn't drink either. He always had to have that clarity for his music. It was not your typical relationship, like never holding hands, never kiss goodbye type of thing. He would do these, I think they're called booty calls, and then be gone. The other part of Arthur was there – I always suspected when he talked about Allen Ginsberg, in fact I think he said something at one point.'

june 1.

arthur —
    enlightenment comes unexpectedly and swiftly. everything seems clearer now — i know i was acting out of human weaknesses & frailities — please forgive me. i'm really happy & feel freer now because i know things will work themselves out. i hope we can look forward to seeing each other in december. i received your postcard (i can recognize your fingerprints anywhere) today just when i was thinking of you — an indication of greater destinies? last night i went with vahideh to hear allen ginsberg michael mcclure & the sufi choir — also a zen priest chanted the hannya shingyo — it all worked to banish all traces of negativity that was in my mind. i guess it was the spiritual cleansing that i needed. i really wish i could share with you this feeling of elation that — words can be put in envelopes but emotions can't. if you can feel it — let it fill you. yet perhaps this separation will confirm our faith. don't try to understand each other — as long as we can feel our heart beats.
                                          my love is eternal — muriel.

— if it is possible — i'd like to hear your voice before i leave — could you call me next sunday (collect) —

Not far from Cheyenne over Red Desert Wyo.
15 Sept 73

Dear Arthur:

Thank yr. soul for helping me out to Kennedy aerport I needed a hand with that fat Cowboy bag.

Oddly on plane to Denver I kept hearing Goodbye old Paint inner ear music — and after last week giggling decline mentioned "I'll even brush my teeth for you" I realized the 14 year old comedy of your precision in words — that is objective, a concrete image taken from life's raw material — it takes a low kind of courage or humor or understanding of basic reality to rely on so delicate a fact & persevere with confidence in your own memories drawn from actual rather than idealized life — to stay put with that real is rare, so that's a rare art you have. I guess the tape-hearing jelled my mind & left an impression without my conscious straining attention. Anyway the tape reeched on plane in head today with a final loveliness & Buddha smallness of the Actual.

See you when I get back to N.Y. — maybe we'll play together at Town Hall — I have an hour's show there Oct 24 at 5-7pm — & will do a little music — then go to Boston oct 26-28 — If you're free maybe we all can drive up there — with Peter who'll be on previous 10 day tour with me — for the Buddha Festival (with Ram Dass Baghvan Das & Rupocha Chögyam, each doing separate evening.)

love as ever,
Allen.

Recent poem from Blake's 'Songs of Innocence and of Experience'

to Yoko ono —
worn scrawl, finger scribble, soul Signature.

Trianon Press, Paris
Printed in France

july 22nd.
dear arthur —

hi again — i just wrote but since i just got your letter — i wanted to write back. thats really great about you going to manhattan (i guess — if thats what i'm expected to say) new york city, huh? i heard there's a lot of weird happenings there (mainly rumors). well, i hope you like it. i don't think i'll like it here — i don't know if i'll stay to finish. did i tell you how long its going to take — one year (2 semesters) and one summer session. i may have a month off for semester christmas (i'm not sure if teachers get the same vacations) — but if i do, i might be able to visit you. the radio station i'm listening to now has an hour of indian classical music every sunday night — mostly ravi shankhar & ali akbar khan. but thats the only indian music i've heard here. today after we went to the beach we stopped at place called valley of the temples which had a has a replica of the byodo-in thats near kyoto. it was really nice except the ponds had green water in it — poor fish & the tea house didn't sell tea — only postcards. there was a big bronze statue of buddha inside and a great bell outside that makes a sound when you push a big wooden log against it. but the fact that it was brought here to be a tourist attraction & not to serve its original purpose as a temple as it does in japan somehow made me very sad. i also had an argument & with this boy from japan about economics and capitalism — he felt that japan isn't doing anything wrong. but i'd still like to go to japan someday —

july 23.

hi — i'm at work now but not hard at work because i'm writing this letter to you. everyone else is sitting around drinking coffee & reading the newspaper. (the middle aged, complacent syndrome) who want to hear another 'funny' thing? this morning i had just picked up this magazine out of a whole stack of magazines which turned out to be a 'psychology today' & inside, there just happened to be an article on frank waters. but i & didn't get to read it all — he really is an interesting person. — wish i could go back to the navajo reservation — i met these 2 really nice girls there — i was supposed to go back & visit them last summer — they lived in a hogan which had only a wood burning stove for heat (no electricity, running water, t.v. or toilet). have you ever been there (ie new mexico/arizona?) — there was also a lot of kids i met — i remember one especially — her name was darlene blue-eyes. — she was a beautiful dancer & could do all these intricate navajo dances about eagles & waving fields of corn.

oskaloosa sounds like a nice friendly place — an old comfortable town? everyone here at work smokes — so by being forced to breathe their smoke its almost as if i was smoking. 2 women here are pregnant — maybe they should read white mule.

so arthur should i keep hoping for a miracle — don't you feel like it'll be an entirely new phase of your life when you move from california to new york? being in hawaii is like being in another world. i know i'm not like how i was in sf — climatic change really makes a difference (environmental too) — its all slowly evolving so i can't really feel it — living at home with parents isn't the most stimulating place to be.

also although you may also think this letter is flat — it really isn't — my thoughts of you filling a 3 dimensional space — & love another dimension in itself — i hope you can feel it even if you can't see it —

love, muriel

In the summer of 1971 Russell had entered Pacific High Studios, San Francisco, with Allen Ginsberg to play cello on pieces that would be released on the collection HOLY SOUL JELLY ROLL over twenty years later. The recording session would eventually lead to an invitation for Arthur to record some of his own songs with the producer John Hammond, the executive who had signed both Bob Dylan and Bruce Springsteen to recording contracts, in New York. Although Arthur informed his parents that he intended to relocate to the East Coast in order to continue his musical studies at the Manhattan School of Music at Columbia University, he had made it clear to Muriel that he was moving to the city to pursue the offer from John Hammond, with whom he was in regular telephone contact.

> Muriel Fujii: 'His parents bought him a brand-new VW to drive across the country to New York. That seemed unusual. People would get five hundred bucks to buy an old piece of rubbish or something, but he was given a brand-new car. He told me when he got to New York it was stripped and eventually it just fell apart on the street.
>
> 'We never talked about our future, but for me, when I graduated, I was going to stay in San Francisco. I didn't want to go back to Hawaii, and I knew Arthur would be going to New York. But my parents came for my graduation and told me that if I didn't come home with them, they were going to disown me. They met Arthur and they were just appalled. My father's second-generation Japanese, typical Japanese man, and, you know, it was just, "No way." All the things that he called Arthur, they were really awful!
>
> 'At that time, I was still naïve, my parents had decided I was going to become a teacher – because that's what all good Japanese girls did in Hawaii in those days. I told Arthur that; I said, "I can't go to New York, I want to stay in San Francisco," and then he said, "Well, come with me. I thought you were coming with me to New York and marry me: let's go," and I just said, "No."
>
> 'I had the good sense to know that I couldn't be with him because he knew exactly who he was and what he was doing and I had no idea, and I knew that if I went with him, I would never have a chance. In the back of my mind, I always thought of John and Yoko. I always thought, "Is this why he was so interested in me?" But he kept trying to get me to move there, and then he even talked at one point of moving to Hawaii, and I was going, "Oh, no way! You would hate Hawaii."'

Letter from Arthur Russell to Muriel Fujii, including notes Arthur made to orientate himself in his new home of Manhattan, New York, 1973.

Muriel,

Hi, riding in a car with some kids — teenagers, two guys from Barre, Vermont. It's a souped up auto, with a tape player playing something by "Steppenwolf", and a vibration that shakes the whole 'mobile at certain speeds. We stopped at a rest stop and turned the engine off. The tape stopped. We went inside, spoke to two old men in the lobby. When we came back, and started the car, the tape started too, and off we went, the two guys in the front seat, drinking beer from the six-pack resting between the two front bucket seats. (the tape just switched to Three Dog Night) Cigarettes, and of course, cigarette smoke.

I went to Hanover, New Hampshire, home of Dartmouth College and Christian Wolff, composer. He teaches there. He's really a good composer, and a beautiful cat. He has a real appreciation for acoustic sounds and natural occurrence. You'd like him, he has two kids and chairs in his house.

It's fall in New Hampshire and Vermont, red, yellow, orange, brown, green. Drinking white grape juice like water. It's very beautiful. (I can barely visualize what it will be like when you come, too bad it won't be fall here) We can go to some very cold places in December, different from Hawaii. (The driver of this car talks incessantly; we're at a gas station and he's still talking. As you can see, the handwriting improved, tho only a little, when the car stopped.

Christian Wolff is really wonderful being, I wish I could go to Dartmouth. Maybe I can.

ALMOST ONE WEEK LATER...

now resting, one leg dangling, the other crossed supporting my notebook, on east side in valuable New York, diamond set. lots of people at a party and me one of them, not asking questions, lots of the kind of shoes that have big thick heels, you know? Denise has some that have leopard fuzz, like a stuffed animal. not asking questions, there's a mask of a man with a small blue hat, a halloween mask, a cigar in its mouth where the paint spreads outside where the cigar is supposed to be. I'll put it on — see? it's the kind of party where people rest on one leg, the other bent and hold a drink with a free hand, a cigarette with another hand. Lots of food, I'm already full. It's the kind of party where it might take a full minute to walk across the room, a big loft. My friends, all girls, have an all-girl rock and roll band and this party is for them, their photographs hanging on the wall. It's the kind of party in which one realizes that where images are made, in New York, that when photographs fade no evidence remains of the food long ago eaten, and now I feel as if I could eat more. But more is there in this case than party food; these girls have an integrity that permeates their life, a strong beat getting stronger, only lower east side puerto rican gutter soul, not this present upper class upper east side wine. The name of the band is Flaming Youth. My dangling leg goes to sleep

40

Don't ever cut your hair, it's too glamorous. I kept thinking I would see your picture in the U Hawaii catalog. (It's very dark in here, except I'm sitting directly underneath the light.) (The record player comes to be drowned out by live tuning up unrelated to the 'slow blues' clanking out of the record player. Colored lights, mike stand, electric feedback. Denise in her leopard shoes says "one, two" in the microphone, electric piano player tests his vibrato through the amplifier.) All the kids pictured were oriental, greenish black & white, I didn't see you. I didn't apply to UH because I had no SAT scores which would have been necessary before Nov. 1st. (The music started can one threat?) Also, the spring semester in Hawaii starts before the Manhattan winter term ends. (large coca cola bottles, the kind with the styrofoam coating "no deposit no refill though they that threw the party pays for the garbage to be disposed of, a big dump somewhere on Staten Island) (A lady from a foreign country who could barely speak english asked me if I was writing an article for a magazine) (The more I see, I find myself wishing it was the fog drifting the mountain, and realize that in a sense it is) (The band is playing their fourth fast number, the party goers sort of bobing up and down loosely with the music) I feel like you sent me the stuff for no reason now. But thanks anyway. (The 'foreign' lady smiled at me and clapped her hands in time to the music.

I should be home working (you see what I might have meant about it taking a minute to get through the room by looking at the last paragraph) on a score and practising for a performance monday in school. (that 'foreign' lady finally couldn't stand it any more and got up and started dancing. Not really knowing how, she sort of steps back and forth to the music. She must be at least fifty, black, and has her hair piled on top of her head. I sort of like her) (I hope that 'foreign' lady (the song just ended) doesn't have a heart attack) (another woman sort of drunkenly asked me if I was writing her biography.)

I'm using my new Pentel super-fine pencil with the extra dark line, I had planned to use it only for scores, but I've been using it for everything, having a full pack of lead confidently in my shoulder bag (the briefcase has been retired.) (there's actually the smell of stage make-up in the air) (it seems that my beginning parentheses are invariably different — shorter than my ending parentheses) (a guy wearing a brown velvet coat just asked, jingling keys or something in his coat pocket, "what's happening?" and a girl sitting down, wearing all denim said "nothing")

Next Day —
At laundromat again, soon it will be December 22. When the band finally came on last night, it was interesting, and I'm sorry for being so opinionated in my write-up. I was just displaced from my "rightful place in line" for the dryers by two people. I'm going to mail this since I had nothing to say in the first place. I'll see you later. Here in N.Y., I guess.

love
Arthur

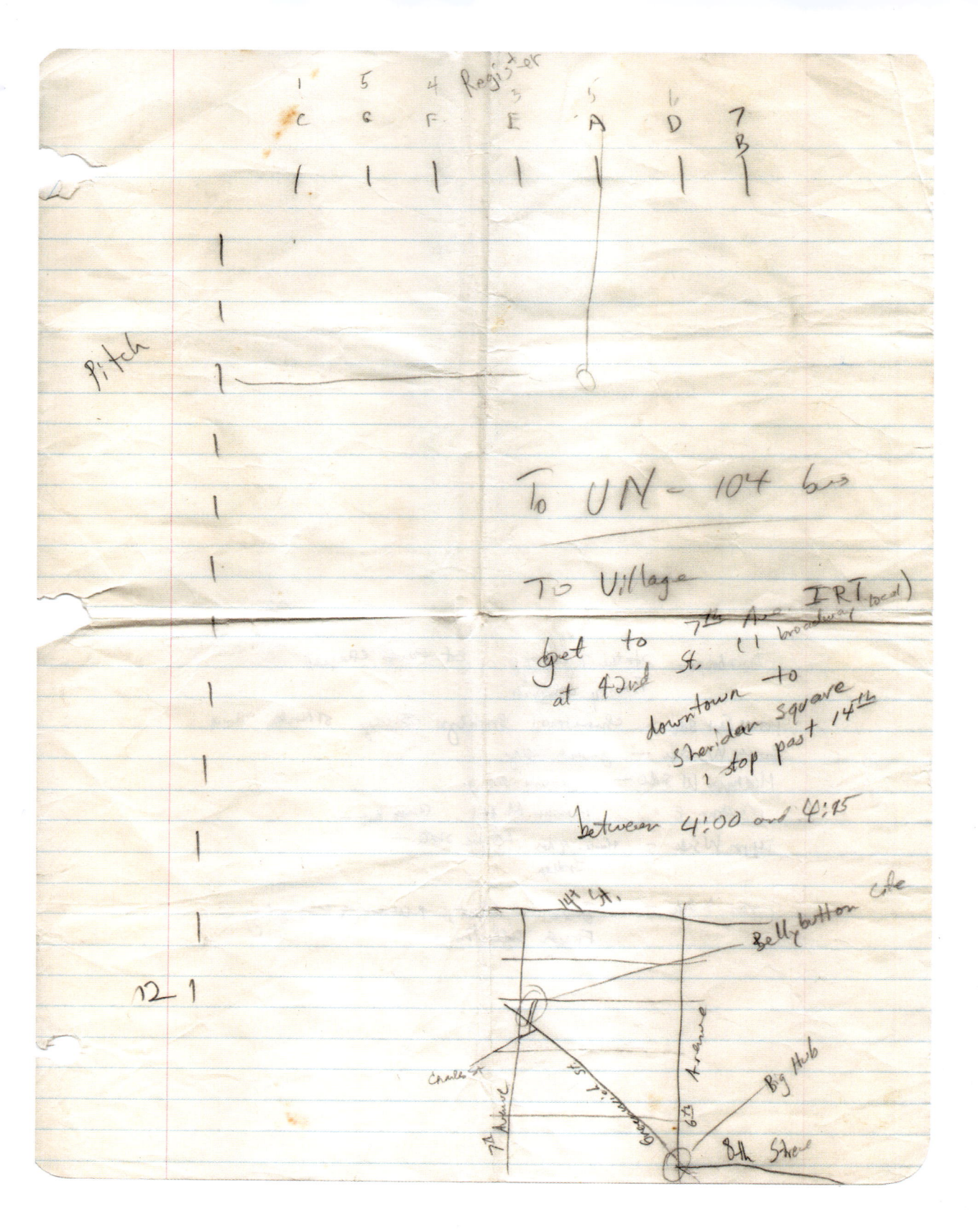

```
    1   5   4  Register  3       5    6
    C   G   F           E       A    D   7
                                         B
    |   |   |           |       |    |  |


    |
pitch
    |


    |                       To UN - 104 bus
    |
    |                       To Village         IRT (local)
                           get to 7th Ave   " broadway
                            at 42nd St.
                                           downtown to
                                          Sheridan Square
                                          1 stop past 14th

    |                       between 4:00 and 4:15

    |
                                        14th St.
                                                      Bellybutton Cafe
12-1
                                                      Big Hub
                              Charles St.
                                                      8th Street
                            7th Avenue
```

Muriel —

Hi, I can not wait. I'm sorry I didn't write you sooner, but last week I was very busy with a piece that was performed at school. I had to play piano in it, and naturally had to work a lot on that. It was the first piece of my own I ever did at the school. The reaction was very strange.

I wrote you a letter about a big party, where a rock band played, a long letter sort of. Did you get it?

later, after phone call

Note (from ancient bottle)

I got a job playing with Alice Coltrane for about two weeks, so I won't be coming back there for a while (but before you leave) It's a tour from Seattle to down here. So will be stopping there.
Take care of ya'self.

love
Arthur

How big is a piece of pie?

Part II

1973-80

Arthur moved to New York City in either late 1972 or early 1973
and gave his address c/o Allen Ginsberg, 408 East Tenth Street.
In correspondence he mentions he was living at the apartment by himself.
The following year Russell stayed at a series of locations, including
some close to the Manhattan School of Music, to which he was admitted
in June 1973. In correspondence to his parents, Arthur emphasises his
dedication to taking classes at the School, possibly with the intention
of securing their ongoing financial support.

L–R: Jack Majewski, Arthur Russell, Laurie Anderson, Scott Johnson, Peter Gordon. An ensemble in which Arthur played drums.

Peter Gordon: 'I first met Arthur at a poetry reading at the Poetry Project at St Mark's Church. Arthur always thought we met at a Cornelius Cardew concert but I'm not sure whether that was right. This was Laurie's band Fast Food. Arthur played drums. I think we might have done a gallery performance or so.'

equal # of loops for
each stein + pound

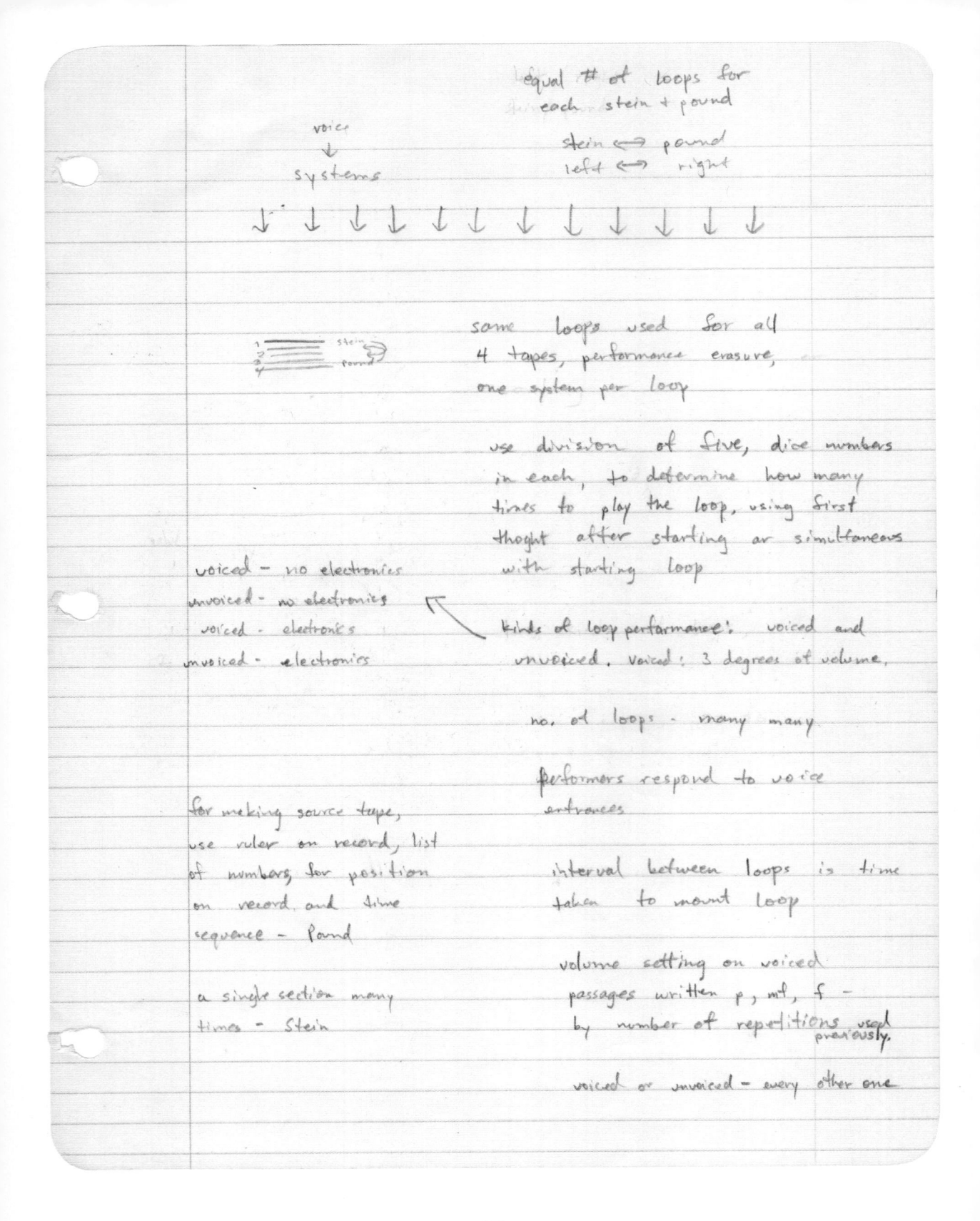

stein ⟷ pound
left ⟷ right

voice
↓
systems

↓ ↓ ↓ ↓ ↓ ↓ ↓ ↓ ↓ ↓

```
1 ─────  stein
2 ─────
3 ─────
4 ─────  pound
```

same loops used for all 4 tapes, performance erasure, one system per loop

use division of five, dice numbers in each, to determine how many times to play the loop, using first thought after starting or simultaneous with starting loop

voiced — no electronics
unvoiced — no electronics
voiced — electronics
unvoiced — electronics

kinds of loop performance: voiced and unvoiced. voiced: 3 degrees of volume,

no. of loops — many many

performers respond to voice entrances

for making source tape, use ruler on record, list of numbers for position on record and time sequence — Pound

interval between loops is time taken to mount loop

volume setting on voiced passages written p, mf, f — by number of repetitions used previously.

a single section many times — Stein

voiced or unvoiced — every other one

Ⓔ Speaker B   Page 5

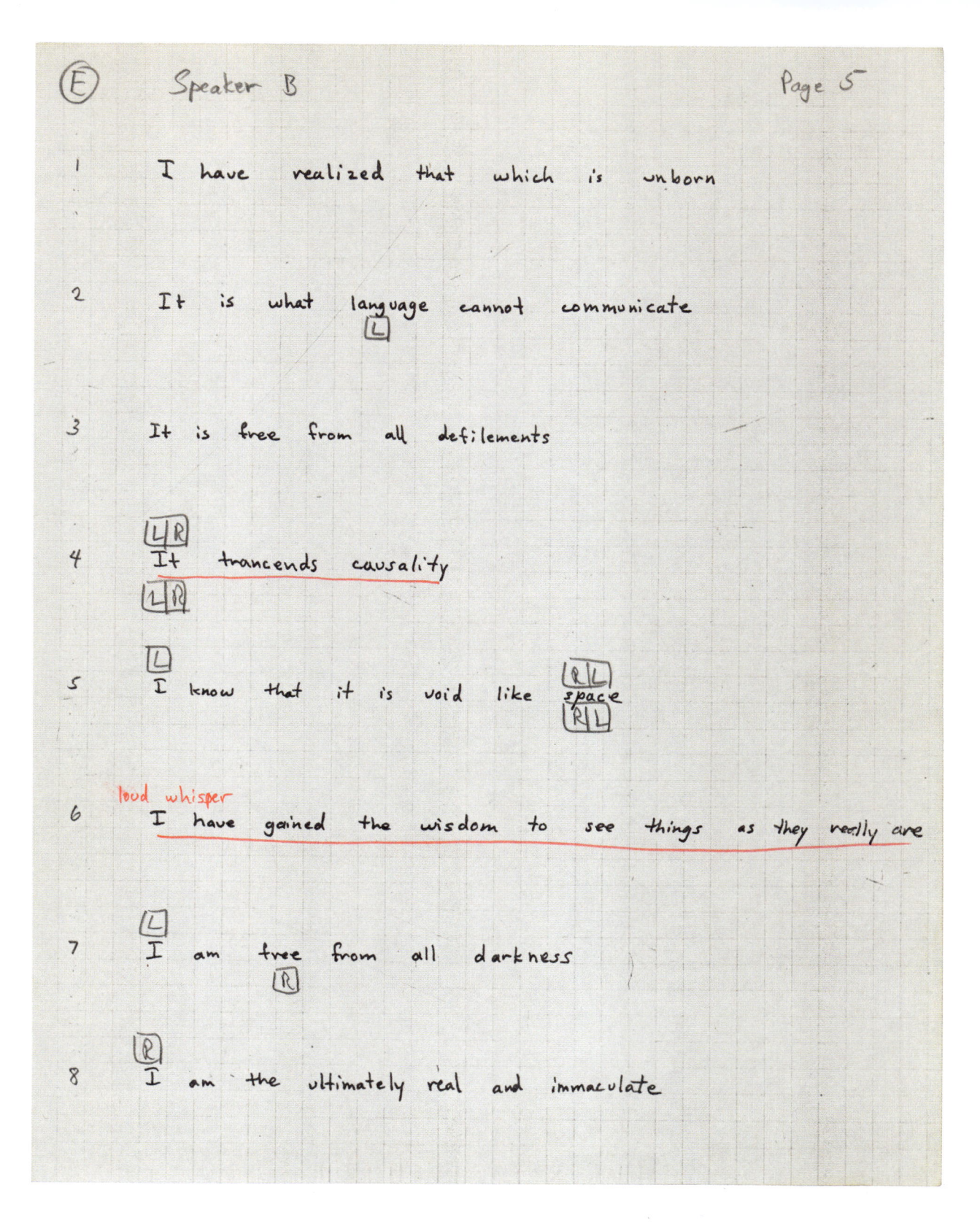

1   I have realized that which is unborn

2   It is what language cannot communicate
                    [L]

3   It is free from all defilements

      [L|R]
4   It trancends causality
      [L|R]

      [L]
5   I know that it is void like [R|L]
                                    space
                                   [R|L]

      loud whisper
6   I have gained the wisdom to see things as they really are

      [L]
7   I am free from all darkness
               [R]

      [R]
8   I am the ultimately real and immaculate

Christian,

    Here's you know what, I hope you can read my writing.
    It's divided in two parts — the Stein/Pound song, a traditional; and City Park, more soloistic. But both are a series of steps, each preceeded by the bass clef sign. (that's how they're separated from each other on the page). As you might remember, each player wears earphones listening to records which have been pre-scratched.
    a number circled indicates number of scratches (③). when music is written with bar lines, a 'measure' is the distance between one scratch & the next.
    I the final 'part', the steps will be represented more or less as you see them here, but arranged on a large sheet of paper divided into sections!

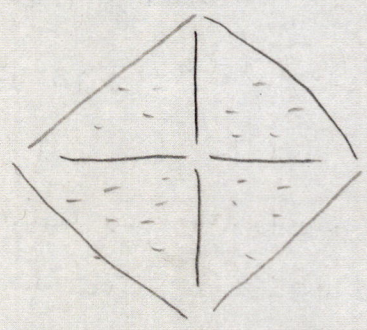

the method used to switch from section to section (between 'steps') is to complex/simple for me to explain here, but it is triggered by the scratches on the record, and may be (?) related to the content of the record. It also relates to every—

(over)

Correspondence between Arthur Russell and Christian Wolff, c.1974, regarding Arthur's studies at Manhattan School of Music.

thing else. I'll explain with my voice, if you want. (I think it would probably be better that way.) Just remember that each step is complete in itself.

I'm sort of embarrassed that you have a scedule you would have to break to come to N.Y.C., but I enjoyed writing the part, and I hope you don't find it too open-ended. Thanks for the interest, any of the steps may be repeated,

                              Arthur

Arthur — perhaps you can still use some of the above instructions. I'm sorry I didn't get to do it, because it looks interesting (and I like to play, especially in a new situation). Tried to phone, but haven't got answer — hoping to hear how the piece worked out. All the best. Will try to do a New York concert in late Spring. Are you still in tune with your 'cello?

                              Christian

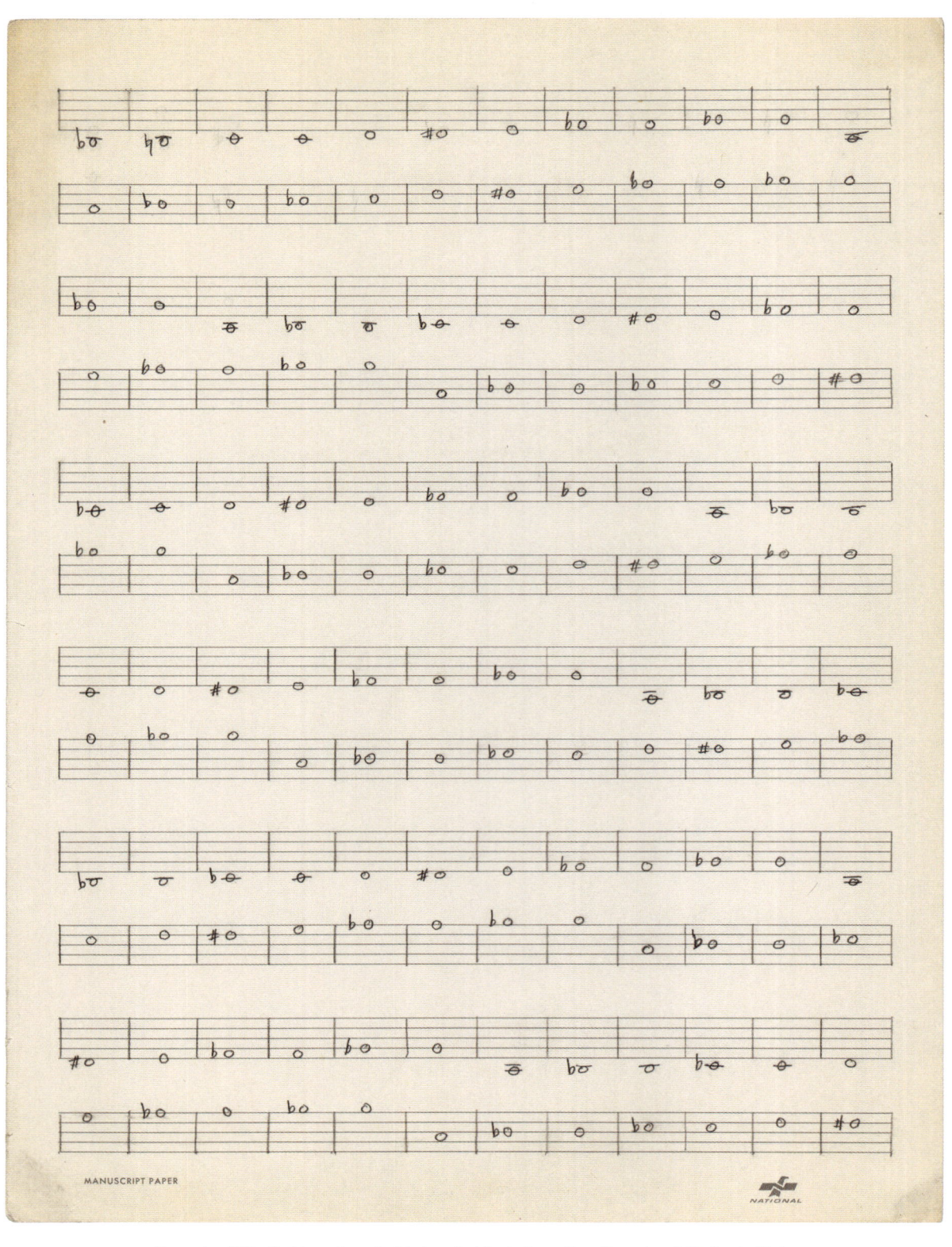

Score for 'City Park', a piece that integrated texts from Ezra Pound and Gertrude Stein with a modular, repetitive score and was intended for broadcast on Columbia University's WKCR radio station.

In an interview Arthur stated: 'I said to [Charles Wuorinen, his composition teacher] the thing that excited me about 'City Park' was that you could pick up the needle anywhere and put it down and it always sounds the same. Not exactly the same, but you could plug into it for as long as you liked, then plug out and then plug back in again without losing anything essential unlike narrative music where your attention is required from beginning to end. He turned to me and said, "That's the most unattractive thing I've ever heard."'

Peter Gordon: 'This score is a way of setting out possible relationships, that something could be composed that's not the tune you're listening to. You'd get different pitch combinations. Arthur was doing a lot of this at the time, it probably came from his studies at the Manhattan School.'

Bill Ruyle: 'This notation of Arthur's was a common way of learning composition that was definitely taught at Manhattan School of Music. It's called species counterpoint, there are species one through five. And species one is having one whole note per measure and then creating a melody that was called a cantus firmus – that's based on a Gregorian chant idea – and then finding notes that harmonise with that cantus firmus in simple polyphony, like two-part harmony. Different rules were arrived at: no parallel fifth; no crossing of parts; no parallel octaves; you can only approach notes in a certain way. I know Arthur was doing that at Manhattan School of Music and I think that knowledge of that kind of system of learning how to write counterpoint somehow influenced his idea of pairing notes together and that's the process he expands later in his work.'

At a Modern Lovers concert at the Townhouse, near Times Square in 1974, Russell met the band's bassist, Ernie Brooks, with whom he quickly started collaborating and founded a group, The Flying Hearts.

That same year, at the age of twenty-three, Russell became musical director of the Kitchen, a video, arts and music space synonymous with the emerging New Music movement. Russell maintained the position for a year. Both he and Brooks lived at the venue intermittently during the course of Russell's tenure. At the Kitchen Russell met a number of musicians he would go on to collaborate, perform and record with throughout his career.

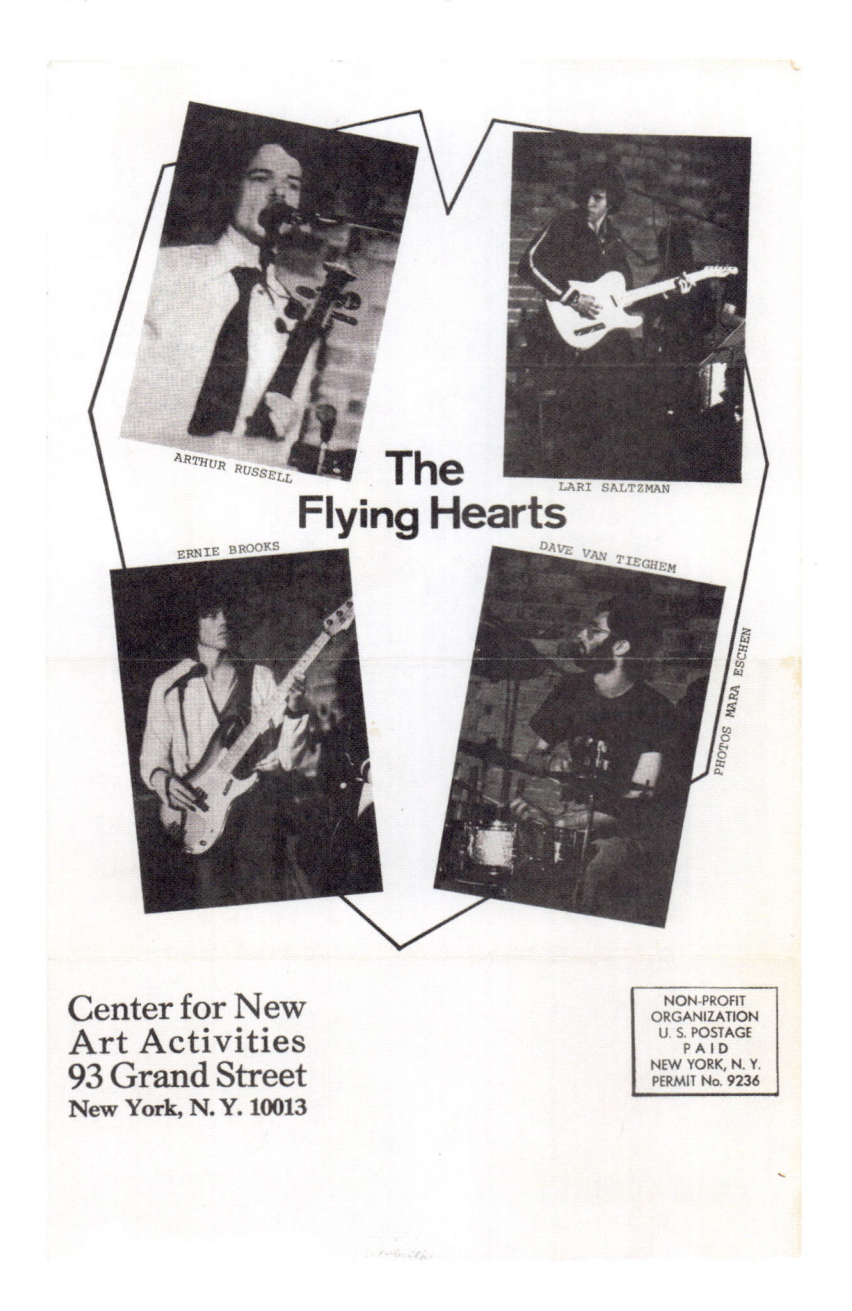

Ernie Brooks: 'The first time I met Arthur was at one of the last Modern Lovers gigs. I always thought there was a big connection between Arthur's song "Time Away" and Jonathan Richman's songs about wanting to meet girls and how he could be in love with them. Another thing they had in common was, if you'd run into them, they would both come up to you and immediately start trying out songs at you; completely different personalities, but both so intense. After that last Modern Lovers gig, Arthur came to see me in Boston and literally moved into my apartment for two weeks and just sat there playing songs.
He asked if I would come down to New York to play and I went to stay with him at the Kitchen. That's how we started playing together. What first got to me about Arthur was the poetry in his lyrics, which seemed to have a similar quality to William Carlos Williams and Robert Creeley. The idea of using simple language to convey something very beautiful.'

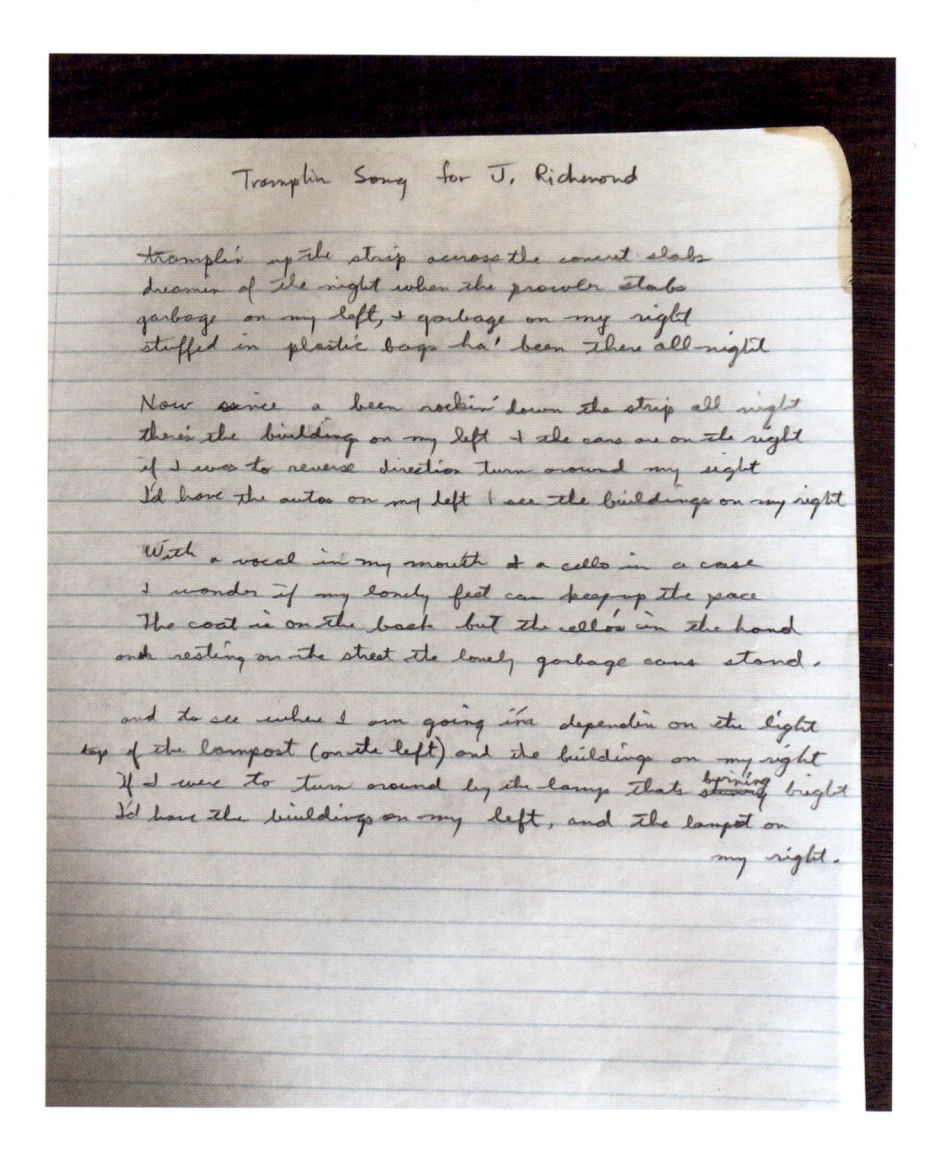

> Ballad of the Lights   Part II
>
> A Young man sits on the bridge
> after night-fall
> and looks across the Hudson to New Jersey.
> He wonders about life
> and he wonders
> if he'll ever get old.
> He sees the lights
> and he wonders if they are talking to each other,
> and he wonders
> if they are talking to him.
> And he asks
> if they are.
>
> His   leisure   hours
> are   spent-in-a-way
> that   mystifies
> his   younger years
>   Thinking hard
> he   has no say
> as-to-what's in his eyes
> or   meets his ears.

'We were in this world of non-profit, arts-funded spaces, a world between people who'd been to music school and people who'd been in the rock world and how it all intertwined. The Flying Hearts also played clubs like the Other End, where we opened for Allen Ginsberg and we performed "Ballad of the Lights" with him. Later on, we also played at the Lower Manhattan Club, but we weren't being showered with gigs. And most of them were free.'

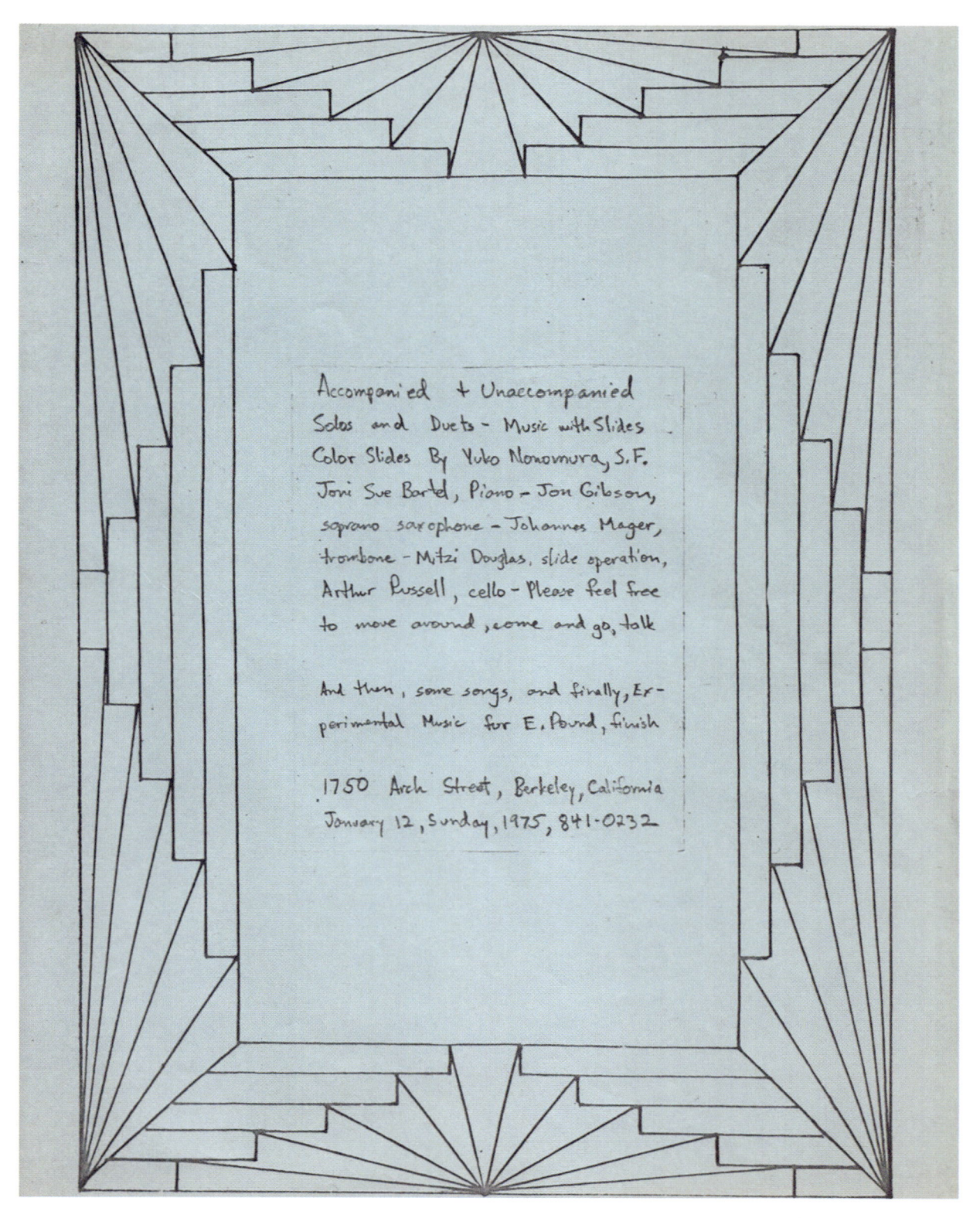

> Accompanied + Unaccompanied Solos and Duets - Music with Slides Color Slides By Yuko Nonomura, S.F. Joni Sue Bartel, Piano - Jon Gibson, soprano saxophone - Johannes Mager, trombone - Mitzi Douglas, slide operation, Arthur Russell, cello - Please feel free to move around, come and go, talk
>
> And then, some songs, and finally, Experimental Music for E. Pound, finish
>
> 1750 Arch Street, Berkeley, California
> January 12, Sunday, 1975, 841-0232

'Please feel free to move around, come and go, talk.'
A return to 1750 Arch Street, Berkeley, California, January 1975.

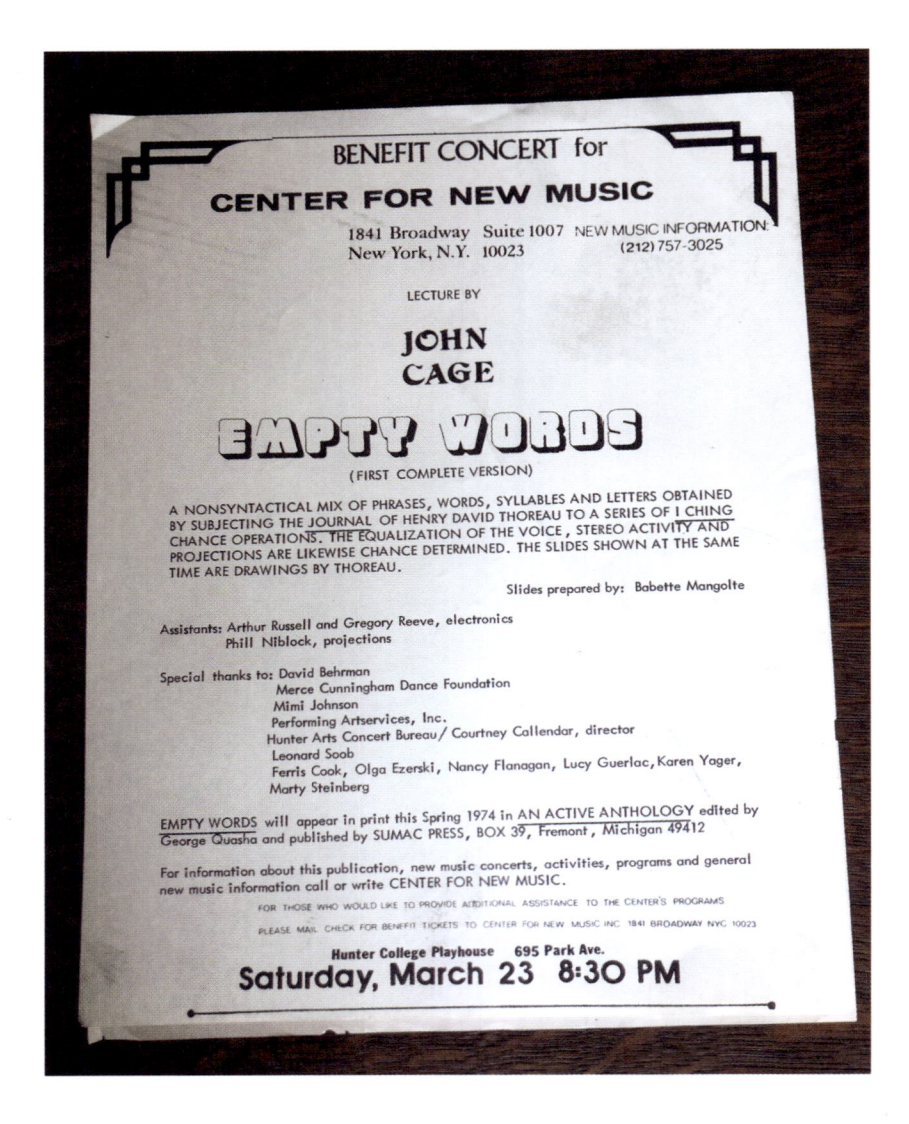

In March 1975, Arthur and several of the musicians he'd met through the Kitchen – including Peter Gordon and Ernie Brooks – took part in a recording session with producer John Hammond and engineer Stan Tonkel at CBS Studios. The offer of this session had been one of the main motivating factors in Russell's relocation to New York from California. The session, which had been postponed, is referred to in a letter from Arthur's father, who offers his son the advice to 'push, but not too hard'.

> Kate Russell: 'My father was a very, very sensitive man, it was hard for him to have a relationship with Arthur, because it was hard to communicate with him, to find a common language. And so, my father found a common language in a business relationship with him. My father was giving him money to help him musically, and my father regretted not giving him more money. But at the time, with this business relationship, he was concerned for Arthur that it wasn't a good business, he wasn't going to be profitable, he was throwing good money after bad.'

CHARLES A. RUSSELL AGENCY
CHUCK RUSSELL - JACK LAMBERSON - ED BUTLER
105 SOUTH MARKET ST.
DIAL: 515 - 673-7376 — OSKALOOSA, IOWA 52577

P.I.C.
PROFESSIONAL INSURANCE COUNSELORS, INC.
(FORMERLY CHARLES A. RUSSELL AGENCY)
Chuck Russell - Jack Lamberson - Ed Butler, C.P.C.U.
105 South Market St. Phone (515) 673-7376
OSKALOOSA, IOWA 52577

(Stamp: NOTHING Has Changed But The NAME)

Your Independent Insurance Agent Serves You First

2-21-75

Arthur Russell
c/o The Kitchen
59 Wooster St.
New York, N.Y. 10012

P.S. Sorry that your recording session was postponed today till 3-12-75. Push but not too hard.

Re: Leasing apt. in New York $1,500 + $300 gift

Here, Arthur, is a check for $1,800 — drawn to you. $1,500 is to be paid back on June 1, 1975 and the $300 is a gift and not to be paid back. It's obvious that the $1,500 represents 100% of your "Fixture Fee" and not the %'age you said you would "Take you up on your 60% offer." I would suggest you took me up on a good deal more (60% of 1500 = 900) Anyway if your not being taken and I'm not being taken then it's a great thing for you and us. As you say you can do a lot more at home — cook, practice comfortably, nearer to work, more secure with your burglar alarm. Good showers, refridgerator, and cook stove. If a table is included then you'll even get off the floor. Instead of the present tennant taking his chairs, bed, rugs, etc, etc, it would be much cheaper for him and you if you would pay him a nominal amt. for them.

It's my understanding that your paying $1,500 to lessee, Steve, $225 security payment and $225 first months rent (April 1975) for a total of $1,500 + $225 + $225 = $1,950. Then in May and each month thereafter you would owe $225 —

A $180/week salary isn't much to pay $225 plus all expenses (elec, heat, etc.) even though you save on eats. Good Luck

Love
Daddy, Chuck

Tom Lee: 'Arthur's dad was business-like but very pursuant of what was going on in Arthur's musical career. His mom was a little more distant, she maybe took the tack of telling Arthur what was happening back home with neighbours and family. At that time she wasn't so emotionally connected. It was still the era of convention. He was a puzzle to his parents. And in retrospect they were very enamoured of what happened, but the fact he'd run away – I get the sense that they were doing the very best they could to help him but it was puzzling to them what was required. A lot of his responses towards them were about how much he was working, he would be promising them he was getting somewhere. He couched everything in terms of what they might want to hear: "I'm taking the cello to get it fixed," "I've met someone at a record company; he seems like a good guy," "I'm taking classes at Columbia."'

Ernie Brooks: 'I knew Arthur's father was giving him money. I was coming from a similar place; I didn't go to graduate school and quickly got into the rock and roll world. If I hadn't stumbled into a cheap rent-controlled loft in Long Island City I would have been destitute.'

```
TO:      Marilyn & Diane
FROM:    Old Liz
DATE:    February 19, 1975
RE:      AUDITION TIME - ARTHUR RUSSELL

This is a confirmation of time booked to audition Arthur Russell in
Studio E, on Friday, February 21, 1975. John Hammond, producer.
Stan Tonkel, engineer.

Setup is incomplete, but we expect at least 6 musicians and track will
probably be mono.

Arthur Russell has been notified of this time and he is responsible for
notifying his musicians.
```

Peter Gordon: 'These were the first recording sessions I did in New York; I'd just moved to town. I was on it, Ernie Brooks, Andy Paley on drums, Garrett List on trombone, Jon Gibson on saxes, Jerry Harrison. I think Stan Tonkel had worked a lot with Teo Macero on Miles Davis recordings. Hammond was expecting, what he wanted to do, was what he did with Springsteen before and Dylan before that: he wanted Arthur to come in with a guitar and play through thirty songs, something like that. So he was a little impatient with us; this was John Hammond who recorded Count Basie and Billie Holiday and he was kind of an imposing figure.'

I'll close my eyes and listen
to hear the corn come out   (darlin')
don't you hear the stars, they glisten
as we go in and out.

(chorus) Will the corn be growing a little tonight
as I wait in the fields for you
Who knows what grows in the morning light
when we can feel the watery dew.

Down where the trees grow together
and the western path comes to an end
see the sign - it says "Clear Weather"
I'll meet you tonight, my friend.

(chorus)

I just can't be there with no other
I know those hills will be true
away from my sisters and brothers
Down through the grasses so new

The air is sweet and steady
and flowers bloom out of sight
I know the sky is ready
Come meet me down here tonight

(chorus)

The fence will not be broken
Our reach will reach just right
The tones that cannot be spoken
will come in the fields tonight

Eli, Eli

Eli, Eli

This arrangement can be superimposed on the same song in Skeleton Songbook

Eli — Eli — Eli — E — A simple dog with ears and nose

I don't know why nobody likes him — there's some people trying to put him away

when he comes up to them they always say go a way go a way please

take him home make him stay

Maybe she would take a walk

even though I just have met her
Together we could maybe talk

or maybe I should just forget her

the only thing she could say is no

best try now when the sky is lighter
I'll just let my feelings show

I'll just go up and invite her.

She might think I'm very strange,
She might think I want to date her,

That would be hard to arrange
Maybe I should ask her later.

Wonder if she knows I'm scared.
Does she know I'm glad to meet her?

Voting with my feelings bared
She'll know when I start to greet her

I'd be cool if she'd refuse
She might think that I don't fit her
I won't show it if I lose
won't be sad I won't be bitter

(margin:) What do any seem to say
Better than just looking at her
So just look into her eye
If she won't come it doesn't matter.

That's what's important to me now

E / C#m / | B / / / | E / E7 / | A / / / |

F#m / B / | E / / / (C#m) (E7) | A / A7 / | D B° / / |

E / B / | C#m / B/D# / | E (A6/4) / / / | (A6/4) / / / / |

I know him real well

chorus   Cm / G / | Cm / Fm / | Eb / D / | G7 / / / | 2x

verse   Cm / G / | Ab/Bb Bb / Cm | Eb / D(7) / | G / / / |

Cm [Ab] / / | Fm Bb Cm / | Fm/G / / / | G / / / |

---

sly out on the street

F / / / | / / / / | Bb / C / | F / [Bb/F] F / |

B / G / | Bb / / / | F / F/G / | G |

F / G / | C / / [G] | F / / / | C / / / |

---

couldn't say it to your face

2/4 Bb/F / | F / | Gm / F / | / / | Bb/F / | F / | Gm / F / |

Gm [C] / / / | Am [Bb] / / / | Bb/F / | F / | Gm / F / | / / |

verse: 2/4 F Dm | / / 3/4 | Am Bb C 2/4 | Eb / | / / |

Am F | / / 3/4 | Dm Bb Am 2/4 | Gm / | C / | / / |

Arthur had been inspired to compose INSTRUMENTALS in 1974, by the photography of his Buddhist teacher, Yuko Nonomura, which attests to the teacher's lingering influence. Arthur wrote he had been 'awakened, or re-awakened to the bright-sound and magical qualities of the bubble gum and easy-listening currents in American popular music'. He had originally intended INSTRUMENTALS to be a major composition performed in one forty-eight-hour cycle; also it was subsequently only performed a handful of times as a work in progress.

INSTRUMENTALS was conceived as a modular piece, in which separate passages of notated melody could be played at random by an improvising ensemble. In a concert setting this form of indeterminacy would allow for a small section of the work to grow into an entire performance; it also ensured that each performance would have its own distinct characteristics and musical elements.

Slides taken by Arthur's Buddhist teacher Yuko Nonomura intended to be projected during performances of INSTRUMENTALS.

ARTHUR RUSSELL - INSTRUMENTALS

Garrett List   Andy Paley   Rhys Chatham
Peter Gordon   Ernie Brooks   Arthur Russell
Jon Sholle   Jon Gibson   Dave Van Tieghem

April 27, 1975 at the Kitchen, 59 Wooster Street, NYC, 8:30 PM, 925-3615, N.Y.S.C.A.

Peter Gordon: 'I'm guessing we did four or five three-hour rehearsals for the INSTRUMENTALS show. I think it was set up at the Kitchen and we'd rehearse during the week and then go and do the show. Arthur was focused on his work, but there were two separate things: for John Hammond he was playing his songs, and then he was also making instrumental music. A lot of the musicians who played at this concert were on the John Hammond sessions. It's pretty much the same band. INSTRUMENTALS was also a way of working out orchestral ideas; as musical director of the Kitchen, in one sense this was part of his day job.'

Ernie Brooks: 'My friend said this performance of INSTRUMENTALS was the best music to take psychedelic drugs to. It was a big sea of sound and we were all different levels of musicians. Jon Gibson and Garrett List were amazing musicians, there were these illustrious musicians and rock and rollers like me, that were struggling to count the changes. The tricky thing about INSTRUMENTALS is because of the methodology of how it was written you get these really odd chord changes. You get five beats then two beats then three beats. I always think of a car struggling up a hill to get into a new gear. Even though the beat stays the same it feels like the speed slows down and speeds up.'

ARTHUR RUSSELL - INSTRUMENTALS

Garrett List Andy Paley Rhys Chatham
Peter Gordon Ernie Brooks Arthur Russell
Jon Sholle Jon Gibson Dave Van Tieghem

April 27, 1975 at the Kitchen, 59 Wooster Street, NYC, 8:30 PM, 925-3615, N.Y.S.C.A.

the kitchen
center for video and music

ENSEMBLE MUSIC BY JON GIBSON   May 16 & 17, 1975

SONG II (1974)

    Barbara Benary..........Violin
    Jon Gibson..............Flute
    Arthur Russell..........Cello
    Ruth Siegler............Viola
    Tom Thies...............Bass Violin
    David Van Tieghem.......Marimba

UNTITLED (FOR FLUTE AND TROMBONE) (1974-1975)

    Jon Gibson..............C flute and G Alto Flute
    Garrett List............Trombone

THIRTY-TWO AGAINST ELEVEN (1974)
    (formerly SOLO FOR SOPRANO SAXOPHONE)

    Jon Gibson..............Soprano Saxophone
    Michael Riesman.........Piano
    Nancy Topf..............Dance

-Intermission-

MELODY (1972,1975)   Parts A, B, I, II, III

    Barbara Benary..........Violin
    Jon Gibson..............Alto Saxophone
    Garrett List............Trombone
    Michael Riesman.........Double Manal Organ
    Arthur Russell..........Cello
    Ruth Siegler............Viola
    Tom Thies...............Bass Violin
    David Van Tieghem.......Vibraphone

    Kurt Munkasci...........Technical Assistance

On the Walter Series and with assistance from Meet The Composer, The National Endowment for the Arts, and Creative Artists Public Service Program.

Special thanks to Philip Glass and Dickie Landry.

59 wooster street / new york city, 10012 / (212) 925 3615

During 1975, Russell and Rhys Chatham, another composer and former musical director of the Kitchen, shared an address at 437 East Twelfth Street, a building in which Allen Ginsberg owned two apartments and whose residents included several poets, among them Richard Hell, then a member of the band Television. That same year Russell would debut his piece INSTRUMENTALS at the Kitchen, a compositional work he would revisit throughout the decade, and which helped forge his reputation as a gifted composer.

The artists couple Steina and Woody Vasulka had founded the Kitchen arts space as a centre for video art in June 1971. Its first location was at Mercer Arts Center, in the former Broadway Central Hotel in Greenwich Village, Manhattan. Rhys Chatham was made musical director the following year, and in 1973 the Kitchen relocated to 59 Wooster Street, where it gained a reputation for video art, performance and as an emerging centre of New Music. As Musical Director for the 1974–5 season, Russell was required to programme the centre's dedicated musical performance space.

Peter Gordon: 'I would see Arthur at the Kitchen a lot. I had heard about it before moving to New York City. In a way it was a bit of a clubhouse. I would perform there every other year. The first set of people I met in New York were at the Kitchen. Steina and Woody Vasulka were video artists and that was really the origin of the Kitchen: music was always connected but video was its thing.'

Peter Zummo: 'I met Arthur in I think the fall of '75 or early '76. I had been in a band in the early seventies named Sunship. I think Peter Gordon and Arthur were aware of the record. No one else had heard it. It's possible we met at the Kitchen; my entry to creative work in New York City was through dance and some artists older than me. Peter was starting what would become Love of Life Orchestra. It was a big band rehearsal situation, a rock rhythm section. There was one studio we used on the corner of Westbeth; I suspect Arthur heard me play there. I had a loft on Twenty-Second Street and that's where he started showing up and yelling for me.'

Jill Kroesen: 'Peter Gordon and I came up to New York from Mills College together. It took about five minutes to get involved with music. It happened really quickly for Peter as well. At that time everyone was so open to everybody, it was an amazing moment if you were an artist and you got there; they opened their arms to you. I don't know where I met Arthur, either at the Kitchen or somebody's gig.'

Lucy Sante: 'I went to the Kitchen all the time, because there were so many different things going on there. When Rhys Chatham became the musical director, it took on a whole new tone, became much less chilly in that way. Earlier, though, it wasn't so much academic as that kind of anti-pleasure business that surrounded conceptual art in the early seventies. It was not materialistic in any way. I saw the Art Ensemble of Chicago there at least three times, saw John Cage perform, saw all kinds of things. I have a distinct physical memory of sitting on those wooden floors on these thin green foam cushions with a sore butt afterwards.'

484 BROOME ST.
TUESDAY THRU SATURDAY 1PM-6PM

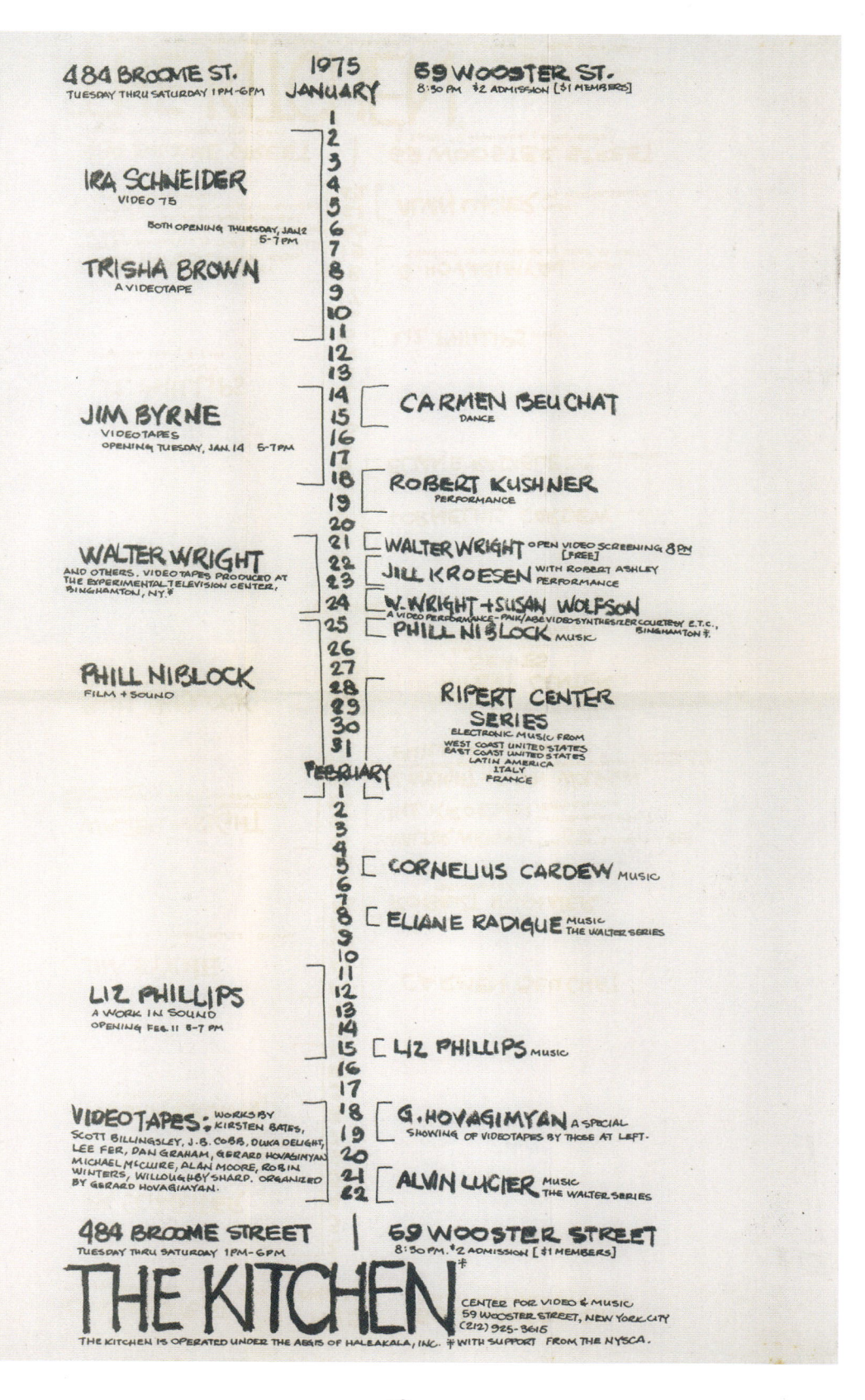

1975 JANUARY

59 WOOSTER ST.
8:30 PM $2 ADMISSION [$1 MEMBERS]

1
2
3
4
5
6
7
8
9
10
11
12
13
14
15
16
17
18
19
20
21
22
23
24
25
26
27
28
29
30
31

IRA SCHNEIDER
VIDEO 75
BOTH OPENING THURSDAY, JAN 2 5-7PM

TRISHA BROWN
A VIDEOTAPE

JIM BYRNE
VIDEOTAPES
OPENING TUESDAY, JAN.14 5-7PM

[**CARMEN BEUCHAT** DANCE

[**ROBERT KUSHNER** PERFORMANCE

WALTER WRIGHT
AND OTHERS. VIDEOTAPES PRODUCED AT THE EXPERIMENTAL TELEVISION CENTER, BINGHAMTON, NY.#

[**WALTER WRIGHT** OPEN VIDEO SCREENING 8PM [FREE]
[**JILL KROESEN** WITH ROBERT ASHLEY PERFORMANCE
[**W. WRIGHT + SUSAN WOLFSON** A VIDEO PERFORMANCE - PAIK/ABE VIDEO SYNTHESIZER COURTESY E.T.C. BINGHAMTON #
[**PHILL NIBLOCK** MUSIC

PHILL NIBLOCK
FILM + SOUND

RIPERT CENTER SERIES
ELECTRONIC MUSIC FROM
WEST COAST UNITED STATES
EAST COAST UNITED STATES
LATIN AMERICA
ITALY
FRANCE

FEBRUARY
1
2
3
4
5
6
7
8
9
10
11
12
13
14
15
16
17
18
19
20
21
22

[**CORNELIUS CARDEW** MUSIC

[**ELIANE RADIGUE** MUSIC THE WALTER SERIES

LIZ PHILLIPS
A WORK IN SOUND
OPENING FEB. 11 5-7 PM

[**LIZ PHILLIPS** MUSIC

VIDEOTAPES. WORKS BY KIRSTEN BATES, SCOTT BILLINGSLEY, J.B. COBB, DUKA DELIGHT, LEE FER, DAN GRAHAM, GERARD HOVAGIMYAN, MICHAEL MCCLURE, ALAN MOORE, ROBIN WINTERS, WILLOUGHBY SHARP. ORGANIZED BY GERARD HOVAGIMYAN.

[**G. HOVAGIMYAN** A SPECIAL SHOWING OF VIDEOTAPES BY THOSE AT LEFT.

[**ALVIN LUCIER** MUSIC THE WALTER SERIES

484 BROOME STREET
TUESDAY THRU SATURDAY 1PM-6PM

59 WOOSTER STREET
8:30 PM. $2 ADMISSION [$1 MEMBERS]

THE KITCHEN *

CENTER FOR VIDEO & MUSIC
59 WOOSTER STREET, NEW YORK CITY
(212) 925-3615

THE KITCHEN IS OPERATED UNDER THE AEGIS OF HALEAKALA, INC. # WITH SUPPORT FROM THE NYSCA.

484 BROOME
TUES-SAT 1-6 PM

SPECIAL SHOWING OF VIDEOTAPES BY KIRSTEN BATES, SCOTT BILLINGSLEY, J.B. COBB, SUSAN ENSLEY, DAN GRAHAM, JULIA HEYWARD, G. HOVA-GIMYAN, MICHAEL McCLARD, DICK MILLER, JOOST A. ROMEU, WILLOUGHBY SHARP, ROBERT KINGSTON WINTERS, JR.

SIMONE FORTI
VIDEOTAPES:
"GRIZZLEYS"
"SOLO #1"
OPENING FEBRUARY 26
5-7 PM

DAVIDSON GIGLIOTTI
"HUNTER MOUNTAIN TWO"
TWO 3-CHANNEL VIDEO PIECES AND 780 DRAWINGS.

VIDEOTAPES:
MARTHA ROSSLER
"SEMIOTICS OF THE KITCHEN"
"A BUDDING GOURMET"
AND
ALAN SEKULA
"TALK GIVEN BY MR. FRED LUX AT THE LUX CLOCK MFG. CO. PLANT, LEBANON, TENN. ON WED. SEPT. 15, 1954."

BERYL KOROT
ONE FOUR CHANNEL AND ONE ONE CHANNEL VIDEO WORKS.

FEBRUARY
18
19
20
21
22
23
24
25
26
27
28

MARCH
1
2
3
4
5
6
7
8
9
10
11
12
13
14
15
16
17
18
19
20
21
22
23
24
25
26
27
28
29
30

59 WOOSTER
8:30 PM $2 $1 MEMBERS

KIRSTEN BATES, J.B. COBB, DAN GRAHAM, G. HOVAGIMYAN, MICHAEL McCLARD, JOOST A. ROMEU, WILLOUGHBY SHARP.

SCOTT BILLINGSLEY, SUSAN ENSLEY, JULIA HEYWARD, DICK MILLER, ROBERT KINGSTON WINTERS, JR.

ALVIN LUCIER STILL AND MOVING LINES OF SILENCE IN FAMILIES OF HYPERBOLAS (1973-74). THE WALTER SERIES AND WITH ASSISTANCE FROM MEET THE COMPOSER.

AMY GREENFIELD NEW VIDEODANCE: COMPLETE AND IN PROGRESS TAPES, PLUS VIDEO PERFORMANCE EXPERIMENT W/BEN DOLPHIN, ANN McINTOSH AND RICKY LEACOCK.

AMY GREENFIELD LECTURE/DEMONSTRATION ON THE MEDIA OF VIDEODANCE AND FILMDANCE. SELECTED WORK FROM 1969-PRESENT.

JULIUS EASTMAN
MORTON FELDMAN
MARCEL DUCHAMP (1913)
PETR KOTIK
JOHN CAGE
THE S.E.M. ENSEMBLE PERFORMS

THE MODERN LOVERS RETURN TO NEW YORK CITY
MUSIC

CONNIE BECKLEY WORKS IN SOUND PERFORMED BY VOICE, RECORDED VOICE, ELECTRONICS & PLAYER PIANO.

THE SCHIZOPHRENIC COALITION WITH THE "MAD" PEOPLE'S UNION. (TAPED & LIVE) PRODUCED BY LEE ROSS.

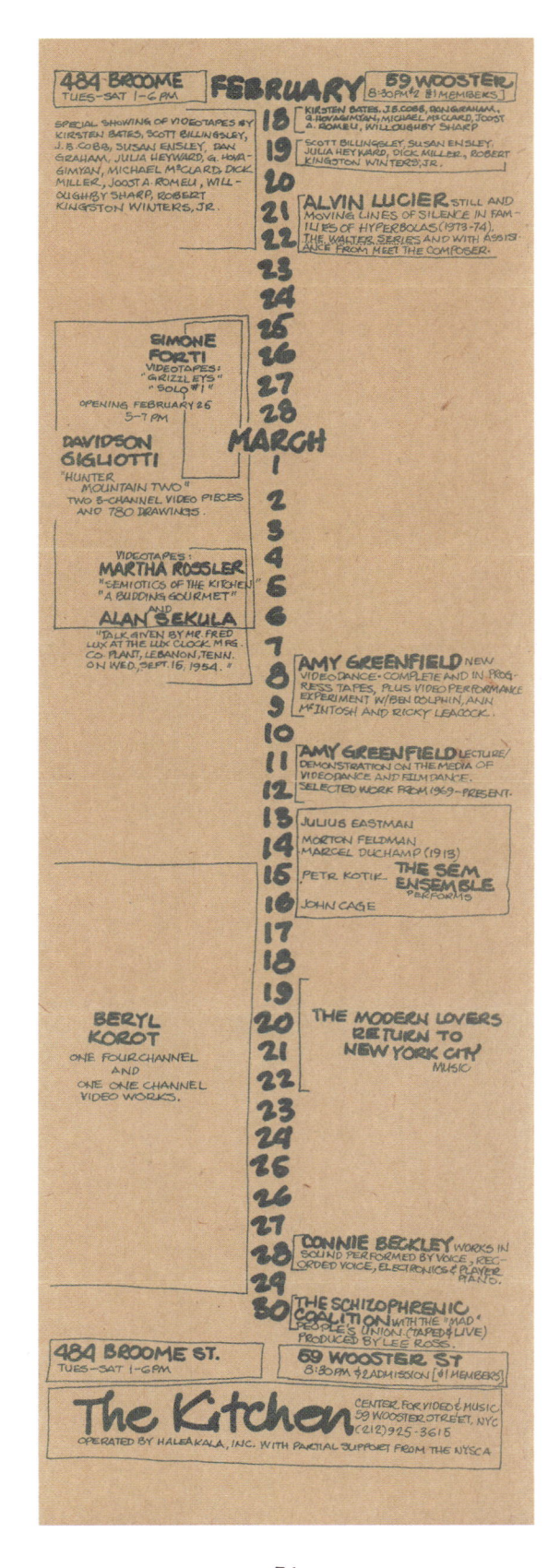

484 BROOME ST.
TUES-SAT 1-6 PM

59 WOOSTER ST
8:30 PM $2 ADMISSION ($1 MEMBERS)

The Kitchen
CENTER FOR VIDEO & MUSIC
59 WOOSTER STREET, NYC
(212) 925-3615
OPERATED BY HALEAKALA, INC. WITH PARTIAL SUPPORT FROM THE NYSCA

exhibitions
484 broome st/tues-sat 1-6pm

eleanor antin — MAY 6-10 VIDEOTAPES: The Ballerina and the Bum (b/w, 54 min.) and The Little Match Girl Ballet (color, 27 min.) Tapes courtesy The Video Distribution, Inc.

jim rosenberg — MAY 7-10 Permanent and Temporary Poetry. An exhibition in conjunction with Jim Rosenberg's concert. See below.

peter campus — MAY 20-24 VIDEOTAPES: His first tape, Dynamic Field Series (1971, b/w, 30 min., courtesy Electronic Arts Intermix, Inc.) and his latest tape, Set of Co-Incidence (1974, color, 13 min., courtesy Castelli-Sonnabend Films & Tapes, Inc.)

steve reich — MAY 20-24 AUDIO AND/OR VIDEOTAPES: An audiotape of his Work in Progress for 21 musicians and singers and videotapes of Clapping Music and Music for Pieces of Wood. An exhibition in conjunction with the concert series by Steve Reich and Musicians. See below.

shigeko kubota — MAY 30-JUNE 7 VIDEO EXHIBITION: Video Poem. "This is my video diary. I found myself in video."

concert events
59 wooster st/$2 ($1 members)

peggy cicierska & andy mannik — SATURDAY MAY 3 8:30PM / SUNDAY MAY 4 3:00PM Five new dance pieces by Peggy Cicierska with live video by Andy Mannik.

jim rosenberg — SATURDAY MAY 10 8:30PM Permanent and Temporary Poetry. A concert of word compositions for Prepared Space, single and mixed voices.

rhys chatham — SUNDAY MAY 11 3:00PM New Leaves. A scored composition for Jim Burton, Jon Deak, Jill Kroesen and Garrett List.

david behrman — TUESDAY MAY 13 8:30PM / WEDNESDAY MAY 14 8:30PM New Music. A concert of live acoustic and electronic music.

jon gibson — FRIDAY MAY 16 8:30PM / SATURDAY MAY 17 8:30PM Ensemble Music. A concert of new works presented on the Walter Series and with assistance from "Meet the Composer," a program of the American Music Center.

steve reich and musicians — TUESDAY MAY 20 9:00PM / WEDNESDAY MAY 21 9:00PM / FRIDAY MAY 23 9:00PM / SATURDAY MAY 24 9:00PM Work in Progress for 21 musicians and singers, Violin Phase (1967) for four violins and Music for Pieces of Wood. A concert on the Walter Series.

the kitchen
59 wooster st/484 broome st/nyc
212 925 3615

with support from the nysca

SYMPHONY
IN FOUR MOVEMENTS (MUSIC: WORDS)

by PETER GORDON

Performed with:

Kathy Acker   Rhys Chatham   Jill Kroesen
Laurie Anderson   Philip Glass   Garrett List
Jim Burton   Scott Johnston   Charlie Morrow
Bob Bielecki   Keshavan Maslak   Arthur Russell

Wed. February 4th 8:30 p.m.
at THE KITCHEN
484 Broome St., NYC — $2 (#1 members)

supported in part by grants from NEA and NYSCA

Jill Kroesen: 'I never saw Arthur as having any kind of ego problem; he was happy to play in other people's groups and performances. I always think of him as slinking back into the shadows and just sort of being there. We rehearsed, we recorded, we went to everyone else's gigs. That was what we just did.
I had so many concerts by my friends to go to that I neglected to go see other things. The audience would be 50 per cent made up of people who knew or who were friends of who was playing, Things were cheap and there were weird jobs to do. It was the luckiest thing ever.

'Everybody would play with everybody else. Peter was one of the people who brought everyone together and was very generous; when he had a record contract he brought his friends along.'

ARTHUR RUSSELL

featuring
ARTHUR RUSSELL, voice cello perc.

Sobossek's
Bowery between Fifth and Sixth
Tuesday March 30
9:00 PM
FREE

Peter Gordon: 'Rhys Chatham was the barman at Sobossek's and he organised these series of concerts by his friends. He had me play happy music on a piano, then at a certain point he'd say, "I want to go home," then I would go into atonal variations. He was really impressed I could clear the place in fifteen minutes, having built up some good tips beforehand. Often there was hardly anybody there. Arthur would feed you songs like "Eli" and "My Sister Knows the Saddest People". It wasn't upbeat bar music that one would necessarily expect. Sobossek himself was a painter, modern figurative stuff, and his work covered the walls. It looked like it had already been there for years. Rhys worked first as a busboy in the kitchen before becoming the bartender.

'Everything was very local between Fourteenth Street and Houston, between Bowery East and Avenue B. This was right before SoHo became SoHo. It was empty at night. You could walk down the street and not see a person anywhere, but you could hear Ornette Coleman coming out of the window of his loft on Prince Street. One of the first things I did with Arthur was when we played with Henry Flynt at 80 Wooster Street, right across from the Kitchen when it was on Wooster. It was all geographically very local. A lot of working relationships with film-makers, artists, people working as bartenders or bussing tables as well were all part of the same community.'

Lucy Sante: 'There were people who never left. There were people who were afraid of going north of Fourteenth Street.'

NOTICE TO DERMATOLOGY PATIENTS

Please note that the Dermatology Clinic is now located within the NORTH TOWER ADDITION to the Main Hospital. Please reference the enclosed materials for assistance in locating Main Hospital Registration where you need to register for this and all subsequent appointments with the Department of Dermatology.

F IOWA
OWA 52242

7, 1976

3/76

Emily: Send this to Charley for her confirmation 7-8-76

Dear Mr. Russell:

An appointment has been rescheduled for you with:

Department of Dermatology--Dr. Radcliffe
on Aug 2, 1976 at 11:00 A.M.

Upon arrival at University Hospitals, please report to the General Hospital Registration. The diagram on the reverse side of this letter will assist you in locating that area of the hospital. Please plan to arrive at the Registration area approximately thirty minutes prior to your appointment time. If you are not able to accept your appointment, please inform the above named department in writing or by telephoning 356-2274 (Area 319).

To confirm your acceptance of this appointment and assist with your preregistration, please complete the enclosed PATIENT REGISTRATION INFORMATION form and return it in the enclosed envelope at the earliest opportunity. Because this information will be used to prepare your medical record, it should be typed or printed. If you have a Hospitalization Insurance Policy, please bring the policy and claim forms with you. You will need to discuss them with the Business Office Personnel after your appointment.

We are looking forward to serving you and will do everything possible to accommodate you during your visit to University Hospitals.

Sincerely,

Mrs. Beverly A. Yoder

(Mrs.) Beverly A. Yoder
Admissions Supervisor

BY/sd

Enclosures

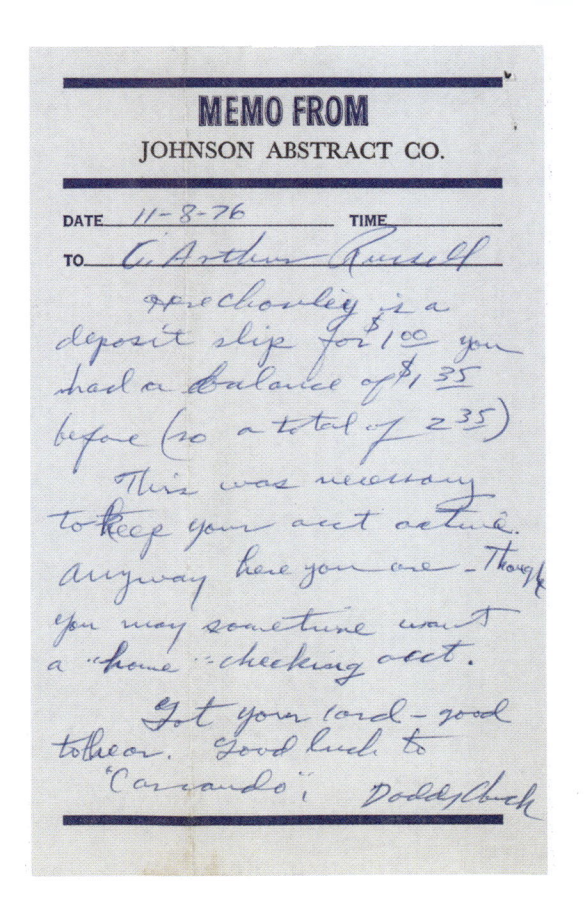

Ernie Brooks: 'Peter had a studio space in Westbeth, I think he may have shared it with The Lounge Lizards. Then The Flying Hearts had a space there as well.'

Peter Gordon: 'Ernie and Arthur could be hyper-critical of each other.'

Ernie Brooks: 'Arthur had an incredibly powerful affect of seeming affectless. It was one of the reasons we had problems getting gigs because it was the punk era, the era of heavy-duty demonstrativeness at places like CBGB. And we were making this gentle sound with gentle lyrics and we were definitely swimming against that tide. INSTRUMENTALS had been a critical hit with the downtown musical community, people like Philip Glass really rated it, but then when Arthur started turning to disco that infuriated some of those people.'

Tom Lee: 'When I met Arthur he would occasionally meet with Ernie to discuss the best possible strategies for dealing with record companies for The Flying Hearts material. While Arthur shared Ernie's enthusiasm for many of the songs they collaborated on at that time, he was also looking towards other projects and interests. Around this same time he and Steven Hall began their Sailboats group, writing songs together and performing at Max's and other such venues.'

Ernie Brooks: 'I basically blame myself for the fact I couldn't keep rehearsing, finishing things, or get the sound right for any of the units I was in with Arthur.'

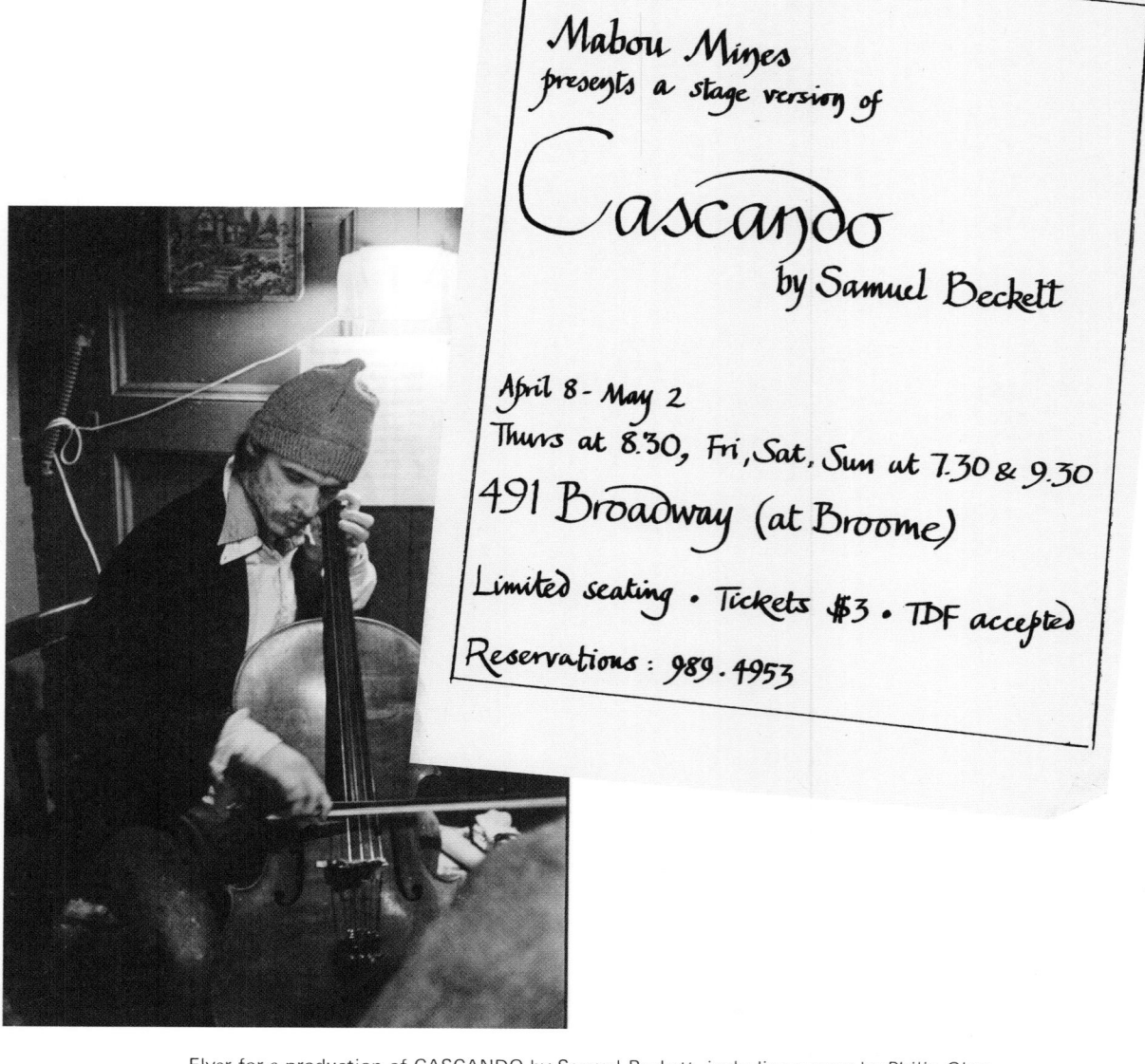

Flyer for a production of CASCANDO by Samuel Beckett, including a score by Philip Glass written for the production's sole instrument, cello played by Arthur Russell.

Philip Glass: 'I was doing a theatre piece for the Mabou Mines, it was some Beckett piece, and I wrote him a cello piece, and he liked the work and was playing it. And I came back about three months later, and I heard it and I said, "Arthur, that's beautiful, but what happened to the piece?" And he said, "No, no, that is what you wrote," and I said, "Arthur, it's no longer what I wrote, it's your piece now." And he thought I was being upset, he apologised and I said, "No, no, no, I think we should put you down as the composer." He had reached the point of transformation. The incremental changes had turned it into this other thing. I love the fact that he did that. And I love the fact that he didn't know that he did it.'

Arthur Russel,
c/o Artservices,
463 West Street,
New York,
USA.

27th September 1976

Dear Arthur,

Thank you for sending us your tape which is enclosed. Unfortunately it is not the type of material we are looking for at present.
However should you have any tapes in the future which you think suitable we would be happy to listen to them.

Yours faithfully,

Linda Gamble
for Simon Draper.

VIRGIN RECORDS, 2, VERNON YARD, 119, PORTOBELLO ROAD, LONDON W11 · Telephone: 01-727 8070 · Telex: 22542

By the end of 1976 Russell had moved from his shared apartment with Rhys Chatham at 437 East Twelfth Street into apartment 38 on the sixth floor of the same building, which he would make his home until his death in 1992. Once resident at East Twelfth Street Arthur rarely played outside New York City. In most instances he was able to walk from his apartment to the venues in which he performed, an activity he undertook on a regular, at times weekly basis.

Peter Gordon: 'We used to joke that the same $50 got passed back and forth between us. There was no dividing line between money and the community. It wasn't like anyone was making any money. We all had different schemes and skills we could monetise, but we came from a shared sense of time and place and a belief and a conviction in something that might be unnamed at the time. Myself and Arthur would talk about shared interests at the time, the connection between the social and the music was something special. It wasn't as overt as saying "this is spiritual" but Arthur clearly had a Buddhist as well as an Indian and Hindustani influence in his music. There was a feeling, the spiritual aspect, not necessarily a religiosity but it had to do with a shared social mission, for common good, that music is necessary, and music might need to change for social reasons. Rent was relatively affordable in the city. There was freelance work at radio stations, cutting tape, some people did proofreading work, Rhys Chatham worked as a bar tender. Arthur was an exception; he didn't have those side jobs. I don't recall him having a job after the Kitchen. Monastic is an apt description of his life, both in terms of his past experience but also in his complete and total belief in his music and nothing else was going to get in his way.

'This sums it all up. I probably paid for Rhys's breakfast, and he cut me a check. Arthur kept everything. Once he moved to East Twelfth Street he never moved. He was there for the rest of his life.'

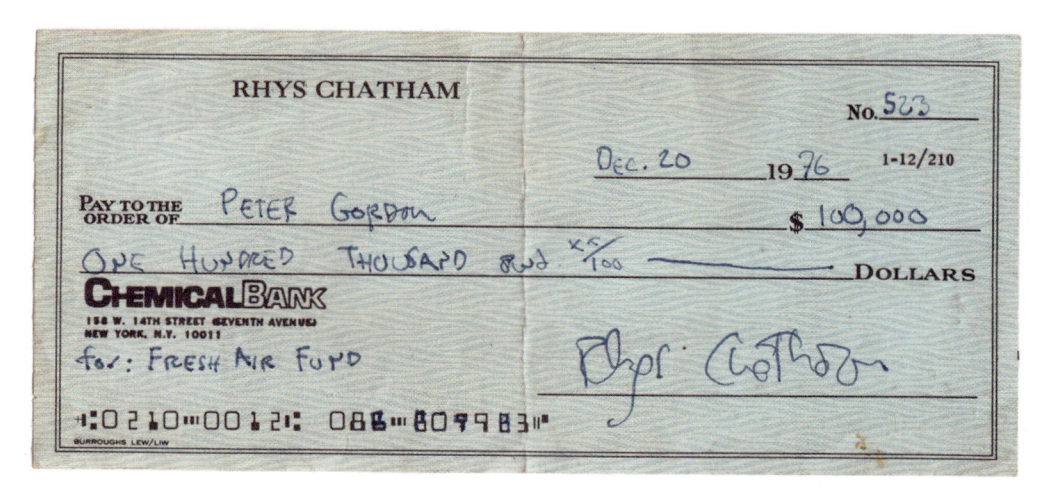

Steven Hall: 'I was starting to go up to New York when I was in high school, visiting various people in 437 East Twelfth, in the Poets' Building, as some people called it. I used to go up and stay with the poet Larry Fagin, and at that point Bob Rosenthal, who became Allen Ginsberg's secretary, was living there, John Godfrey was on the top floor and Arthur was soon to live on the top floor, and Richard Hell was there.

'We were definitely at the nexus of all these people and different styles, and people being open and very open sexually as well. There were a lot of casualties from the hippy-flower free-love scene who had sort of gone full-speed – literally on speed, most of them – and burned themselves out. And Allen had this saying, "The only good thing about money is you can throw it at problems until they go away, otherwise money is useless." Allen's big thing about making money was so that he could support and help his friends. He had this incredible nurturing thing, and he sort of took Arthur under his wing, as well.

'But very quickly, Allen grew to respect Arthur as a teacher himself, so actually, Arthur became Allen's teacher. Because Allen was like a big kid in terms of his musical knowledge and his approach to music, and Allen was very open and honest about that.'

Lucy Sante: '437 East Twelfth Street, the building was on six floors. There were seven apartments per floor and each had a different layout. And it's the same whenever I go there, it looks like it has the same cracks in the walls that it had then, all these many years later. I first lived there in '79. The apartments in the front of the building tended to be kind of big. Allen Ginsberg's, of course, was huge, because he had two apartments put together.

'I moved to the area in '78. I lived on St Mark's Place for a year and a half. By the time I moved to Twelfth Street it was all over, but when I was on St Mark's, there was a whole year of fires to the east, every night. It was just astounding, and they just became weather. I remember going to a cook-out in somebody's back yard on Fourteenth Street, and we watched a building burn as we ate our hamburgers, and by the time the fire department showed up, it had been burning for twenty hours; there was nothing left to burn in it, seemingly.

'We were in our early twenties, so it was no big deal, really, after a while. A bigger problem occurred a few years later, really around '81, '82, which was the peak of heroin, and there were heroin spots within a few feet of really any short walk from the building in a couple of directions, and that was the only time I was ever mugged, by a guy who followed me into the building one day who didn't have enough money, just an amateur, and I made a lot of noise and my neighbours came running and he ran away. But that's the most danger. The danger was less from crime than from people that you knew and loved destroying themselves.'

Peter Gordon: 'There were always a lot of issues with that building.'

Lucy Sante: 'When I moved in, the building was nominally owned by this elderly Eastern European couple – I forget whether they were Polish or Ukrainian – who actually lived on my floor, but they were old and battered and they really couldn't deal with it. And when I moved in, the tenants had just been awarded the building in a rent strike, but the court ordered it turned over to a receiver to pay off the debts, and the receiver was the one who sold it to the first shark in 1982. So, you know, we never got legal notices of anything.

'I remember my rent, I had a two-bedroom apartment, and the figure I have in my head is $162 and I don't think it went up much – it might have been $142 when I moved in and $162 when I moved out, but it didn't move that much.

'The super was called George, he was Polish. His real name was Zbigniew, and he did his best. He was a drunk who liked to pick up young Dominican prostitutes on Saturday night, but he was a really decent guy and he didn't have much to work with. The building was falling to ruin as we watched. We were all thinking that it was going to collapse or something just irreparable was going to happen before it ever got gentrified.'

Tom Lee: 'There were three or four times when I saw Arthur as I was coming home from work. I lived on Avenue A and I saw him more than once on the telephone at the Gem Spa. I saw him another time in a bar which I was in with some college friends and Arthur came in. And I went back to that bar every other day because I was driven; it turned out he only went to that bar to use the bathroom. Then another time he and Steven Hall were walking down Avenue A to the Tisch School of Arts, which is part of NYU, and I followed them in there. I was spotting him for a few weeks in the East Village. I was smitten, so finally one night I was coming from Hurrah's by myself and walked across St Mark's Place and I went into the Gem Spa and there he was, buying an ice cream. I just thought to myself, I have to do something. So I introduced myself and walked with him for a while.'

Steven Hall: 'The first apartment I had there when I first moved after high school was literally on St Mark's Place, where Arthur and Tom met at the Gem Spa. I was in that building above the shop, and that was $90 a month, the rent for us moving in there. When I first met Arthur, I was living in that building, and then I moved to Twelfth Street between Second and Third, so I was like two blocks across from Arthur and Allen, and also, when you went across First Avenue at that time, you were going into a danger zone, because that was where the Puerto Rican gangs were in control, and then the next block, Avenue A, was the heroin zone. There were little candy stores – there was one on Tenth Street, on that block, I think there was another maybe on Eighth Street – where you would go in and buy weed from the Puerto Rican gangs, and it was all pretty much in the open at that point.'

Tom Lee: 'I think Arthur's parents had visited the apartment before he and I were together. They were aware it was a tough place, which it was. They weren't terribly close in that regard; when I first met Arthur I was under the impression he and his parents were estranged. There were intermittent phone calls – later on I'd realise that most of their phone calls were about money – but they followed his trajectory very closely, they were asking how things were progressing. They were pleased when they saw a copy of "Kiss Me Again", any item Arthur could show them, something like a little notice in BILLBOARD – that was enthralling to them. Even though they loved his music, a challenge to them was the staid Republican town they lived in; they didn't have a way to explain to their friends what Arthur was up to. Even if he got good notices, it was for a strange song. It was a challenge.'

'I moved around the city in '78 and I lived right around the corner from Arthur and my brothers would visit from New Jersey. And they were so excited that they could go round the corner to what was a candy store and there'd be one of those sliding windows that the guy opens up and they'd put their twenty bucks in and get a bag of pot. They thought they'd gone to heaven. It was that acceptable. Moving there was all about the cost. I was working at a silk screen place and was always asking for leads for apartments. People would walk up and down St Mark's Place and ask anyone sitting on stoops if they had any leads. That was the protocol of the time and that's what I did. When I met Arthur I was somewhat naïve about gay culture in the city. I was cautious but intrigued.'

Lucy Sante: 'The candy store, along with the sadly departed Gem Spa, were twenty-four-hour institutions, but especially in the seventies, it was pretty much shut down at night. I mean, you'd go to clubs or parties, and you'd leave your house at midnight but there was really not much open. There were still twenty-four-hour record stores in Harlem and barbers' shops and twenty-four-hour things around Times Square, but down there, not so much. It was twenty-four-hour definitely for some people, but not for shopkeepers or restaurateurs as much.'

Steven Hall: 'Facing Tompkins Square Park there was the Odessa Restaurant, which was an all-night Ukrainian restaurant, which was great; Arthur and I used to hang out there. You could go and have a chicken soup with rice and just sit there for a couple of hours and talk about music.'

Tom Lee: 'Aside from the hours when Arthur and Steven Hall would smoke pot and walk around the Village looking at guys, he was up every day and laser-focused on working on his music.'

Steven Hall: 'The type of weed that we were getting was not really very strong, I mean, compared to what you get now. So you could smoke it all day with not really much of an effect, except the naughtiness of it, I think that's a big factor of it. And the idea of walking around and looking at guys is really something that we shared very deeply in terms of an almost religious idea of looking for inspiration as well as excitement: they would be the same thing. I think it was sort of getting ready for the day's work, which was usually something that Arthur had been working on maybe the night before, or something that was ongoing that we'd been discussing. We'd go to his place and get settled down into work: listening to takes of something we'd done a few days before; talking about approaches of what we might be doing that day.'

Lucy Sante: 'There were a whole bunch of Ukrainian restaurants, they made no concessions to fashion; they did not put modern art on their walls. The Ukrainians owned large portions of the neighbourhood at the time, and they wielded the greatest economic power. Odessa was one of them.'

Jeb Loy Nichols: 'I arrived in the summer of '79 when I was seventeen years old. After a year or so I moved to Eleventh between A and B, a block away from Arthur. We ate at Odessa or Kiev nearly every night. Me and my friend were the first white people to move back on to that block; it was entirely a Puerto Rican community. Our kitchen wasn't hooked up in any meaningful way, so we were without the means of cooking for the first six months. Places like Odessa on Tompkins Square were the cheapest places to eat; you'd get big plates of pierogi for next to nothing.

'When we moved in, we were broken into seven times in the first two weeks. We got to the point where we just left our door open because there was no point closing it. We used to come down the steps and there would be the guys and girls who lived in our building reading my books and wearing my clothes, and they would say, "Hi, how you're doing?"

'After that sort of four-week trial by fire, we were okay – and we really were okay. It was an absolutely brilliant place to live. As much as there was a great community we didn't hang out there because there wasn't all that much to do.'

Steven Hall: 'There were homeless and a lot of heroin addicts in Tompkins Square Park. There always had been a lot of heroin addicts there, and that was in the middle of the heroin-selling area, so it was very dangerous to be there at night. It was really easy to get into trouble if you wanted to, but Arthur, because he did play around and he didn't want to be seen too much in the immediate local places, because he wanted to be more discreet, and mostly because the music in the West Village was so hot, we used to head over there. The other club that I was going to at that time, which was famous because it had a jukebox in the dark room, in the groping room, was the International, which was also called the Stud, and that was a place where you could meet Asian guys, so that's where I met my first Asian boyfriend, in that dark room. Arthur and I would go into there to listen. We'd hide out in the dark room and listen to "Kiss You All Over" by Exile. That song was like the first song where rock and disco came together.'

Tom Lee: 'I wasn't so interested in the gay bars. It probably saved me.'

How'd the D.C. opening go?

2 P.M.
Thursday
26, Feb.

Arthur — If you're back in time + have strength, we're recording this weekend, if you can come up, great — with cello — also need yr. drum rythms.

ZBS RD 1 Fort Edward N.Y.
12828

518- 695- 6406
695- 3960

Call if you can. Trains + buses go up To Saratoga Springs arr. 1:30 we pick you up
Trains 9:30 AM — Bob Rosenthal
477-2487 Can advise on transport.
We record with Jon Sholle David Amram
         Sat-Sun   Sun
and Steven Taylor recording + Editing Sat Sun Monday + Tuesday.   Allen (Ginsberg)
   I'll pay etc.

Show other Eve
Sat Nite
March 5
1977

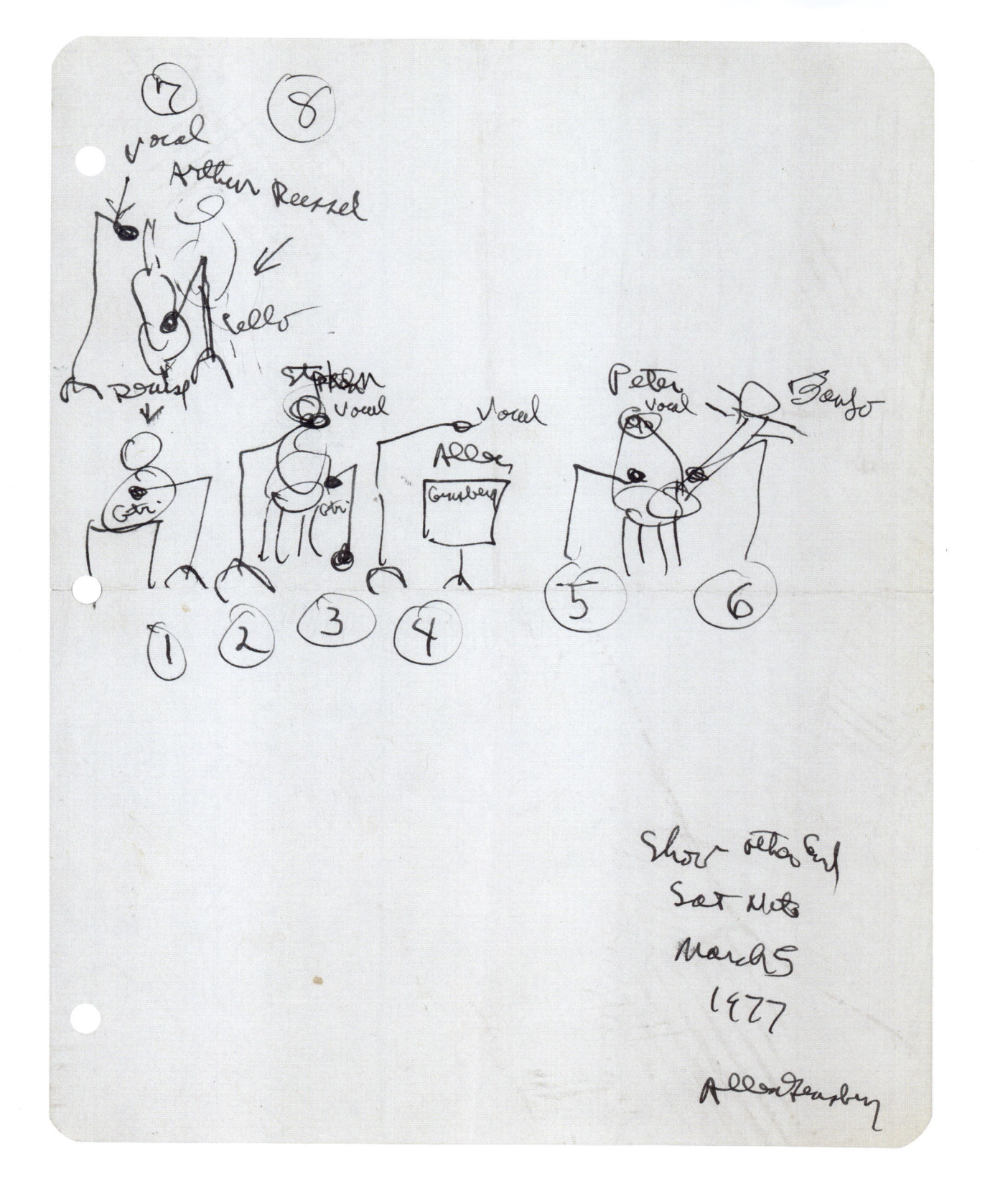

Allen Ginsberg

In May 1977 INSTRUMENTALS received its second performance at the composer Phill Niblock's Experimental Intermedia Foundation; the players were credited as 'The Flying Hearts and other musicians'. A month later the piece was once again aired at the Franklin Street Arts Centre, also known as Franklin Furnace, during a month-long residency by Peter Gordon's Love of Life Orchestra in which Russell played cello.

> Ernie Brooks: 'Arthur could happily play with other musicians' bands. Peter had scores for everybody; Arthur was a great reader. It was easy for him to drop into it. He could be so laid back, but at the same time he had very strong aesthetic ideas about everything. In some ways he was shy, physically shy and retiring but at the same time he could be so insistent and obsessive.'

Poster for the Love of Life Orchestra residency at the Franklin Street Arts Center, also known as Franklin Furnace, June 1977, including performance of INSTRUMENTALS Part 2.

> Bill Ruyle: 'For this performance Arthur told me he just wanted me to keep time playing steady eighth notes using Dave Van Tieghem's instruments that were strewn on the floor. These were mainly found instruments – mallets, ashtrays, debris – and Dave would do the same thing and then at the coda of each section he'd move to the drum set and that would be more of a groove section. And that would develop. That was my first experience of playing with Arthur. Franklin Furnace was where Arthur asked me to be part of INSTRUMENTALS and it was recorded; part of it was released on the LP later.'

Following the Franklin Street concert Russell was invited to travel to Italy by Tony Pagliuca, leader of the group Le Orme, to explore writing songs together.

Ernie Brooks: 'Arthur did want to go places, to an extent. He jumped at the chance to go to Italy. But in New York, outside that small little circle of places that was open to music that was different, it was hard to get gigs.'

Selection of seven-inch singles purchased by Arthur Russell while visiting the band Le Orme in Italy, at the invitation of its leader Tony Pagliuca. Although the trip proved fruitless in terms of a collaboration it produced one of Arthur's most tender songs, 'Oh Fernanda Why?'

*When I stood in the grass in my shoes
like a foreigner in the nature I love
It's so, so hard to tell if its really ~~really~~ true
It used to be the two of us, but now its three
see the mind makes faces
see the mind makes faces in the mirror at me*

Tuesday, May 9, 1978, 8:30 p.m.

THE ORCHESTRA OF NEW YORK

THE KITCHEN CENTER
484 Broome Street
New York, N.Y. 10012

"Fruit de la Lumière" by Ralph Jones

"(   )" by Arthur Russell

"Tone Death with Orchestra" by Rhys Chatham

    with Nina Canal & Rhys Chatham,
    electric guitars; Peter Gordon,
    tenor sax; Robert Appleton, drums

"Overture & Finale in C" by Alan Lloyd

violins: Tatiana Feigin, Boris Barkin,
        Clara Zahler, Susan Krongold
violas: Sarah Ricketts, Roberta Hankin
cello: Gabriel Morales
bass: Deborah Newmark
horns: Melissa Coren, Rodney Hytonen
trumpet: Nashta Olarte
flute: Kevin Hosten
oboes: Theodore Baskin, Pamela Epple
clarinets: Stephen Hart, Robert Yamins
bassoons: Charles McKracken, David Miller
percussion: David Frost

        Julius Fastman, conductor

The Orchestra of New York is administered by the
Brooklyn Philharmonia and funded by CETA.
Paul Dunkel, Music Director; Maurice Edwards,
Administrator; Brian Bruman, Coordinator

The Kitchen Center is supported in part by the National Endowment for the Arts, a Federal
Agency, and the New York State Council on the Arts.

It is thought '(   )' by Arthur Russell may have been a performance of INSTRUMENTALS Volume 2, played by The CETA Orchestra of New York the Comprehensive Employment and Training Act under the administration of the Cultural Council Foundation, conducted by Julius Eastman. No recordings of the concert are currently available, although eyewitnesses attest to the fact Julius Eastman was disappointed that Arthur arrived forty-five minutes late for his own performance.

Peter Gordon: 'There was a lot of arts funding that went through the CETA programme. Julius [Eastman], for some of the early ensemble works by people like Rhys Chatham and Glenn Branca, was really quality control. He was a meticulous conductor and musical organiser. He would like to have a good time and go to the bars at night, but he had the discipline of a highly trained classical musician, which he maintained and he brought to the scene.'

Bill Ruyle: 'I played in a concert of Jon Gibson at the Kitchen and Julius was on piano. I remember in that concert Julius also conducting a piece, really conducting it, in a very animating fashion. I have no doubt at all in Julius's capabilities and talents. He was an amazing pianist and vocalist, classically trained.'

Peter Gordon: 'I lived in a storefront on Sixth Street and folks would drop by and Julius would come and hang. I showed him a score I was working on and it had a bunch of repeat signs and he said, "Peter! Repeat signs! No! Write it out, this is lazy compositional technique." He would have these titles that are unspeakable nowadays in some of his work (EVIL N——R, CRAZY N——R, and GAY GUERRILLA, c.1979) but the music was meticulously composed and performed. In terms of his polytonality there was a motor drive to it, he had done a lot of work as the male vocalist with Meredith Monk in her ensemble and had been on the recording of Peter Maxwell Davies' EIGHT SONGS FOR A MAD KING, which was mainstream contemporary music.'

Prior to his move to the new apartment on 437 Street in 1977 Arthur had, for the first time, experienced the powerful and unifying vitality of a dancefloor. Louis Aquilone, a boyfriend, suggested that he and Arthur visit the Gallery, an invitation-only disco situated in SoHo run by Nicky Siano, an acquaintance of Aquilone and energetic presence in the city's underground nightlife. At the Gallery, Arthur witnessed the transformative energy of a beat played through a powerful sound system. Contemporary testimony is unreliable and it is tempting to eulogise Arthur's exposure to the spiritedness of the Gallery and overstate its significance. He certainly experienced some form of epiphany while visiting the club. A set of principles that had hitherto defined Arthur's consciousness – the ability of music to transcend the here and now; his belief in its ability to convey powerful emotions and engender the dissolution of the self, to be replaced by membership of a collective whole – coalesced around him in the darkness of the dancefloor. A disco, Arthur realised, was a space that contained both the repetition of minimalist composition and the consciousness-raising properties he had previously encountered in the drones of Indian music. This new environment of communal joy was also one in which tonal music could have a beneficial, socially positive effect on its attendees, and in the extended twelve-inch releases played by the DJ songs could be freed of the conventional strictures of composition and time.

 Russell would continue to return to the Gallery and began to explore other clubs across the city. According to those who attended dance spaces with Arthur, which he continued to visit until his illness incapacitated him from doing so, he rarely took to the dancefloor. Arthur's interest was in experiencing the clarity and authority of the sound system and the effect it had on those blissfully congregated in abandon beneath the speakers, lost to its frequencies.

A demo tape of early Talking Heads recordings. Arthur played cello on an acoustic version of the band's debut release, 'Psycho Killer', which was included on the B side of the US 7" single version.

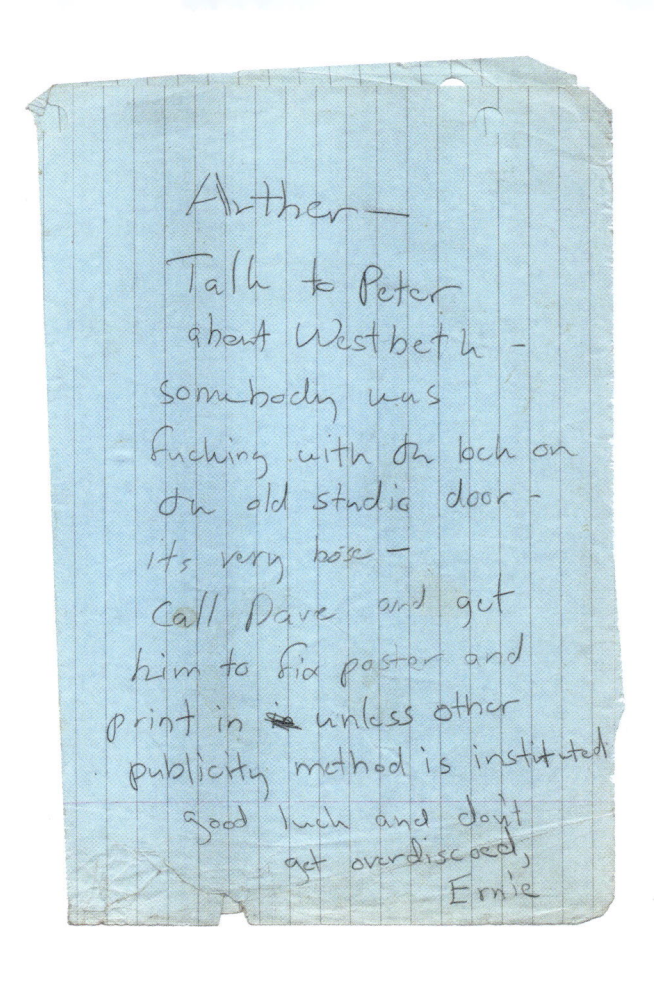

> Arther —
> Talk to Peter about Westbeth — somebody was fucking with the lock on the old studio door — it's very bad — Call Dave and get him to fix poster and print in unless other publicity method is instituted. Good luck and don't get overdiscoed,
> Ernie

Ernie Brooks: 'I guess when I wrote this note Arthur was getting ready for a weekend of disco. I was always ambiguous about that because I knew I wasn't a funky bassist. I was adequate for the weird stuff in The Flying Hearts, but not much more.'

Peter Gordon: 'The crux of what Arthur and I had been getting at in 1975 was that there were certain generative processes that were useful but they being used to make what Philip Glass termed "creepy music". On the other hand, you could use these similar processes and attitude to make music one could want to hear, or take things further, make people dance. The first time I heard Giorgio Moroder, I thought, "Wow, once you get the groove going you can put anything on top of it." I remember hearing this at gay dance clubs like the Stud, when the DJs started extending beats. By freeing the music from the song structure per se, it could go in any number of directions, including music you could dance to.'

Steven Hall: 'At that point, the repetition in both Philip Glass and Steve Reich's work was very much related to the patterns in disco music coming from African drumming and Indian raga practice, so there was a lot of cross-over in that way, and that's where Arthur thought things were really happening.'

Ernie Brooks: 'Arthur would play the bass part for "Kiss Me Again" on the keyboard for literally hours at a time in my apartment. He was fascinated with riffs, he wanted heavy duty studio guys on that record. He talked about disco constantly.'

Jill Kroesen: 'It was sort of a weird thing when Arthur started doing disco stuff.'

Phill Niblock (composer, owner of the Experimental Media Foundation): 'I didn't particularly like that kind of music. In fact, one of the most amazing things about Arthur was that he had this other side.'

Nicky Siano's Gallery party, which Arthur had attended towards the end of 1976, was partially modelled on David Mancuso's Loft, one of the first spaces to prioritise sound, warmth and a relaxed social environment for its mixed clientele, as fundamental properties necessary for communal dancing.

Will Socolov (co-founder, with Arthur, of Sleeping Bag Records): 'I'd been going to the Loft for a long time, my father was a lawyer, he lived in Brooklyn Heights. That's how I got into the whole music scene, through my father, he wasn't only David Mancuso's lawyer but did a lot of work for the Loft. David had been arrested for drugs, that's how my father met him, he represented David.'

Rome Neal (actor, collaborator with Arthur): 'The Loft had something special about it because it was one of those all night into Sunday afternoon places. When people were going to church you were on the subway going home. It had a different festive appeal, it had big balloons all over the place, it had a humungous mirror ball, great sound and there was food being fed to the people: fruit, snacks, all kinds. It was really a wonderful party environment. A very friendly place.'

Jeb Loy Nicols: 'I knew about the Loft and tried to go about half a dozen times but you just couldn't get in if you didn't know someone. I actually got in one night because Mancuso had come in to Record City where I worked and he'd bought a stack of records. He recognised me and gave me a pass, and I still almost didn't get in even with the pass, because it was such a set clientele. With the Loft, it was however many people it held, those people came every time. It was incredible. It was everything people say it was. The sound system was unlike anything I'd heard in New York. I used to go to Negril [in the East Village] a lot and that system was amazing, but Mancuso's was light years ahead. There was no fringe hipster element at the Loft, it was really pure.'

In November 1977 Arthur and Siano began to work together on a disco single, 'Kiss Me Again', released the following year and credited to the band Dinosaur. Arthur would further explore the potentialities and urgency of dance music even as his commitment to other musical practices remained ongoing.

1

I．

Here I run uptown
As fast as I can
I want you beside me
Yes that is the plan

Oh baby
Oh baby
In the lions den
Oh baby
Oh baby
Here we are again

II．

I need you beside me
The best love that I gave
The wind blows
The clouds wave
Am I a woman/ or a slave

Before me in danger
I strain to hear
The world is so smoky now
But I see you so ~~clear~~ cleaR

shoup

* My visions are real   4x

III． * Oh baby   oh baby
Here we are again   4x

II

Oh baby is this the woman
   I want to be
The door is unlocked
The windows are open
Every time you're face to face
   with me

Kiss me
Kiss me again   3x

How lucky
This love takes
A strange new kind of twist
Hey maybe I'll find out
Learn what I have missed

Before we were lovers
Sparkle in your eye
Now I have love that lives
Alone up in the sky

I sometimes believe you
Wait for you to call
I'm leaving it up to you
You don't care at all

The first time the last time
I'm much too confused
What happened to me this time
I want to be used

Shoup

My visions are real

Oh baby
oh baby
Here we are again   3x

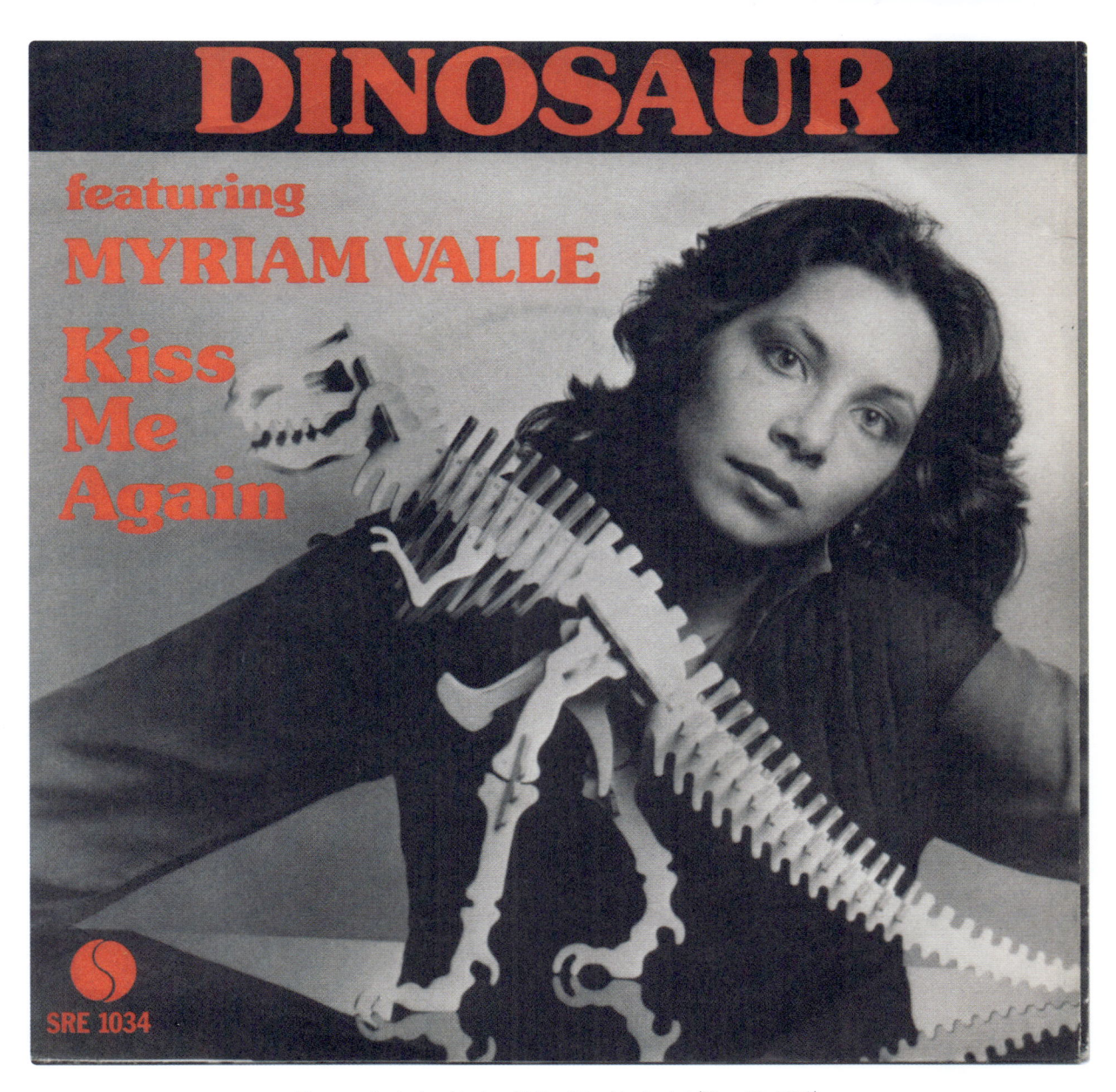

Dinosaur featuring Myriam Valle, 'Kiss Me Again' (Sire, 7", 1979).

While working on 'Kiss Me Again', Arthur continued to attempt to secure funding for a recording of INSTRUMENTALS. He also began work on a new piece, 24 > 24 MUSIC, that married his compositional interests and techniques with the steady beat of the dancefloor.

```
KISS ME AGAIN

Guitars:  David Byrne, Larry Saltzman
Basses:   Bob Babbitt, Wilbur Bascomb
Drums:    Alan Schwartzberg
Percussion: Sammy Figueroa
Trombone: Peter Zummo
Alto Saxophone: Peter Gordon
Piano:    Frank Owens
Organ:    Arthur Russell
Violin:   Henry Flynt
Cello:    Arthur Russell

Vocals:   Myriam Valle, Jennifer Jacobson

Produced by Arthur Russell and Nicky Siano

Recorded at Sun Dragon's, NYC
Engineers: Michael G. Ewing, Tom Duffy

Remix by Jimmy Simpson  Sigma Sound Studios, NYC
Engineer: Andy Abrams
```

Production notes including personnel for the 'Kiss Me Again' recording session at Sun Dragon studio, November 1977.

Peter Gordon: 'With "Kiss Me Again", clearly the song was there, but there wasn't a chart with chord changes in the studio, it was more like, "Play this riff here." Me and Peter were doing overdubs, punching in and out so we didn't need a chart. It didn't feel like a pressured environment. Sun Dragon was a local studio that had a big aquarium – Arthur liked spending time there because of that.'

Peter Zummo: 'I enjoyed that because it was nice way to use alternative positions and major seventh chord implications. I had a background in jazz and R'n'B already, so a steady beat and a groove; I'd always been trained to put the note anywhere on the beat.'

Dinosaur, 'Kiss Me Again' (Sire, Promotional 12", 1979).

Instrumentals is a sound composition conceived as a continually changing work-in-progress, presented with the visual accompaniment of of photographic wall projections by Yuko Nonomura. The first concerts of Instrumentals took place in Berkeley, California and New York City in 1975. At these initial stages, one component of a performance was the combining a sense of "bubblegum" musical sound with the current modes of "avant-garde" musical practice and thought. These earlier Instrumentals concerts consisted of a more or less continual recycling of a multi-purpose musical content: small segments drawn from a long sequence, any full performance of which could take more than 48 hours. Whether composed or improvised, it was encouraged that the arrangements change from concert to concert, with the concepts, or the mode of musical practice and thought, changing somewhat as well.

Consequently it's appropriate that the record, "Instrumentals Vol. 2" (Another Side 8401), presented, necessarily, without the benefit of Yuko Nonomura's photography, include different concert recordings, distinguished from one another by recording dates listed on the label. These later recorded versions leave omitted the drums of the earlier version (Instrumentals Vol. 1)(Chatham Square SFCSL145). But they show a different movement or sequence, and hint at the "bubblegum" of the future.

                                                Arthur Russell
                                                Arthur Russell

May 13, 1978

Nancy Vandenberg
Beard's Fund
9 West 57th Street
New York City

Dear Nancy,

John Hammond suggested I write to you, and apply to Beard's Fund. As a project I propose work on a composition which has appeared in several versions. The most recent of these was performed by the CETA Orchestra, but as I was not satisfied at the performance I choose to overlook this particular version, and suggest the following:

A.
1) To prepare a new version of this composition, "Instrumentals" $1000
2) To rehearse it with musicians of my choice $1500
3) To record "Instrumentals" preferably "live" in performance, or in a studio setting compatible with the players $1500

    Total project cost $4000

Up to now, three versions of "Instrumentals" have been prepared for performance. For my intentions, I've come to feel the raggedness and spontaneity of live performances exceeds the interest of finished product, and yet it's my desire to prepare the performance situation as thoroughly as possible.

Melodies were then derived from this array of pitches, and sequentially illustrated, moving forward in the array, or down the columns as shown in Xerox Two. These melodies were set out in the same order and manner (by ear) as the columns of "companion notes" already explained, using each successive of these "companion notes" as a starting point, then moving freely, but always forward, from there, drawing lines from note to note. Xerox Two is a copy of the line drawings of these melodies from the ten columns on the first page of the first stage (Xerox One). Numbers above the notes indicate the relative duration that they will have in the actual performance.

The melodies starting from the successive notes in a column of "companion notes", primary melodic material, were then recorded sequentially and without interruption or demarcation on score paper, reproduced partially here in Xerox Three. Recorded also were the melodies which had as their starting note each of the notes in the primary melodic material as illustrated in Xerox Two. In this way, for each of the melody notes in the primary melodic material, a melody was recorded above it on the page. These then became potential voices of harmony in the actual performance.

The final score, Xerox Four, was then orchestrated by ear from the materials previously recorded (Xerox Three)

This process (Xerox Three and Four) is carried out with each of the ten columns of "companion notes".

Each musician is supplied with his part from my orchestration as in Xerox Four and the primary melodic material transposed to fit his instrument as well. So he can play either of those, or the chord changes resulting from the processes of Xerox One, Two, Three, and Four are there so he can improvise off those if he wants to.

What we have then is a long series of chords continuing without interruption or demarcation. In the actual rehearsal, this series is played in its entirety into a tape recorder. When it's played back, whoever's interested, usually the musicians, listens and decides what short sections he or she would like to have abstracted from the whole series to be played as a repeated, short "module". The results of this is what you hear (in an edited version) on the tape of the concert at the Kitchen, April 28, 1975.

The rehearsals, despite their apparent simplicity, turned out to be tedious in some ways, asking the musicians to do things they weren't really accustomed or prepared to do. But after it was all over, it seemed worth the trouble. The performance at the Kitchen showed what three or four rehearsals could be expected to yield. In that performance about half the production expenses were provided by myself, the total being about a thousand dollars. Most of that was musicians' fees, and that could probably be economized a little in the future now that I have some idea of the problems involved.

Most of any money I receive for this effort in the future would be used to pay musicians for rehearsals, which would be important if the project were to be realised well or probably even at all.

Because in this case it is important not only for the musicians to learn the music, but also, in a performance situation, to be able to accept the color slides as an unconscious input, something I've found is not as hard as it sounds considering the quality of Mr. Nonomura's work. But even with that, it would take many rehearsals to accomplish it.

I'd like to ~~thank~~ acknowledge Yuko Nonomura for the photographs he provided, which in all stages of production have been and will be a parallel, albeit static, input to "Instrumentals."

I'd like to thank also Phill Niblock (of Experimental Intermedia Foundation), Jim Burton (of The Kitchen Center), Rhys Chatham (of The Kitchen Center, 1978), NYSCA, NEA, and the CBS Foundation.

As of now ~~only~~ two reviews of "Instrumentals" have appeared in local papers (the <u>Village Voice</u> and The New York <u>Times</u>) and these are available on request, as well as the various scores and tapes ~~(212-677-1437)~~.

or <u>B</u>. The writing, rehearsal, and recording of an entirely new piece. Projected cost: $4000

                                          Sincerely, yours,

                                          Arthur Russell
                                          437 East 12th Street
                                          New York, N.Y. 10009
                                          212-677-1437

I hope that I have provided the relevant information to initiate consideration by the Fund of sponsoring one of my projects. Should any further information or materials be necessary please contact me at the above address.

Arthur Russell
437 East 12th Street
New York, N.Y. 10009
April 26, 1978

A proposal for the recording of the work by me entitled <u>Instrumentals</u>

```
10 musicians @ 120 dollars each---------------------------------- $1200.00
10 hours of recording studio time @ 100 dollars per hour--------   1000.00
Estimated cost allowance for tapes and materials----------------    300.00
                                                                  $2500.00
```

Draft of application to
Kitchen-Rhys

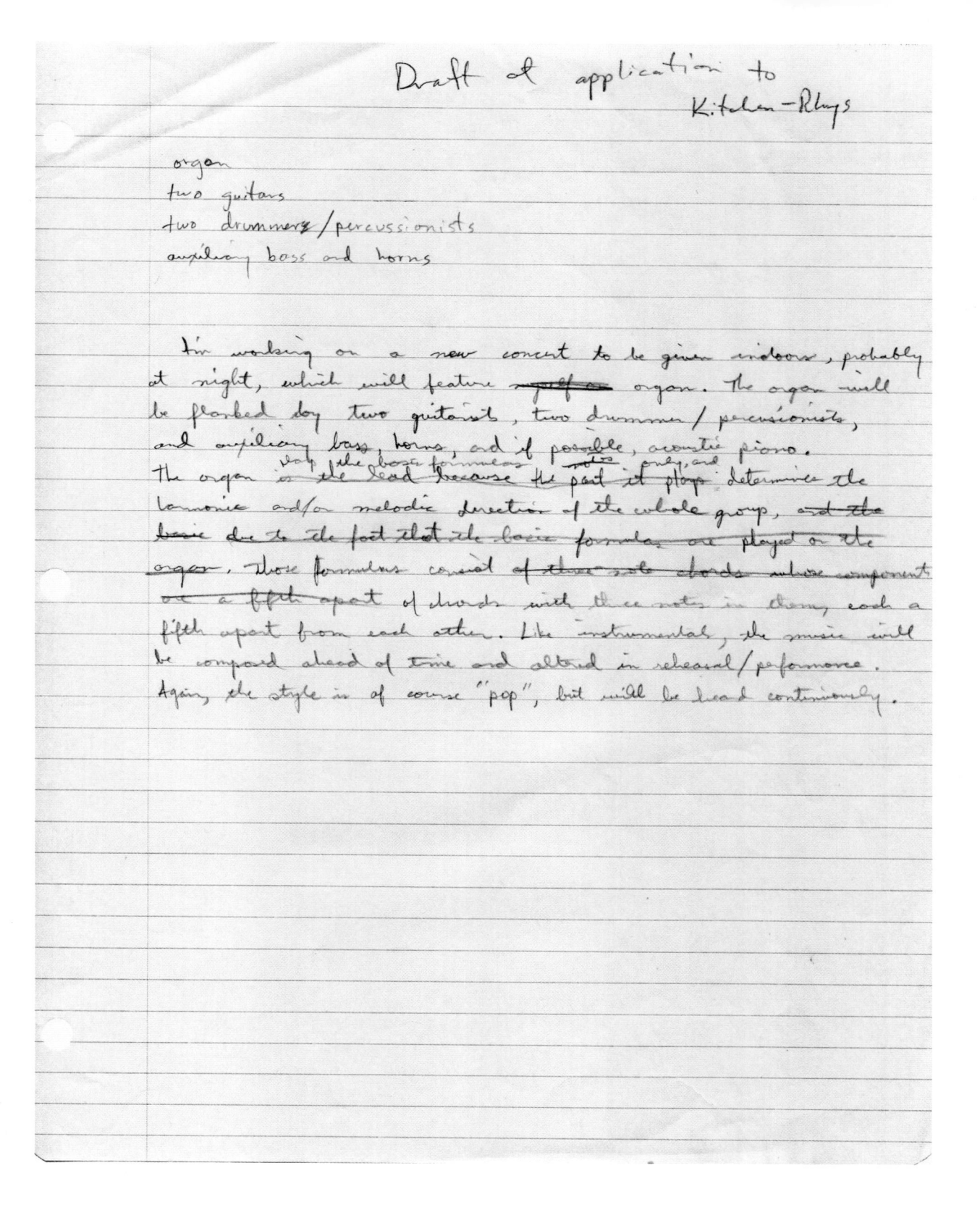

organ
two guitars
two drummers/percussionists
auxiliary bass and horns

I'm working on a new concert to be given indoors, probably at night, which will feature ~~self~~ organ. The organ will be flanked by two guitarists, two drummers/percussionists, and auxiliary bass, horns, and if possible, acoustic piano. The organ is ~~the lead because the part it plays~~ basically the bass formulas only, and determines the harmonic and/or melodic direction of the whole group, ~~and the basis due to the fact that the basic~~ formulas ~~are played on the organ~~. Those formulas consist of ~~three solo chords whose components on a fifth apart~~ of chords with three notes in them, each a fifth apart from each other. Like instrumentals, the music will be composed ahead of time and altered in rehearsal/performance. Again, the style is of course "pop", but will be heard continuously.

Flyer for a two-night residency performance of 24 > 24 MUSIC at the Kitchen, April 1979. The drawing of Arthur Russell was made by his friend Joel Sokolov. A recording of the performance on 28 April 1979 (the second of the two shows) was released by Audika Records in October 2021.

Peter Zummo: 'The recording of this show is really cool. Two nights, which is interesting. I don't remember memorising any of the key melody lines at the time. As I recall my role was more of a free agent.'

Peter Gordon: 'It sounds like a jam, which it is. I think part of the concept was you set up the structure and everyone responds within it.'

Peter Zummo: 'The piece is looped melodies which is mostly Arthur. Then Larry coming in on the guitar. The chord pattern, cool organ chords, which are ninth and inverted ninths, that's a twenty-four beat pattern. The melodies, the first one is twenty-four and the rest are not necessarily. So there is a chord sequence that loops and every other chord is root, fifth, ninth, no thirds, no sevenths and then the next chord is root, ninth, fifth, in close formation, so it goes open–closed, open–closed as written but it definitely expands. That's very organised, it's very polytonal, but if you look at the melodies they relate as they go along.'

```
APRIL 16 1979

ON FRIDAY APRIL 27 AND SATURDAY APRIL 28 AN ENSEMBLE OF MUSICIANS
LED BY THE COMPOSER WILL PERFORM NEW MUSIC BY ARTHUR RUSSELL AT
THE KITCHEN, 484 BROOME STREET, RESERVATIONS 925-3615. THE PIECE
IS TITLED " 24 to 24 music " AND WAS WRITTEN FOR INSTRUMENTS
INCLUDING TROMBONE (PETER ZUMMO), KEYBOARDS (JULIUS EASTMAN) AND
VIOLINCELLO.

CHARLES ARTHUR RUSSELL WAS BORN MAY 21 1951 IN OSKALOOSA IOWA.
HE LIVED IN SAN FRANCISCO FROM 1968 TO 1973 SINCE WHEN HE HAS
RESIDED IN NEW YORK CITY. IN 1974-75 HE SERVED AS MUSIC DIRECTOR
OF THE KITCHEN, PRESENTING THE FIRST POP MUSIC EVENT THERE (JONATHAN
RICHMAN AND THE MODERN LOVERS). SINCE THEN HE HAS WORKED WITH THE
ROCK BAND THE FLYING HEARTS, AND HE IS THE COMPOSER/ARRANGER/PRODUCER
OF THE DISCO GROUP DINOSAUR WITH A RECORD ON THE SIRE LABEL.

RUSSELL HAS PERFORMED WITH LAURIE ANDERSON, JOHN CAGE, ALICE COLTRANE,
JON GIBSON, PETER GORDON, GARRETT LIST, JACKSON MACLOW AND CHRISTIAN
WOLFF, AND HAS APPEARED IN THE PLAY CASCANDO WITH MABOU MINES, PLAYING
MUSIC BY PHILIP GLASS.

IN THE SPRING OF 1978 RUSSELL CONTRIBUTED AN UNTITLED PIECE FOR
BAROQUE ORCHESTRA TO THE CETA ORCHESTRA OF NYC SERIES AT THE KITCHEN.
OTHERWISE THIS IS THE FIRST PERFORMANCE OF HIS MUSIC IN NYC SINCE A
MAY 1977 PERFORMANCE OF HIS PIECE "INSTRUMENTALS" AT THE EXPERI-
MENTAL INTERMEDIA FOUNDATION, WHICH EVENT PROMPTED ROBERT PALMER TO
SAY "THAT THE MUSIC OF THE SOHO MINIMALISTS AND PROGRESSIVE ROCK
MAY BE COMPATIBLE...MR. RUSSELL'S PRESENTATION...SUGGESTED NOT
JUST A FURTIVE EMBRACE, BUT A REAL MERGING...THIS IS A FASCIN-
ATING DIRECTION, ONE THAT DEMANDS FURTHER EXPLORATION." (NY TIMES
MAY 6 1977).
                                    INFORMATION: DON MURK
                                                 677-1437
```

Steven Hall: 'I remember the audience dancing at this show and I remember that being a really big deal. And also some people not being sure if they should dance or not, because it was the Kitchen, but then eventually, everybody got it. And I think a lot of that had to do with Arthur just being there, and sort of giving people permission to explore that side of things.'

Rome Neal: 'This show was Arthur doing his other music. That was quite wonderful. It was more experimental, it had that free flow about it. When I went to the Kitchen to perform with Arthur he brought a different sensibility. It was different. It seemed like it was free form and in a way it was free form, but more so it had that spacey feeling about it, that airy experimental New Music feeling.'

The Kitchen Center for Video and Music

press release

ARTHUR RUSSELL

24 TO 24 MUSIC

April 27th & 28th, 1979   8:30pm
$3.50 / $2.00 / TDF Music
The Kitchen Center, 59 Wooster Street
Reservations: 925-3615

On Friday and Saturday, April 27th and 28th, at 8:30pm, The Kitchen Center will present the premiere of a composition by Arthur Russell. 24 to 24 Music is an evening-length piece for trombone, 'cello, keyboards, electric bass and drums. Musicans assisting the composer include Peter Zummo and Julius Eastman.

This performance of 24 to 24 Music is Arthur Russell's first public performance of his music in almost two years. Russell came to New York in 1973, after studying extensively on the West Coast ('cello with Andor Toth Jr., Stephanie Beal, Margaret Rowell and at the San Francisco Conservatory of Music; world music with Ali Akbar Khan and G. S. Sachdev; composition with William Mathieu). In New York, he studied composition with Charles Wuorinen and Bulent Arel and directed the music program at The Kitchen (1974-75). As a 'cellist, he has performed Philip Glass's music in Mabou Mines' Obie-award winning Cascando (Public Theater, 1975-77). He has also performed with Laurie Anderson, John Cage, Alice Coltrane, Jon Gibson, Peter Gordon, Garrett List, Jackson MacLow and Christian Wolff. Performances of Russell's own music have taken place at Berkeley's 1750 Arch Street, The Kitchen, Sobossek's NYC and the Experimental Intermedia Foundation. He is best-known for his composition Instrumentals (1975), written to accompany the viewing of slides by Yuko Nonomura.

+ + + + + + + + + + + + +

Upcoming performances at The Kitchen Center include "Acoustic Space Measurement," a composition by the Austrian composer H. Lugus (May 15th, 8:30pm; detailed press release forthcoming). For information on performances and exhibitions at The Kitchen, please contact Joe Hannan at 925-3615.

484 Broome Street between West Broadway and Wooster, New York City

19-Oct-79

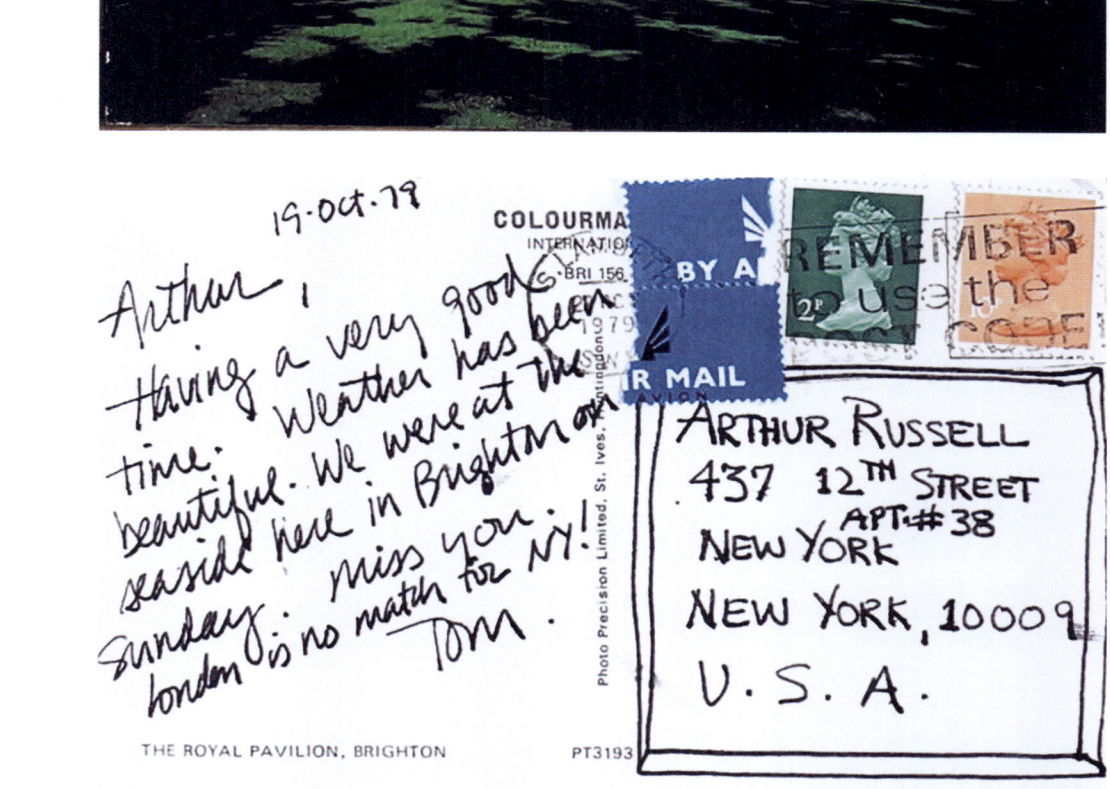

Arthur,
Having a very good time. Weather has been beautiful. We were at the seaside here in Brighton on Sunday. Miss you. London is no match for NY!
Tom.

THE ROYAL PAVILION, BRIGHTON

Arthur Russell
437 12th Street
Apt #38
New York
New York, 10009
U.S.A.

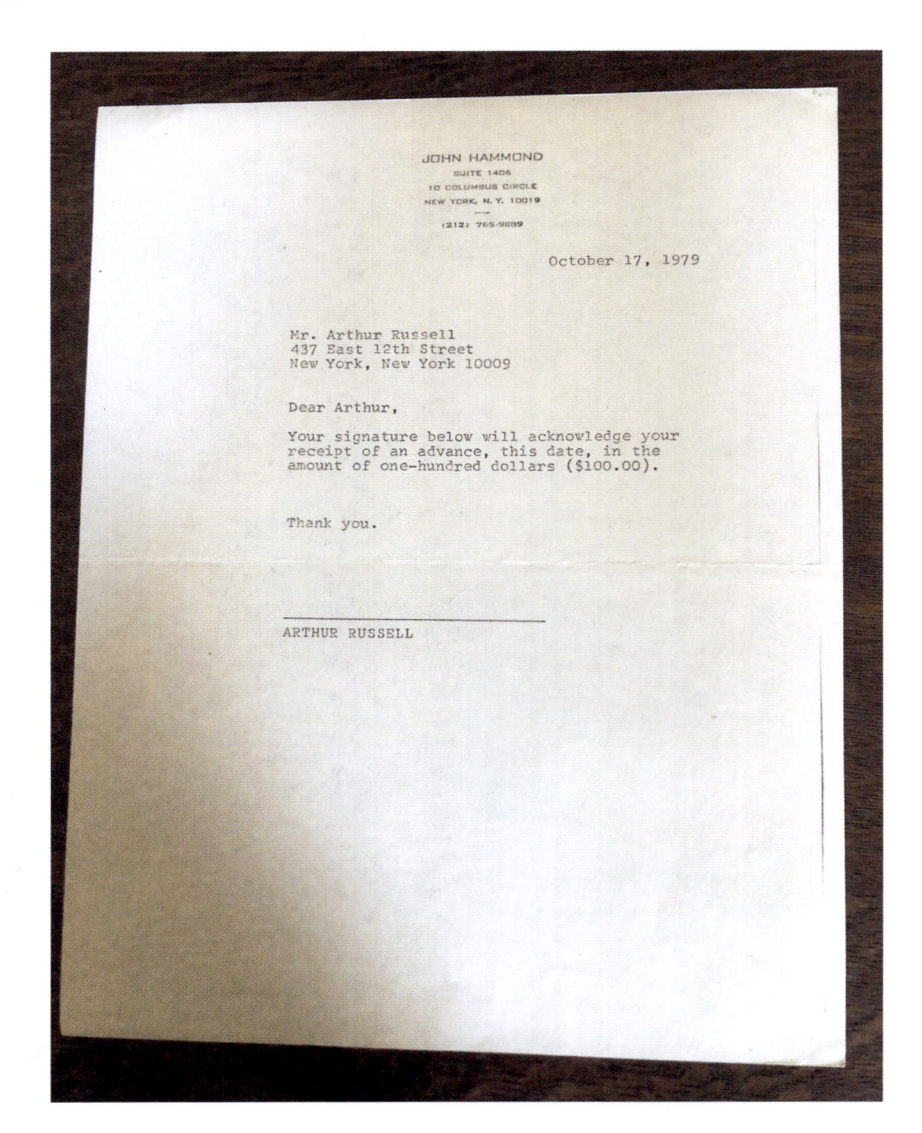

> JOHN HAMMOND
> SUITE 1406
> 10 COLUMBUS CIRCLE
> NEW YORK, N.Y. 10019
>
> (212) 765-9889
>
> October 17, 1979
>
> Mr. Arthur Russell
> 437 East 12th Street
> New York, New York 10009
>
> Dear Arthur,
>
> Your signature below will acknowledge your receipt of an advance, this date, in the amount of one-hundred dollars ($100.00).
>
> Thank you.
>
> _____
> ARTHUR RUSSELL

At the end of the decade, a final correspondence and advance from John Hammond. This memo is thought to be in relation to a demo session for Flying Hearts songs that included Ernie Brooks and Joyce Bowden.

Joyce Bowden: 'I first met Arthur at a studio session. Ernie suggested we all got together and I chose the studio, Rock Bite in Midtown, and Arthur arrived in painted boots. I had a friend I had been working with called John Scherman; he and I had been working on folk songs together and he had told me about Ernie and this "strange cat" called Arthur. He gave me a cassette of some of the Flying Hearts material and it was kind of a life-changer, how it affected me personally when I first heard it. It was material that was so honest and true. Arthur was smart and analytical but had a feminine spirit.'

Stills from a film shot at Hallwalls Contemporary Art Center, Buffalo, New York, c.1979.

Arthur Russell and Peter Gordon, California, 1979.

Jill Kroesen: 'It was hard to get hold of Arthur so I had to write a letter to get him to call me. It's not like you saw him everywhere. We'd see him at parties, but he'd just sort of be there, in the corner. He wasn't a gadfly running around town. He'd place himself in one spot and give off his good vibes. He was an incredible person to collaborate with, he got stuff and was always very present.'

JILL KROESEN
24 Fifth Avenue
New York, New York 10011
Telephone: (212) 982-9577

~~Dear Dear Arthur~~

Dear Adr

Dear Arthur,

Call me up.

Love Jill

Part III

1980–86

1980 was the year in which Tom Lee moved into East Twelfth Street to live with Arthur Russell. They would remain living together in the sixth-floor apartment for the rest of Russell's life. During that time Lee worked at a printworks and framing studio located a few blocks uptown. As well as providing security for the couple, the job allowed Lee to produce his own work and to help Arthur with designs for a myriad of flyers, posters, prints and record sleeves for the various configurations Russell performed and recorded under.

In the first half of the new decade Arthur would continue to experiment within dance music idioms. Building on the experiments of 'Kiss Me Again' and 24 > 24 MUSIC, he would issue a series of records and collaborations under the names of Loose Joints and Dinosaur L, which were met with approval both on the city's dancefloors and its boom boxes.

Tom Lee: 'When we first met, Arthur was cutting all the edits of "Is It All Over My Face?" like a madman. The pieces of tape were hanging on the walls of the apartment everywhere.'

Alison Salzinger: 'The apartment would have been a slum if anyone else had lived there. The landlord did not maintain the building, but Tom made it beautiful with all his artwork and Arthur had all his tapes, rows and rows of tapes that he was endlessly splicing and editing.'

Peter Gordon: 'Tom and Arthur had a beautiful connection.'

DUBBED BY

FRANKFORD/WAYNE MASTERING LABS

1697 BROADWAY, NEW YORK, N.Y. 10019
212 - 682 5473

33 1/3 rpm   THE FADES

POP YOUR FUN

10/5/79

'Arthur could appear modest, but he wasn't modest about his own work. He was always very active in trying to establish business networks with record companies.'

Tom Lee: 'He could seem upset by the way the record company people would respond whenever he took a meeting with them. He took these interactions very personally. His perception of how things transpired would affect his mood and interactions between Ernie, Steven or Will, depending on who was involved.'

Steven Hall: 'It was very significant that Ernie Brooks was a Harvard guy, I was a Columbia guy and Arthur desperately wanted to be taken seriously. Early on, Arthur thought he wasn't attractive enough to be a pop star, but he desperately wanted to be a pop star, and then there were two poles of his personality: of being shy and then being totally dominant and controlling when he needed to be, in the studio or in some kind of professional situation. He could spend three hours listening to two different takes of one track, not being able to decide which was the best, and then turning to me, if it was during the day, or turning to Tom at the end of the day, and saying, "Which one is the best one?" And more often than not, Tom would be right – Tom always had great taste – so that was a big part of their relationship.'

Peter Gordon: 'Arthur was always very shy on stage. Whether with Love of Life Orchestra or even with The Flying Hearts he'd keep his head down. He was very self-conscious about his acne and he was very shy. Even when he's there in the photos, it's hard to find him in the picture. His paranoid side would come out in different ways, sometimes totally off the wall. He had no need to be paranoid, he was so talented.'

Steven Hall: 'Arthur had a very complicated relationship with the people he worked with closely, because he thought that they were trying to take advantage of him. He had a phrase which I've often quoted, which is, "Sometimes paranoia is justified." He thought that "Miss You" by the Rolling Stones was something that they had stolen from him, that they had taken one of his drum tracks – because I think there were people he'd worked with at Warner Bros who also worked with the Rolling Stones – or they had taken a bass line that he had done and they had developed it. He thought Talking Heads were taking advantage of him, that they had gotten a certain sensibility from him that was very subtle but was very successful, and he felt slighted in that way. He also had this relationship with his close friends, like with me. Sometimes, he would accuse me of stealing ideas from him. But I think if he hadn't got sick, I think all of that would have been taken care of by his ongoing success, because I think it was inevitable, that he was working in so many areas, that any one of them could have taken off.'

Tom Lee: 'Philip Glass was one of Arthur's lone supporters. One of the dozen or so people who would show up at Arthur's concerts, especially at Phill Niblock's place. They were pretty sparsely attended. Some people from my job would turn up, maybe people who were working at Phill's, there were a few occasions when it was over twenty people there, but never many more.'

EXPERIMENTAL INTERMEDIA FOUNDATION

MARCH 1980

ARTHUR RUSSELL — SAT 1 NOON
AN UNNAMED NOONTIME

CHARLIE MORROW — MON 3 9PM
THE ROLE OF MEMORY

DARY JOHN MIZELLE — THU 6 9PM
INFORMATION STRUCTURES: MUSIC FOR VOICE, INSTRUMENTS AND COMPUTER

ALLISON KNOWLES — SUN 9 9PM
GEM DUCK, AN OPERA IN FIVE GRAYS AND SIX ACTS

RUTH ANDERSON* — MON 10 9PM
CENTERING THROUGH SOUND, WITH EVA KARCZAG, DANCE

PHILL NIBLOCK — FRI 21 9PM
MAY PIECES FOR CELLO FOR DAVID GIBSON FOR THE FIRST DAY OF SPRING

WITH SUPPORT FROM THE NEW YORK STATE COUNCIL ON THE ARTS
*WITH SUPPORT FROM CAPS COMMUNITY SERVICE PROGRAM

224 CENTRE STREET AT GRAND — $2.50

Experimental Intermedia Foundation flyer, March 1980. The venue was located in Phill Niblock's SoHo loft space.

As the 1980s commenced, an unrivalled decade of cultural cross-pollination developed momentum in downtown Manhattan and Arthur would produce consecutive releases suffused with its energy. He recorded these singles both with the aim of hearing them played through the seductively powerful sound systems of club spaces such as the Loft or the Paradise Garage and with the knowledge that dance records had the potential to be lucrative. These tracks, which confirmed his reputation as an innovative and sui generis dancefloor producer, were released under various aliases: 'Kiss Me Again' by Dinosaur was followed in 1980 by 'Is It All Over My Face?' and 'Pop Your Funk' by Loose Joints. In 1982 Dinosaur L (rather than the previous Dinosaur) released the epochal 'Go Bang #5'. Arthur would also utilise the names Killer Whale and Indian Ocean later in the decade. The decision to use such aliases was invariably a consequence of the fast-turnover street economy in which dance singles operated and Arthur's mood on any given day. The changing names reflected both his capriciousness and music business expediency.

> Mustafa Khaliq Ahmed: 'At the time I was working with James Mason, I was the percussionist on his album RHYTHM OF LIFE. While I'm recording with James, Arthur comes into the studio, because he worked about five or six blocks away at this place called Westbeth and this was down in the Village, but Arthur's looking for spec time, he's looking for all of these smaller independent studios to record his work. He comes into the studio and he's there and he's listening to a session that I'm working on. And this guy, he comes up to me afterwards: "Yo, I really like what you do, it's like you're the dude, you're the dude."
>
> 'Now, I'm like a deer in the woods who comes out and there's all these lights. I'm looking for opportunities to play. I had no formal music education and that's how it was, and Arthur, he was very different to the R'n'B, jazz situations that I had been exposed to, and yet it was very exciting that he could hear my voice. That's how we met: we met at downtown Studio, on Christopher Street, so that would have been about 1979.'

In the late 1970s and for first half of the 1980s Arthur's dancefloor recordings shared a rotating set of musicians, as well as remixers. The foundations for Dinosaur L and Loose Joints releases was laid by Arthur's favoured studio rhythm section of the Ingram Brothers: Butch (bass), Jimmy (keyboards), John (drums), Timmy (congas) and William (guitar), most usually at recording sessions held at Blank Tapes studio in Midtown. Here they were joined by collaborators and friends constituting alumni from the Kitchen/New Music confluence including Peter Gordon, Peter Zummo, Julius Eastman and Jill Kroesen; a group of musicians and composers with distinct individual careers who were content to play each other's material, either in the recording studio or at concerts held in a network of clubs, theatres and performance spaces usually located downtown. The tapes of their work in the studio with Arthur were then passed on to a network of professional remixers for further collaboration, including such luminaries of mixing-desk dexterity as Larry Levan, François K. and Walter Gibbons.

Mustafa Khaliq Ahmed, Arthur Russell, Frank Katz
and Peter Zummo in rehearsal c.1980.

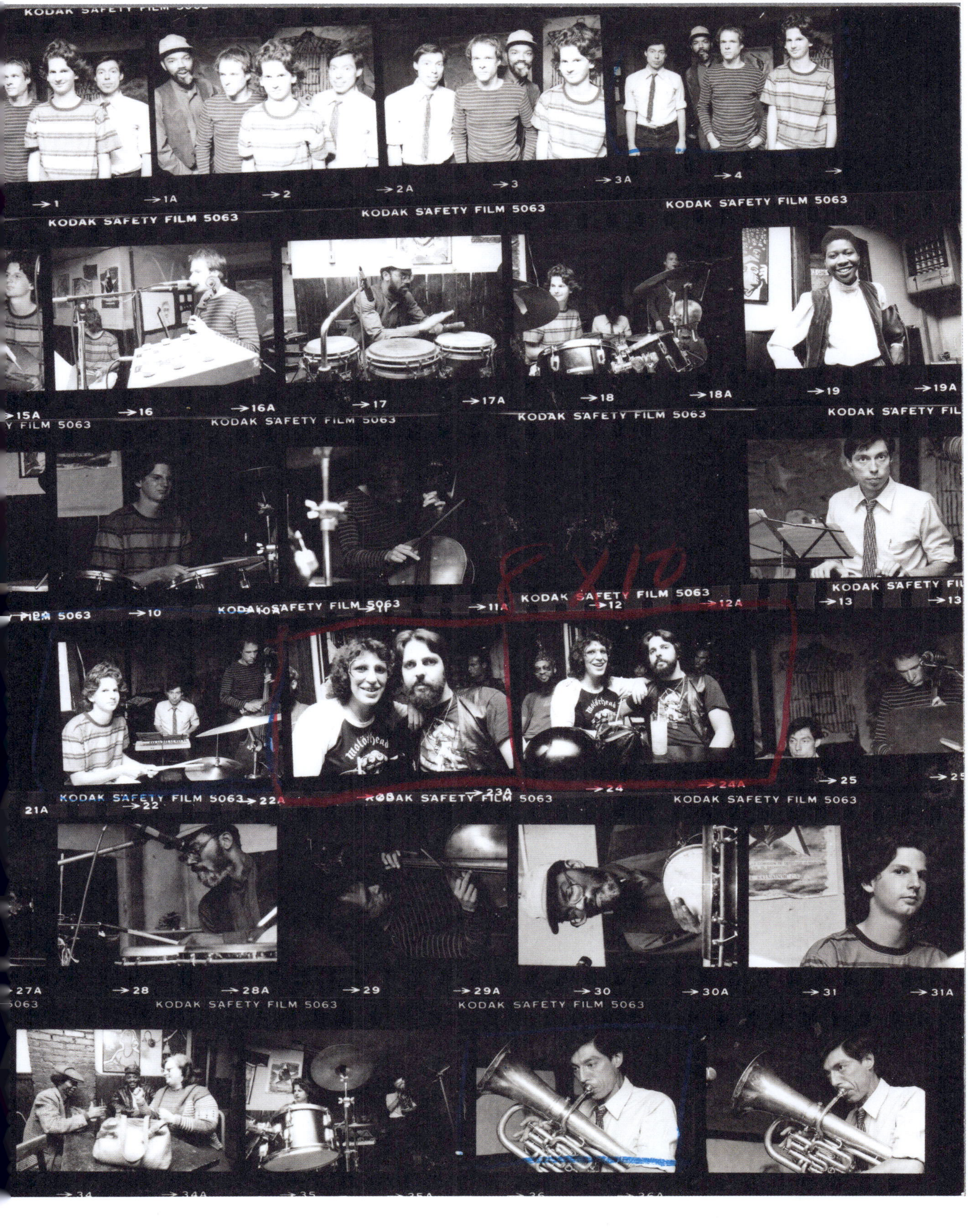

2x [1 Caught Me   Caught Me
      Love Dancin
      Sound now seek and you will find
            It's many friends   catch the wave
                                  catch the Love wave
            Feel it up   catch the wave
                                  catch the Love wave

Is it all over my face?

   You Caught me Love Dancing

Is it all over my face
   I'm in Love Dancin

And Springing out the Same

   Send one now at seven

      Feel it out
      Catch the love wave now
      Feel it out
      Catch the Love wave

Loose Joints, 'Is It All Over My Face?' (West End Records, 12", 1980).

Loose Joints, 'Is It All Over My Face?' (West End Records, 12", 1980).

Will Socolov: 'The music for those singles was done by the family from Philly, the Ingrams. They backed Patti LaBelle. The thing Arthur loved about the Ingrams is that it was a family. He said, "They vibe off each other, Timmy and Jimmy." He said the most difficult to deal with was Butch, because Butch was older and he didn't have the energy, he was like strictly business. Timmy and Jimmy, maybe Johnny, those guys, when Arthur would jam with them, he said those guys took off and they were really into it. Arthur I know loved to work with the Ingrams because he felt that they just worked together.'

Peter Zummo: 'I was aware of the music as projects. In the studio, whether the session was called Loose Joints or Dinosaur, it could have been either. Dinosaur L took different forms and if that was the name of the band of the time, then that was the name.

'I only had vague notions of what would happen with the recordings I just made or was making.

'A name would be chosen, "This is Dinosaur L," but the material dovetailed with other projects and bands from earlier and would be revisited in the future. That's not an unusual process. It's more creative than what a lot of people do. The process was just ongoing: working on the music, now we can play at the club, who's going to play? What shall we call the band? The motivation was the continuation of the experiment. We were attracted to each other because musicians could do much more than render A to G on the score. What's the next step?'

Mustafa Khaliq Ahmed: 'I played with Arthur on sessions in Blank Tapes every now and then. But I'm not sure I was involved with him on the sessions for those singles, because the original Loose Joints were a group of studio musicians, the Ingram Brothers. They did the original stuff – Arthur hired them, however that happened; Arthur either had funding or something for them to do that. But those guys were not going to play in the little clubs and so forth and so on, because they were on a higher level, in terms of where they were, and so I'm the guy that came in to be the real embodiment of that, and once the Ingrams went on to their regular thing, that's how he found me. He went out looking for guys to replace the Ingram Brothers. I had to learn all of the Loose Joints stuff and so forth.'

Peter Gordon: 'I don't know what the difference was between Loose Joints and Dinosaur L. I don't think Arthur thought there was a difference. It was to do with business entities and record companies and things like that. I think it was similar to Parliament and Funkadelic, it was interchangeable. They were both working from the same raw materials. Whenever there was full moon Arthur would be in the studio one way or another. It wasn't like they were special full-moon sessions, but he'd be sure to be working.'

The sessions at Blank Tapes also featured Steve D'Acquisto, a charismatic DJ who had met Arthur at the Loft and was determined to see the music recorded in the studio released on a reputable label. D'Acquisto duly approached Mel Cheren of West End Records, arguably the premier record company in New York releasing music for the dancefloor.

> Steven Hall: 'Steve D'Acquisto had the magic ear. Steve D'Acquisto could hear a hit: he had that ability, which in a way is a kind of genius which very few people have. I mean, usually people who have that ability end up running huge record companies.'

The studio takes for 'Is It All Over My Face?' included a male and a female vocal version and numerous subsequently released recordings that evoke studio spontaneity verging on pandemonium. According to associates of Steve D'Acquisto, he would invite people he'd met on the street to visit the studio to participate in the musical energy. However, for all Arthur's adherence to the philosophy of first thought, best thought – one D'Acquisto shared with a vivid enthusiasm – there was a foundational order to the recording sessions.

> Peter Zummo: 'I didn't see too much chaos in the studio. When I was there, there may have been a band or a rhythm section in the live room and I was stuck off in a corner, but often it was just me and Arthur. One time I was in his apartment either rehearsing or recording – I didn't always know where it was going – when the phone rang and he came back in the room and said, "Now look, some really weird people are going to come up here now." So I just waited and worked with the equipment. I don't know who they were but they may have been some of the people who sang on "Is It All Over My Face?" All I knew was: "Are you doing anything Friday night? Can you come to the studio around eight?" There'd be music on the stand or there wouldn't. Arthur liked it when it was getting out of hand because that's when things get good, but that only happened because he set it up with many layers of process and the writing, recording and overlaying and happy mistakes. It was analogue and we all wanted to see those little red lights lighting up and the needles going into the red.
>
> 'I know people want to inject mystery and magic into the recording sessions but at some level it was just a skill, engaging in the process. Yes, we wanted to take it up a notch, we all wanted to get off, but the beat was good.'
>
> Lucy Sante: 'I was friends with Nan Goldin at that time, and I still sort of am, but I dated her for a week back then, and she was just starting to do her slide shows and one of the prize numbers she used was "Is It All Over my Face?" I thought this was the most amazingly explicit disco song I'd ever heard, and it was only later I found out it was Arthur, and I knew Arthur as this cello guy who played with Allen, seemed very peaceful, did not seem like the sort of person to put out this scabrous disco, you know?'
>
> Tom Lee: 'People infer a sexual element in the lyrics of "Is It All Over My Face?" But I always thought it was genuine joy. I remember it was a phrase Arthur and his father used, like – "Is it obvious?" Perhaps I was naïve!'

Peter Zummo: 'The female vocal version of "Is It All Over My Face?", the first time Arthur played it to me I said, "What is this? What are those notes?" I was really taken with it. "Those aren't notes," he said. "It's a woman I met from Brooklyn." And I said, "That is it!" Arthur had studied Indian music and he was aware of notes that were shapes, not just notes. Regarding his disco releases Arthur would say, "The whole thing is about trying to keep your head above water in Midtown."'

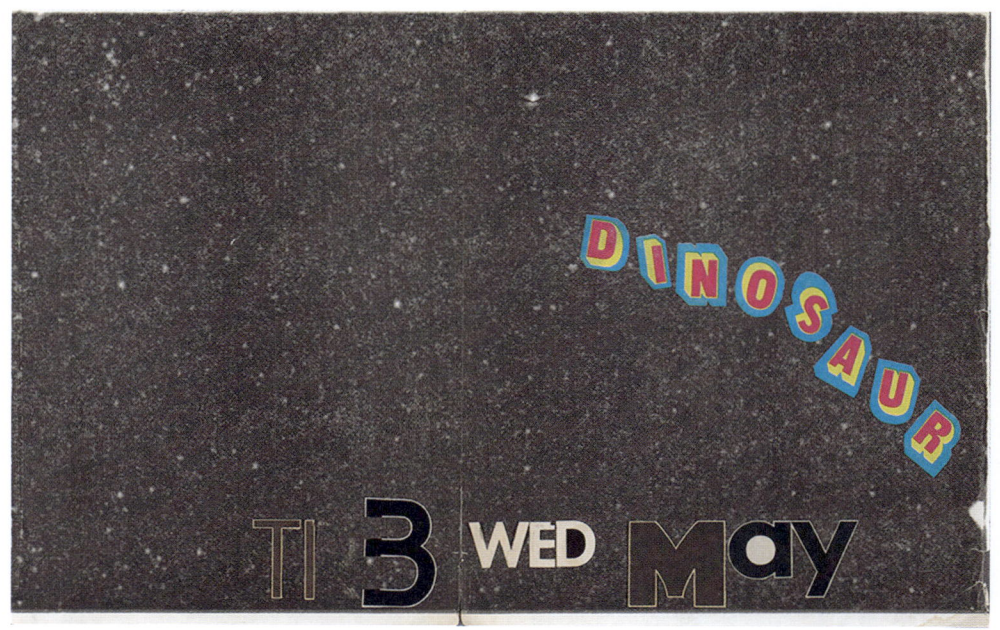

In the late 1970s two clubs had opened in Manhattan that reflected the new interdisciplinary and interpersonal social energy of the city. The Mudd Club was located at 77 White Street in deepest Manhattan; further downtown, Tier 3 was a smaller club at 225 West Broadway.

> Lucy Sante: 'I was a Mudd Club regular for the first year or so of its existence, and then I switched my allegiance to a club called Tier 3, which was this tiny little club in Tribeca where the major British acts often played, in this intimate space, before playing the much larger Hurrah's in town.'
>
> Peter Gordon: 'Tier 3 was a great place.'

Among the UK bands to make their USA debut at Tier 3 were The Raincoats, The Slits, The Pop Group, Delta 5, Young Marble Giants, A Certain Ratio and Bauhaus. The club's DJ booth was painted by Jean-Michel Basquiat along with a mural on the wall between the bar room and the main stage room.

Two years later Dinosaur would play the Mudd Club as Dinosaur L, accompanying Allen Ginsberg. The show was a benefit for Dudjom Rinpoche and also featured Afrika Bambaataa and the Rock Steady Crew.

The incipient No Wave scene of sometimes atonal, confrontational guitar music was also becoming synonymous with downtown and was a form of music Arthur avoided.

> Peter Gordon: 'Arthur wasn't into what they called No Wave or punk. Musically it didn't really do it for him. Arthur had, I think, a visceral response to the nihilism and the death energy and anger. Arthur's music was always positive.'
>
> Jeb Loy Nichols: 'There was an undercurrent in New York at the time, a mix in that world of people living on the Lower East Side who were really outsiders from the place they came from, and they didn't come to the city to be horrible, to be punks: they wanted to come to New York and not be bullied or behave like the people who had made them want to leave their hometown. I have visions of my mind seeing Arthur walking around with his headphones and thinking, That's the Loose Joints guy.'
>
> Will Socolov: 'I don't think punk was one of the styles Arthur was crazy about, there was something hard about it that didn't appeal to him.'

Loose Joints, 'Pop Your Funk' (B side of promotional copy of 'Is It All Over My Face?')
(West End Records, Promotional 12", 1980).

BEATWAVEOLDWAVENEWWAVE
RAP

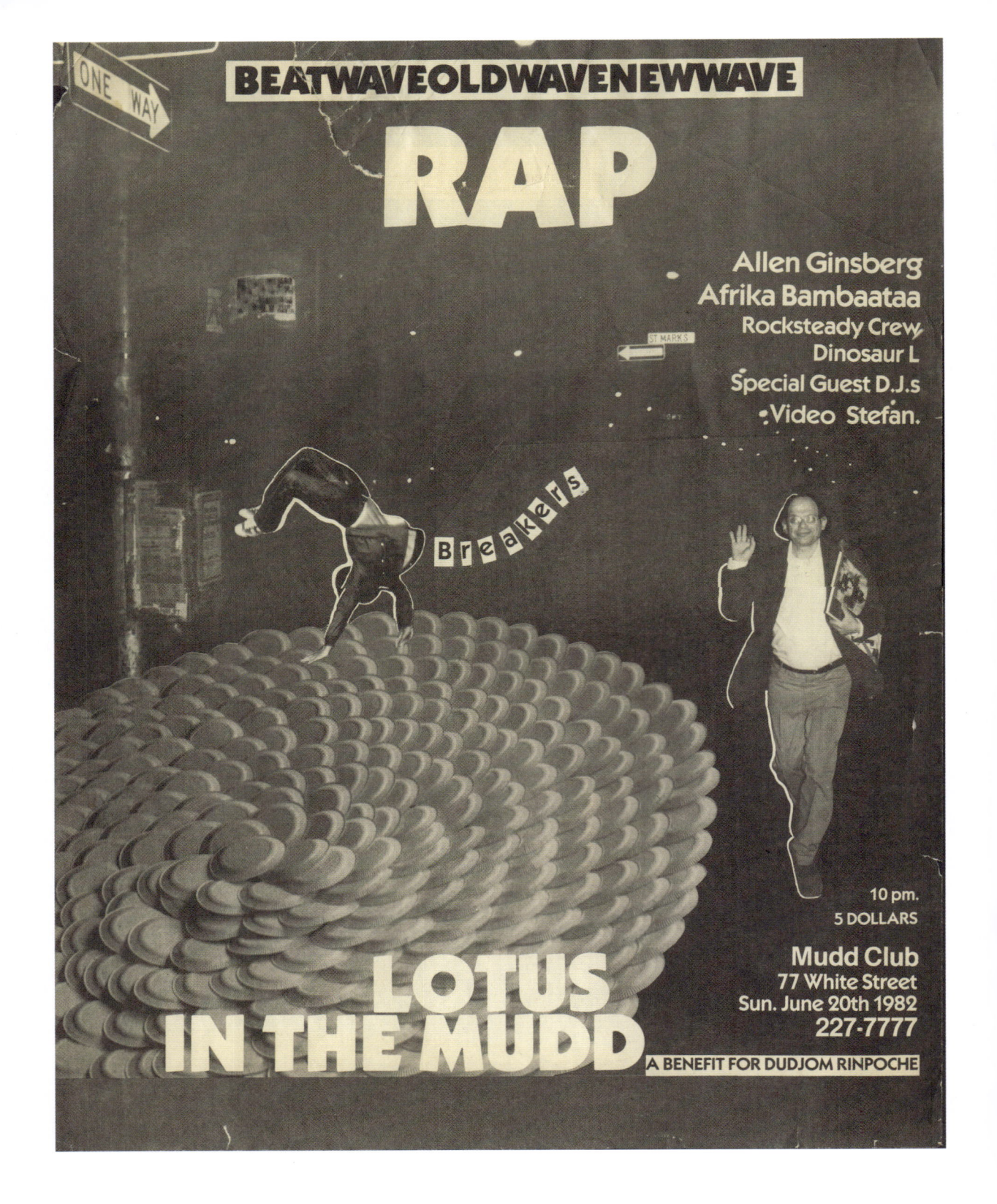

Allen Ginsberg
Afrika Bambaataa
Rocksteady Crew
Dinosaur L
Special Guest D.J.s
Video Stefan.

Breakers

LOTUS IN THE MUDD

10 pm.
5 DOLLARS

Mudd Club
77 White Street
Sun. June 20th 1982
227-7777

A BENEFIT FOR DUDJOM RINPOCHE

Peter Gordon: 'Arthur and I used to go to Union Square Park to buy loose joints and hear Loose Joints coming out of the boom boxes. I remember wearing a pair of black hard ball shoes that had black soles. One of the kids we were buying from asked me if I had been in Spofford, which was the youth detention centre, because they were like the shoes they wore there. Arthur was always paying attention to what was coming out of the boom boxes and cars passing by. As well as experiencing music in the clubs, a big part of hearing music was in the car or the park. There were times when you couldn't walk through there without hearing Loose Joints or Dinosaur L. And WBLS (the most popular black music radio station in NYC, with an extensive audience) on a Friday or Saturday night was pretty awesome.'

Steven Hall: 'Arthur knew that the disco records he had done were huge hits, and that he had been ripped off by the gay mafia: Mel Cheren at West End. He went after Mel, and that's like going after the real Mafia; Mel was the real gay mafia at that time, he was dangerous.'

Peter Gordon: 'The Mob was very strong in NYC at the time, so in some areas of the record business you may have still had that influence, whether at West End or the distributors or through licensing arrangements. But it is in those times in between paradigms when creativity can flourish. There wasn't a new paradigm that was set up yet but the old one was dying. At these points the bottlenecks are loosened and you have creativity going on in all sorts of areas. In business as well as the arts.'

Will Socolov: 'Arthur and I went to a lot of clubs, because that was his research. We went to Nicky Siano's clubs, we went to the Buttermilk Bottom, which is where Arthur's friend Walter Gibbons played. But I never saw Arthur dance. He was always more listening to the music, or he would sort of like be in his own little world, walking around, moving, but not really dancing.'

Tom Lee: 'For Arthur, the purpose of the visit to places like the Loft was to witness his song come on, to hear what it was doing coming through the PA. And sooner or later we'd turn around and go home.'

Kate Russell: 'At the discos, Arthur was collecting his own kind of information. I think he was there studying humankind and listening.'

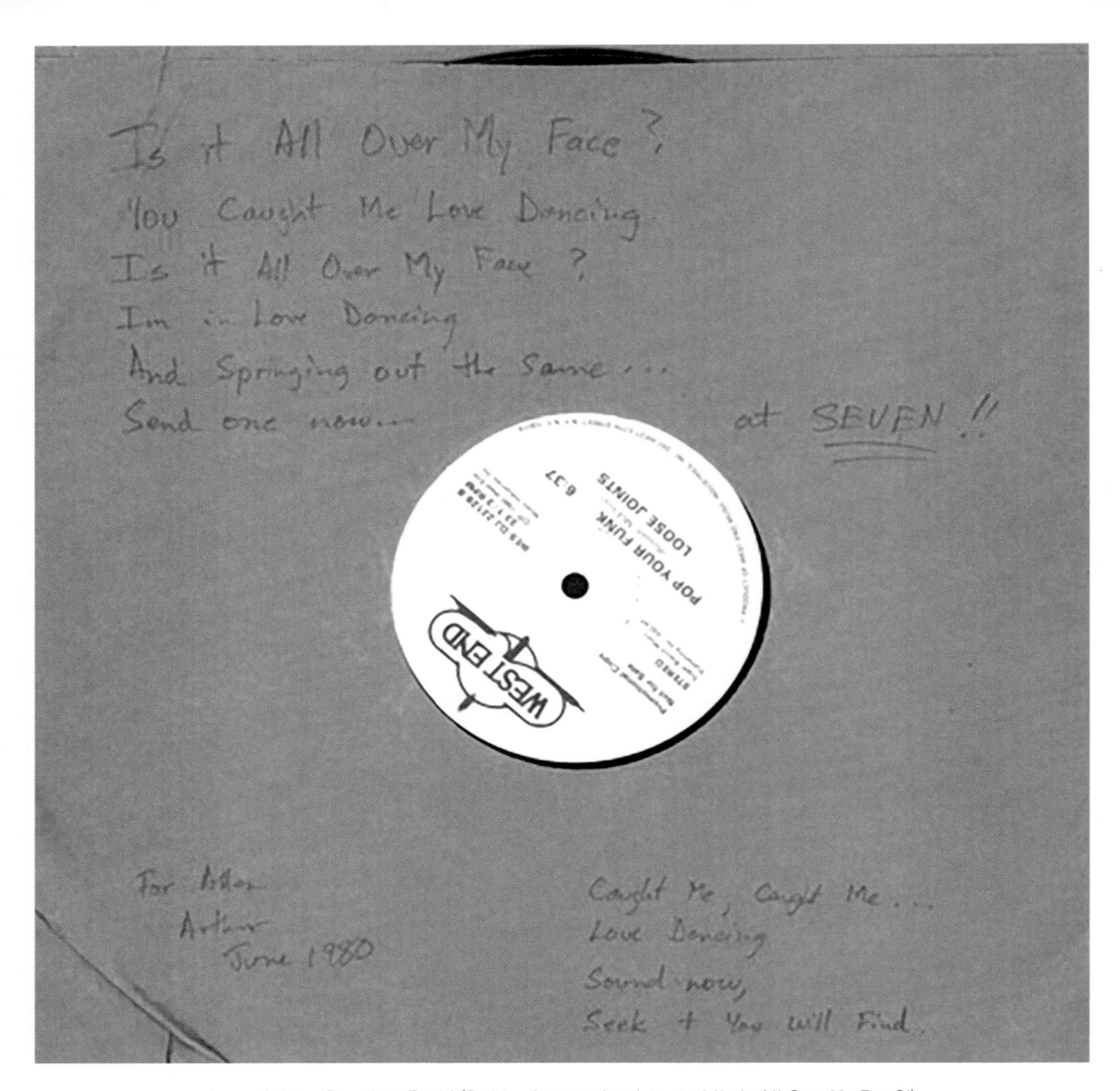

Loose Joints, 'Pop Your Funk' (B side of promotional copy of 'Is It All Over My Face?')
(West End Records, Promotional 12", 1980). Inscribed with the lyrics to 'Is It All Over My Face?'
written by Arthur for Allen Ginsberg. 'For Allen, Arthur, June 1980'.

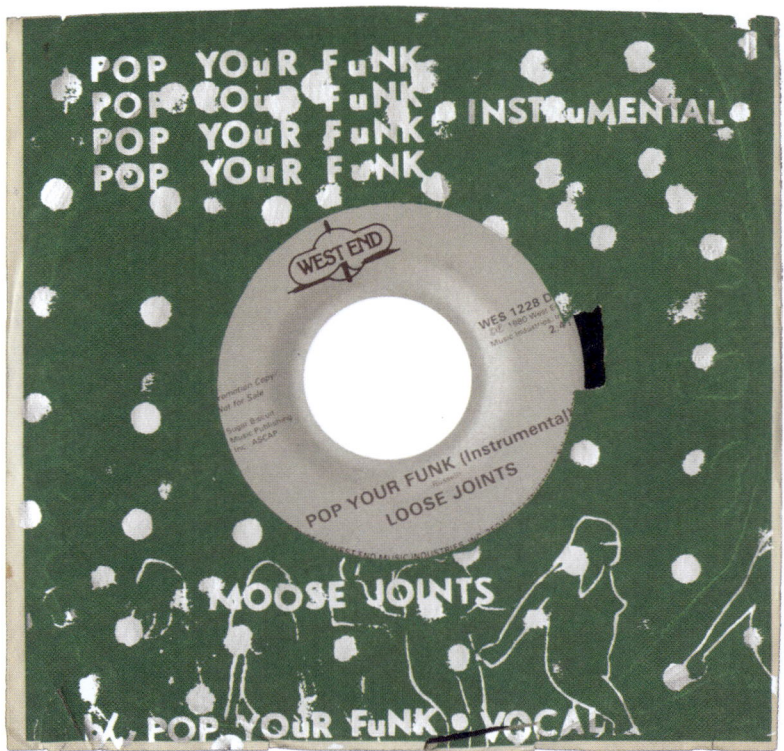

Loose Joints, 'Pop Your Funk' (West End Records, Promotional 7", 1980).
Coloured sleeves hand printed by Tom Lee.

GARDEN STATE RECORD PROMOTIONS & DOCKS

We Got
Loose
Joints

Performing Live!

"Is it all over my face?"

SATURDAY, NOVEMBER 8 - 11pm.
At DOCKS 776 BROAD ST NEWARK, NJ
Adm. $5. w/flyer - $6. w/out
100 Free Records & Buffet
DJ. GEORGE

WEST END Records

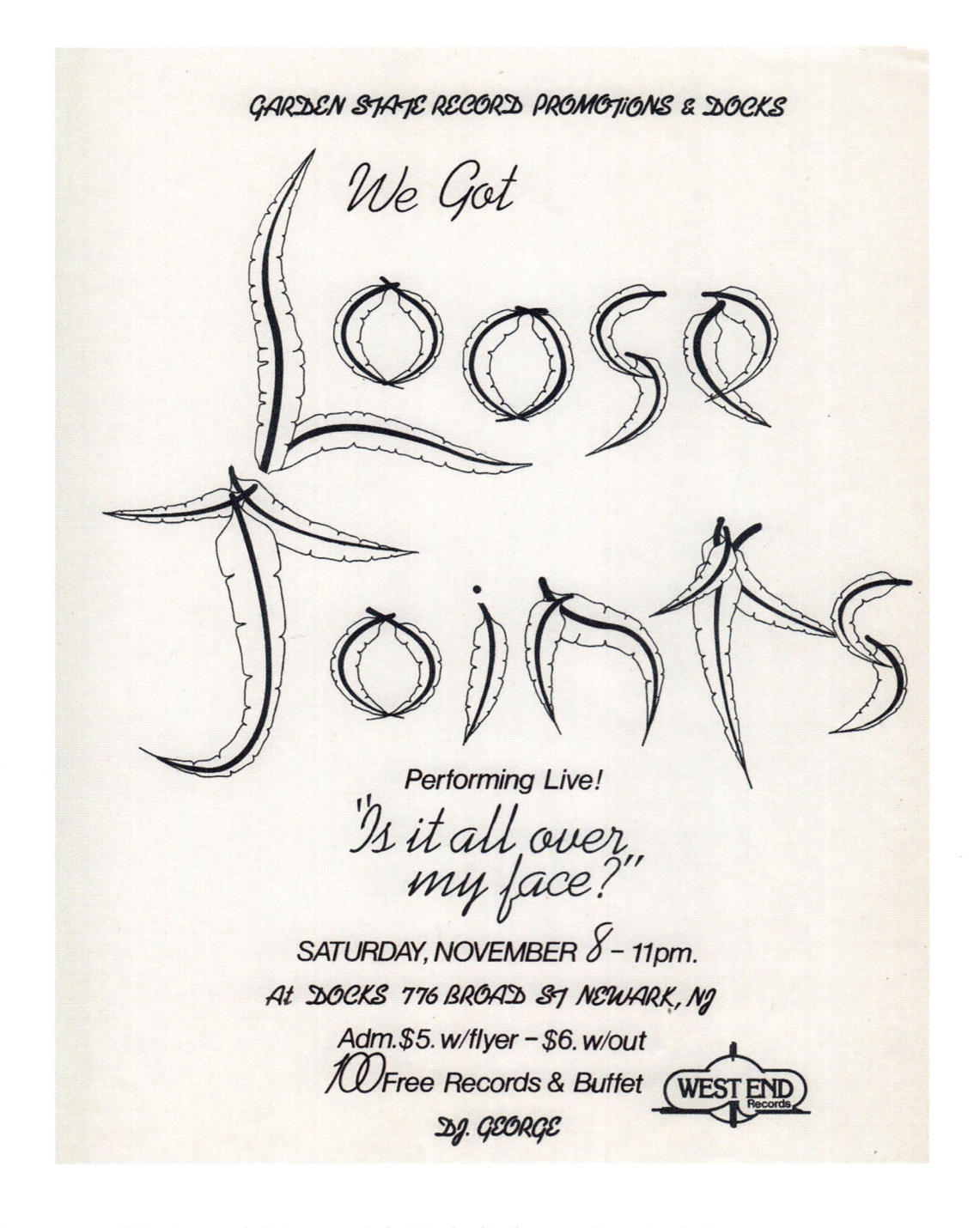

The success of the Loose Joints records led to invitations and contracts to play PA-style (public appearance) concerts at various nightclubs, known within the dance music industry as track dates. Although comparatively well paid, these showcases were more suited to a vocalist singing live along to a tape of their current dancefloor hit than a cellist attempting to play along to a backing track.

ARTIST ENGAGEMENT CONTRACT

AGREEMENT made this __1__ day of __December__ 19 __80__,
between __Loose Joints__ (hereinafter
referred to as "ARTIST") and __Fantasia Club__
(hereinafter referred to as "PURCHASER").

It is mutually agreed between the parties as follows:

The PURCHASER hereby engages the ARTIST and the ARTIST hereby agrees to perform the engagement hereinafter provided, upon all of the terms and conditions herein set forth, including those hereof entitled "Additional Terms and Conditions."

1. PLACE OF ENGAGEMENT __Fantasia Club__
   Exact address __120 20 Queens Blvd., Kew Gardens, N.Y.__
2. DATE(s) OF ENGAGEMENT __December 6, 1980__
3. HOURS OF ENGAGEMENT __1 show at 12:30__
4. REHEARSAL(s) __check in time__
5. FULL PRICE AGREED UPON: __$500 plus sound and lights__

All payments shall be paid by certified check, money order, bank draft or cash as follows:

(a) $ __250. dep.__ shall be paid by PURCHASER to and in the name of ARTIST'S agent, not later than __immediately__

(b) $ __250 bal.__ shall be paid by PURCHASER to ARTIST not later than __in cash before show__

(c) Additional payments, if any, shall be paid by PURCHASER to ARTIST not later than _____

PURCHASER shall first apply any and all receipts derived from the engagement herein to the payments required hereunder: All payments shall be made in full without any deductions whatsoever.

6. SCALE OF ADMISSION __500.__

Troy Entertainment Agency, Inc.
600 Old Country Road, Suite 305
GARDEN CITY, N.Y. 11530
(516) 741-2101
LICENSED/BONDED

Return all signed copies to agent:

__Loose Joints__ (ARTIST)
By _____
__Fantasia Club__ (PURCHASER)
By _____
Address: __120 20 Queens Blvd. Kew Gardens, N.Y.__
[signature]
Phone: __212 793 1000 Adam or Bob__

THE ABOVE SIGNATURES CONFIRM THAT THE PARTIES HAVE READ AND APPROVE EACH AND ALL OF THE "ADDITIONAL TERMS AND CONDITIONS" SET FORTH ON THE REVERSE SIDE HEREOF.

Peter Zummo: 'I did very little playing like that. I remember Arthur inviting me, but you never knew when or what was going to happen.'

Tom Lee: 'Arthur would do these shows at club. They were quite goofy. He brought the cello and the tape of the song and it would be a twenty-minute thing.'

Peter Gordon: 'These were borderline lip-sync gigs. $500 was very good. Arthur might have a singer or percussionist with him.'

Peter Zummo: 'Arthur would turn up and play his cello over a tape and maybe take a vocalist along. These were live playback shows. $500 was good money for a PA in 1980, and it was always nice to have contracts!'

Ernie Brooks: 'Because I had a vehicle I somehow got roped in to driving Arthur around to these very heavy-duty, mostly African American gay clubs. Arthur would get on stage and try and plug in his cello and it would start feeding back and the audience didn't want any of that. Arthur would always have problems with technical stuff, syncing with the drum tack, but $500 was a lot better than the hat going around some of the venues we usually played.'

Tom Lee: 'Arthur drove this car, a vintage Chevy, out from Iowa. Arthur's father gave it to him. Arthur then traded the car with Bob Blank at Blank Tapes in exchange for studio time. Arthur always had a need for studio money and knew Bob was interested in vintage cars.'

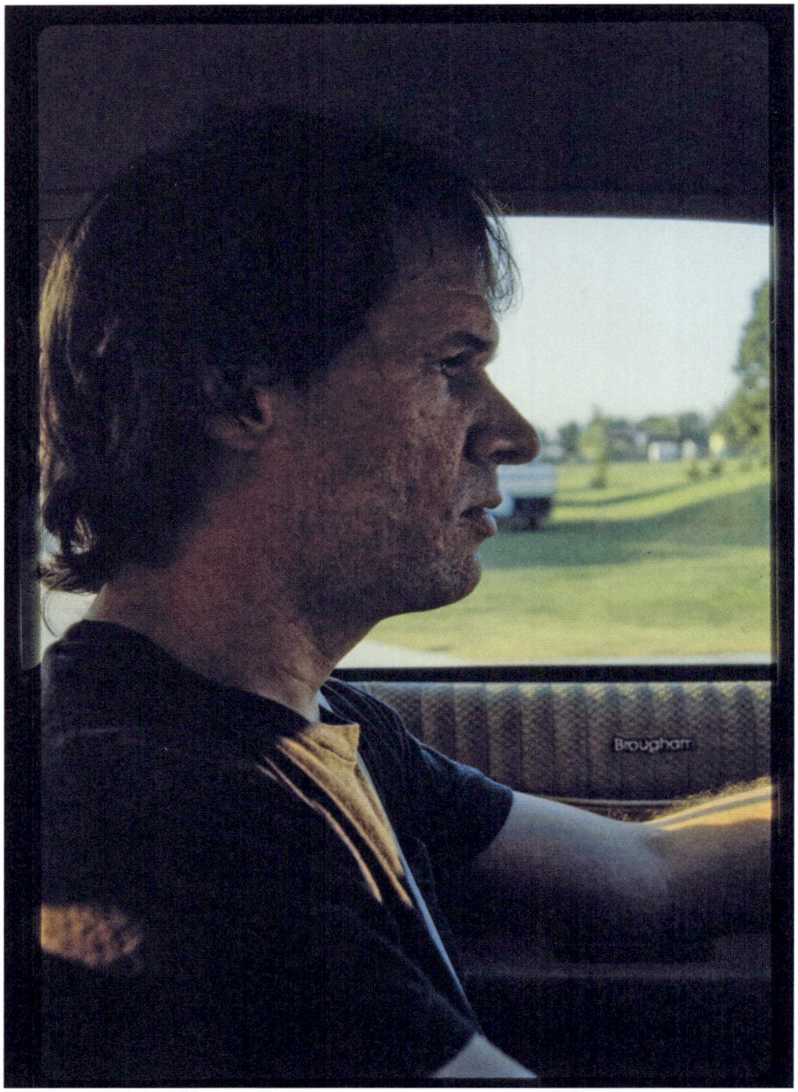
Brougham

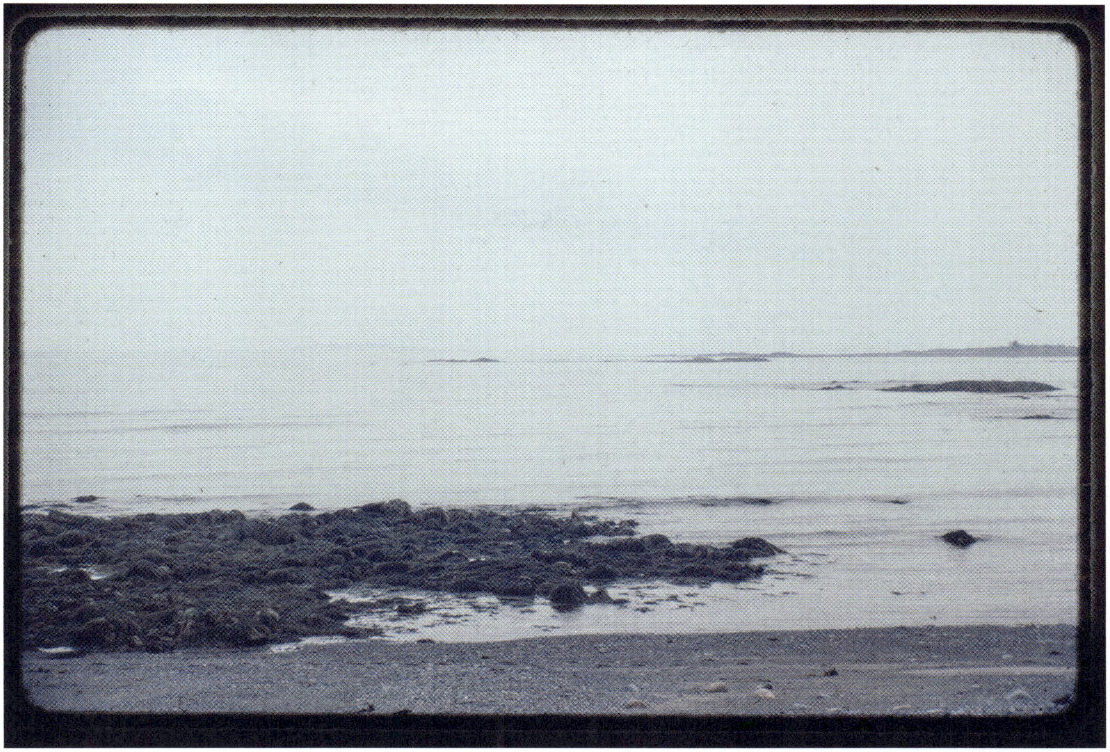

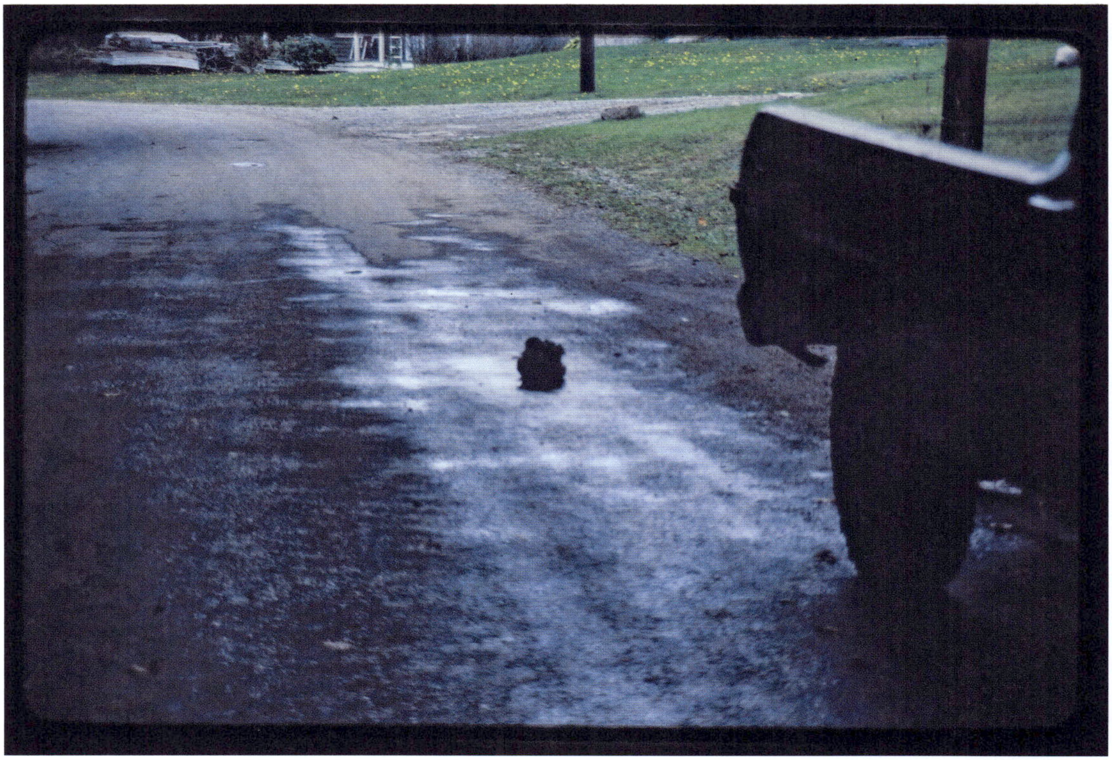

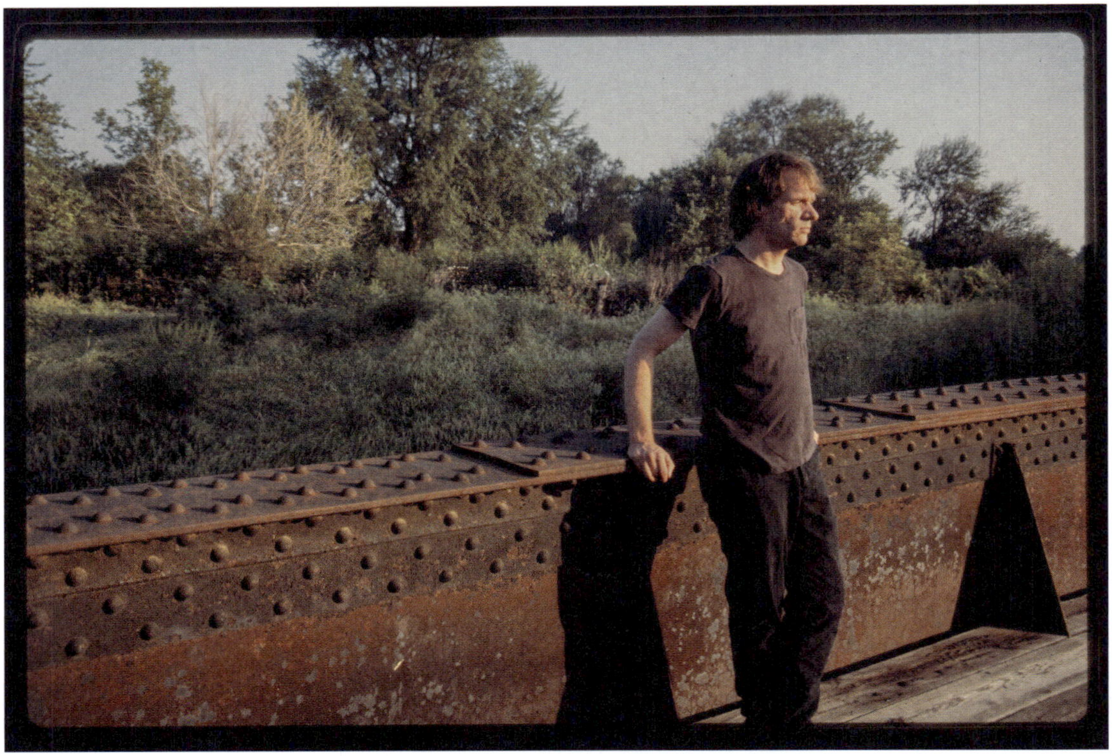

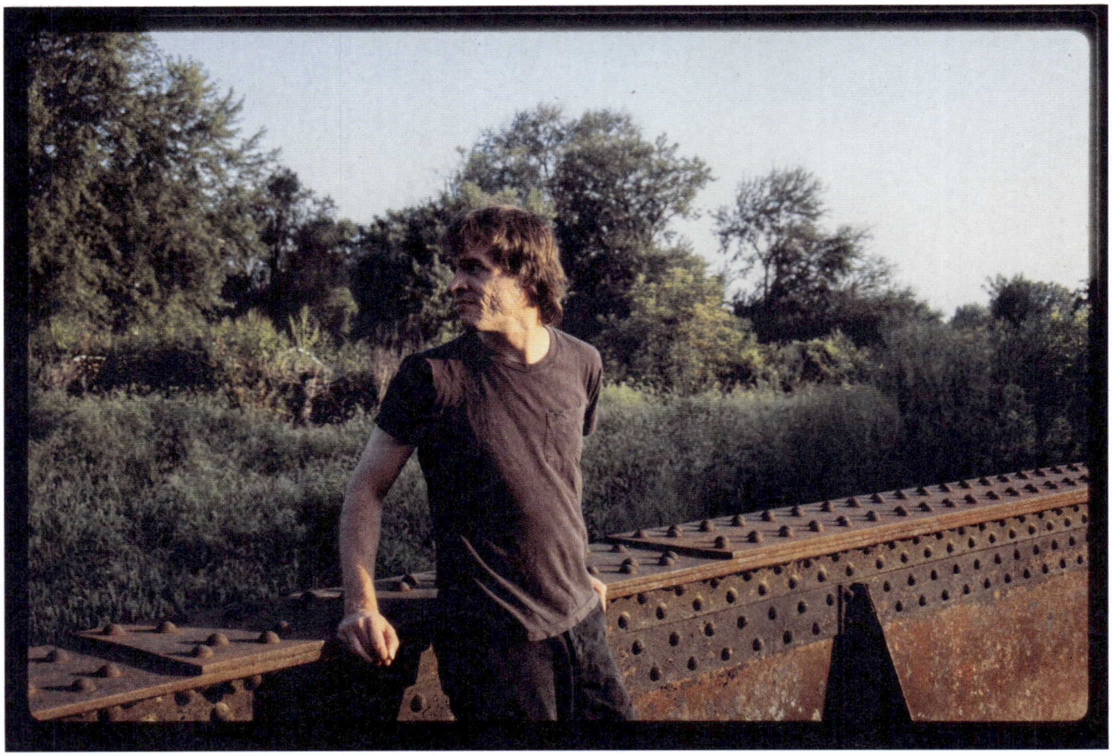

Tom Lee: 'This is where we washed the Chevy, near my brother's house in New Jersey.'

```
BLANK Tapes INC. Recording Studios
              37 West 20th Street   Telephone
              New York, N.Y. 10011  212 255 5313

                                            INVOICE
                                            N⍜  6180
Arthur Russell                              1/20/81
437 E. 12th St. No. 38
New York, NY  10009


1/20/81   Ordered by Arthur Russell      "Arthur Russell"

3 Hours of 24 Track Studio Time (Studio C) @ $75.00 per
hour                                                        $ 225.00
Studio Tape Charges:
    3 Reels of ¼" Tape @ $25.00 per Reel                      75.00
    1 C-90 Cassette Copy                                       8.50
                                                             308.50
                                        Sales Tax             24.68

                                        Total              $ 333.18


              Paid in Full
              Ck # 135
```

Tom Lee: 'Most of his studio time as well as new equipment was supported by his parents. It seemed at times awkward for him to ask them, but he would persist.'

Will Socolov: 'Arthur hustled people who had studios. He was on his own, trying to get studio time, because Tom wasn't rich, he wasn't rich, so he dealt with people like Bob Blank.

   'Arthur had a passivity to him and making records, producing records, you've got to make a lot of decisions, what works, what doesn't and he sometimes compromised with people just because he thought that was his Zen philosophy of getting things done: the problem was, it definitely hurt some of the projects he created.'

BLANK TAPES

C CK D

Date _____ Time _____ To _____
Bill To _____ P.O. # _____ Engineer _____
_____ Ordered By _____
_____ Artist-Product _____
Tel. _____ Mail ☐ Pickup ☐ Deliver ☐ Approved By _____

	QUANTITY	UNIT	TOTAL	REMARKS
Studio A - B - C				
Mix 1 - 2 - 4 - 8 - 16				
Studio Tape Charges				
Tape Copies 3" 5" 7" 10"				
Tape Copies 3" 5" 7" 10"				
Cassettes				
Editing or Leadering				
Copying Time				
Production				
Pulsing				
16 Mag Trans				
Masters Mono/Stereo 7" 10" 12"				
Processing				
Pressings 7" 10" 12"				
Labels				
Discs 7" 10" 12"				
Shipping - Packing - Mailing				
Postage				
Messenger				

Steven Hall: 'Arthur's whole thing when he got into the disco music was focusing on the drums, and finding these amazing drummers and falling in love with them, like Rob Shepperson who was the drummer for Tirez Tirez. Arthur was totally obsessed with this guy's drumming and particularly with his bass drum sound, and then Arthur and Bob Blank would spend sometimes five or six hours tuning the bass drum and getting the mic position right, getting the EQ right, and they both shared that obsession. Bob Blank was kick-drum and bass, that was what he got, and that was what Arthur tasked him to do. And everything else, Arthur could basically produce on his own, apart from when it got to something that was very technical in terms of editing and sampling, because that was a new thing.'

British airways

Flying between _____
and _____

Waco
Dec 25 '80

Dear Arthur

I stole this off B.A. I really really like the last tape I got. I have played it over many times here in Texas and I think it is perfect for the new play — I am not clear about which music should go into parts A B C. I think that there should

be a distinct dif. in
each section —

Sorry to have been
so hectic before leaving
— Anyway thanks
— Best wishes for a
Merry Christmas —

HAPPY NEW Year!!!

Much love
Bob

In 1980, Arthur was approached by Robert Wilson to write the music for his new opera MEDEA, based on the play by Euripides. Wilson had initially wanted to repeat the successful collaboration he had made with Philip Glass on the production of EINSTEIN ON THE BEACH. Glass had existing commitments and suggested that Wilson consider working with Arthur. Although justifiably excited at the prospect of working with Wilson and aware of the potential transformation in his career that might occur, Arthur found the process difficult and as the writing and recording of MEDEA progressed, relations between Arthur and Wilson deteriorated.

Bill Ruyle: 'From the correspondence it appears Robert Wilson was very keen on what Arthur was doing and the notes indicate that Arthur had a large-scale plan for the music for MEDEA, both for the instrumentation along with a chorus and how it would be performed. What I have gathered from records of the recording session is that Arthur was finding it very difficult to meet the deadline and the needs of Robert Wilson to have pieces to rehearse with the cast. In any case, Arthur recorded a lot of music for MEDEA and not all of it was used. He recorded instrumental music for MEDEA and he also had music for the chorus.'

Steven Hall: 'The big break with Robert Wilson was just a huge heartbreak for him, because he thought he'd made the big time then. That was exactly what he wanted to do, but the pairing was like two magnets repelling each other; two great geniuses. I love Robert Wilson's work. And in a way, it was a perfect pairing: that piece was only performed once, and it was Arthur's greatest work. Arthur never worked on anything else so hard and never poured so much energy into that, in a way that broke him, because he thought that would have put him up with Philip Glass, Steve Reich.'

Peter Gordon: 'Collaboration takes a certain type of energy at that level. I'm surprised Arthur's music wasn't taken up by more choreographers back then. The Wilson collaboration really traumatised Arthur. But someone could say to Arthur: "We want something coloured red." Arthur'd come in and try to explain why green is so much better than red.'

Bill Ruyle: 'Julius Eastman was working closely with Arthur on MEDEA, not just rehearsing the musicians but rehearsing the singers as well. From the rehearsal tape I've heard Julius was very capable of playing this music that was not in the most user-friendly notation. He ended up not having a live instrumental ensemble playing for the MEDEA workshops: it was pre-recorded music plus actors and a chorus singing primarily in Greek, occasionally accompanied by a pianist on stage. Arthur had musicians in the studio with him, the bulk of the music was recorded in the studio almost always with a click track. There'd be a core group and then there'd be overdubbing, and Julius was there for all those recordings helping co-ordinate them. Most of the material was recorded in stages; it wasn't a whole ensemble in a room at the same time. Of this large amount of material, some of it was used for MEDEA, not all of it but large portions of it.

'I've heard recording of more than one workshop performance. Those workshops happened and I think Arthur barely got the tapes of them to Robert Wilson in time for either the rehearsals or the workshop performances, I think he completed the studio recording the day before the performance. They were done at a studio called Secret Sound in Manhattan. It was all really down to the wire, and you can see in the correspondence there was tension with Robert saying, "Arthur, get this done."'

Ernie Brooks: 'At one level Arthur's misadventures with Robert Wilson were funny. It upset Arthur, but he kept saying, "I know I'm doing the wrong thing. I know I'm fucking up." I said, "Yes, you're fucking it up, to the point you're infuriating Robert Wilson." At some point people thought, As talented as Arthur is, he makes everything too hard. Arthur could be so laid back, but at the same time have very strong ideas about almost everything. In some ways he was shy but he could also be insistent and obsessive.'

Bill Ruyle: 'I played glockenspiel on a session and I had no idea what it was. He said, "Play only the notes that have asterisks either above or below them." There was a click track and Arthur was somehow counting along and indicating the measures of the bars, the notation was just whole notes, one whole note per bar. To me Arthur almost always seemed a little under duress, so at that time I didn't really know anything about the project and I didn't have a sense he was struggling. I did have a sense that when we did that overdub it was just one pass, one and done and no going back to make corrections, so there was, I think, a time crunch.'

Tom Lee: 'It was an extremely frustrating time; Arthur hired his friend Kirk to work on the score. They worked in our home. Arthur had built shelves in the apartment so each instrument had their own individual score that could be housed in their own compartment. He had gone to the lumber yard to get the materials to make the shelves. It was a big production for a few months, they did it as a work in progress at the Kennedy Center in DC, I think to raise more funds. I was with Arthur there. At the rehearsals, Bob wasn't happy with the music. Arthur needed some feedback but there was no communication.'

Bill Ruyle: 'There was a parting of ways. Arthur had ideas about doing things a certain way and apparently Robert Wilson had other ideas and they couldn't come together. I think there was frustration from the Wilson camp dealing with Arthur, saying he's not getting us stuff on time, when music comes in late there's not any chance to collaborate further, there's not a chance to work with it and mould it – and this is a common story, this sort of thing happens a lot.'

Tom Lee: 'The impression I got is they were equally frustrated with each other. It affected Arthur deeply. He struggled with the time frame of something like that. After it was over, he didn't dwell on it that much. But there he was working on MEDEA at the same time as he was going into the studio to remix one of his pop songs with Ernie; there were so many compartments in his head.'

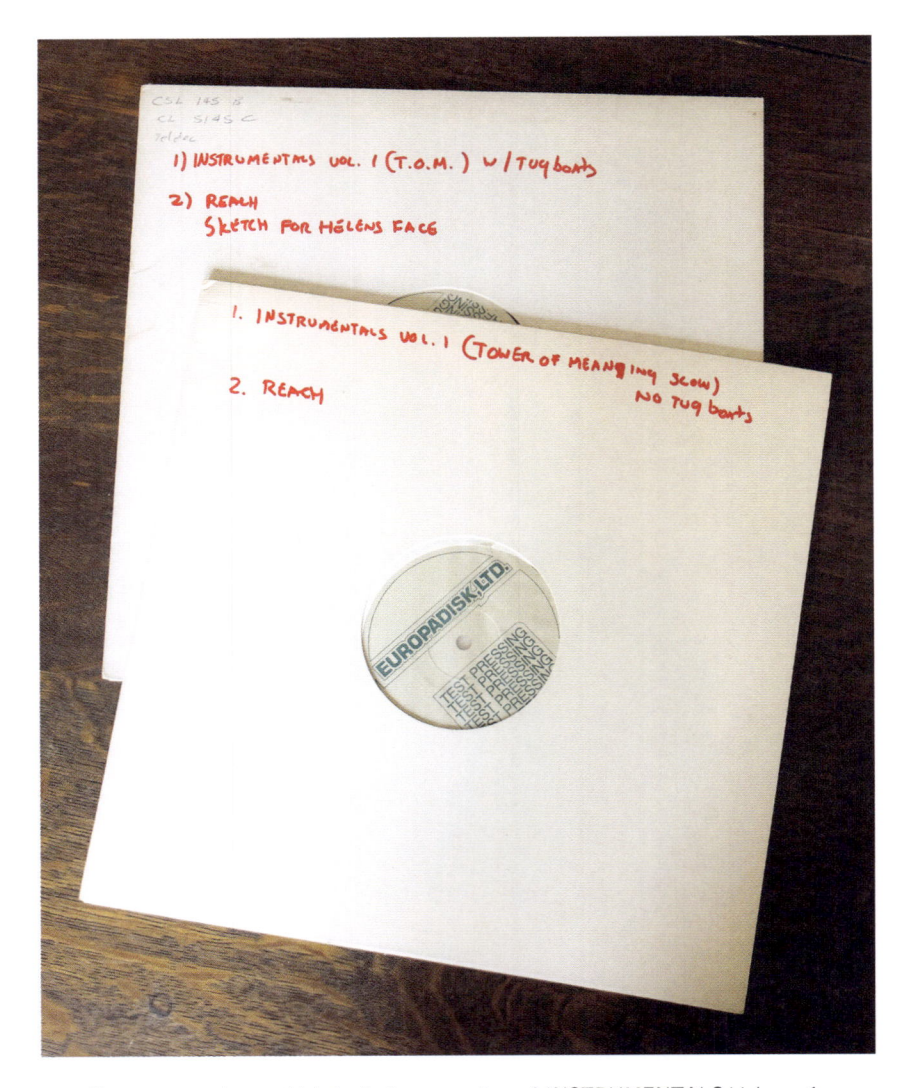

Two test pressings, which include a recording of INSTRUMENTALS Volume 1, 'Reach' and 'Sketch for Helen's Face'. One recording features the sound of tugboats; c.1981, both unreleased.

The recordings of tugboats speak to Arthur's love of water and the sound of water in particular, from which he continuously drew great comfort and inspiration. In an interview Arthur stated: 'There's something about water that does it to me. I have to live near water. I couldn't live in the centre of the continent. I go to see the Hudson river nearly every day.' He would also regularly take the Staten Island ferry to spend time on the water. In the East Twelfth Street apartment, Arthur would place a battery on a note on his keyboard in order to produce a drone that replicated the rhythm and noise of the ocean. He would also switch on a food blender to create a similar effect. Arthur's connection to water began during childhood. From the ages of around nine to twelve, his bedroom contained three fish tanks stocked with black mollies, neon tetras and angelfish, some of which he bred. The tanks were, according to family members, 'a complex affair', that included 'heaters, pumps and lights'.

The Musical Theatre Lab and The Byrd Hoffman Foundation

present

Euripides' Tragedy

MEDEA

in Prologue and Five Acts

Direction and Design

ROBERT WILSON

Music

ARTHUR RUSSELL

Production Design

Adaptation	Minos Volonakis
Transliteration	Athena Voliotis
Costume Design and Scenery Supervision	Kristine Haugan
Lighting Design	Jeffrey Nash
Choral Director	Gene Paul Rickard
Production Stage Manager	Joanne McEntire

Cast

Medea	Sheryl Sutton
Nurse	Caroline Thomas
Jason	John Nesci
Creon	Ari Petros
Tutor	Alexander Reed
Children	Paul Prappas, Scott Robinson
Aegeus	Rome Neal
Messenger	Terrell Robinson

Chorus

Evelyne Barton, Ann Borchert, Andrew Gold, Maria Hagisavva, Manolis Koutsourelis, Rome Neal, Lola Pashalinski, Ari Petros, Paul Prappas, Scott Robinson, Terrell Robinson, Lynn Swanson, Athena Voliotis

Choral Music Arrangement	Gene Paul Rickard and Robert Wilson
Choreography, Act IV, Scene A	Manolis Koutsourelis, Lynn Swanson
Scenic Construction	Brian Lago
Scenic Artist	Michael Rizzo
Properties	Beth Hirsch
Mask Design	John D'Arcangelo
Costume Assistant	Cristiana Senni
Visual Consultant	Ann Wilson
Hair Stylist	Diane E. Stokes
Assistant for Transliteration	Manolis Koutsourelis

Musical Theatre Lab

Production Manager	Paulette Laufer
Technical Coordinator	Peter Lang
Technical Director	Owen E. Parmele
Master Electrician	Robert A. Mond
Crew	Mary Nelle Osborne, Brett Turner, Rodney Wallace

> Dear Bob,
>
> Last night I dreamed we somehow broke the ice again and became friends. Everyone was there + was very angry. You performed a puppet show, I had to go to the bathroom and you thought I was being rude.
>
> I know you'll probably tear this up. I never wanted to hurt your show, I was struggling with my inability to go faster. I always thought that you would be pleased in the end, but now I'm sorry; you are angry.

Rome Neal: 'Arthur and I came to be good friends. He came to some of my events and knew I wanted to be an actor. He said to me, "Rome, I'm going to be doing a play by Robert Wilson at the Kennedy Center and we're going to be auditioning people at the City Center in Manhattan, I think you should go out and audition for it, I think you could get a part." I auditioned and out of what felt like a thousand people I got the part of Aegeus. Unfortunately, Robert wasn't happy with the music Arthur presented to him. I appreciate Arthur for bringing me on board for this because it actually got me my Equity card. Arthur got me into the actors' union.'

Peter Zummo: 'Arthur invited me to come and audition for the chorus of MEDEA. It was just him and Bob Wilson standing there. And Bob Wilson said, "Just sing something." I thought they'd be handing me a score and asking me to sing what was on the page, which I would be comfortable with. Instead, I had to think of a piece to sing. The only thing I could think of was "The Star-Spangled Banner". Apparently, it was quite embarrassing, and Arthur said, "Why would you do that? Why would you do that?"'

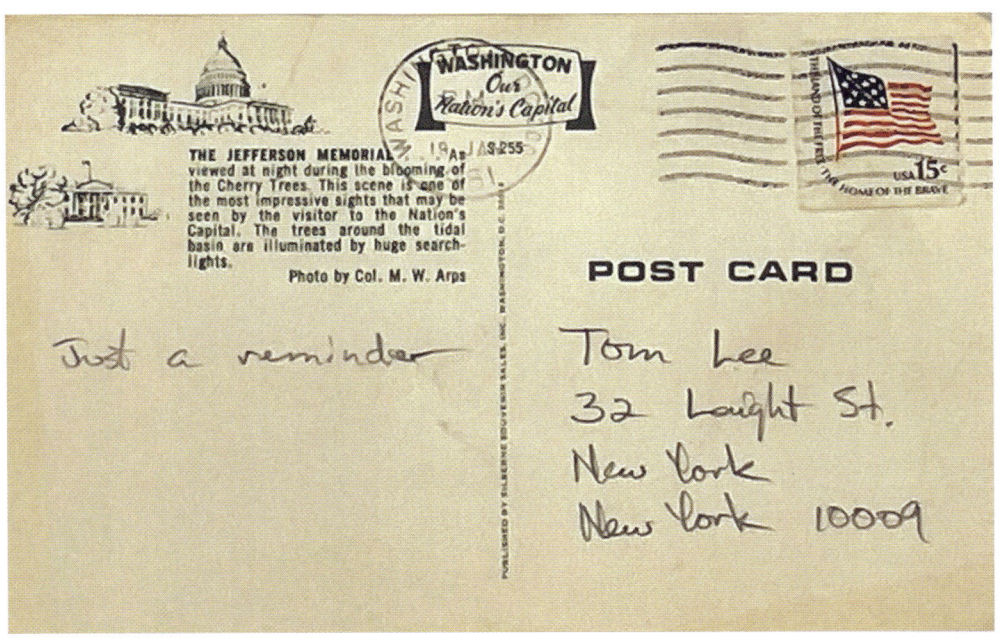

THE JEFFERSON MEMORIAL viewed at night during the blooming of the Cherry Trees. This scene is one of the most impressive sights that may be seen by the visitor to the Nation's Capital. The trees around the tidal basin are illuminated by huge searchlights.
Photo by Col. M. W. Arps

Just a reminder

Tom Lee
32 Laight St.
New York
New York 10009

In 1983, Philip Glass released Russell's composition, now titled TOWER OF MEANING and conducted by Julius Eastman, on his label Chatham Square, in an edition of 320 records.

> Tom Lee: 'Occasionally we'd go out to breakfast on a Sunday morning, to one of the local places and we'd run into Phil[ip Glass] on the street. This happened more than a few times. I would step aside and Arthur and Phil would have this intense conversation, usually about the fact Phil wanted Arthur to release something on his label.'

> Arthur
> Before I leave I'm listening to a few tapes to decide which ones to borrow and right now my ears have on the one from your concert of 3·1·80 at Phil Niblock's. Well I like it very very much and it should be on at least one side of an album (and some page(s) of the score could be on the cover and the date could be the title of the album) bye.
> T.
> Also have you seen my red sweatshirt around here. I've misplaced it
> And also file these tapes rather than leaving them on the floor — like this
> And Julius Eastman is at the Kitchen Jan 30th — Fridays.

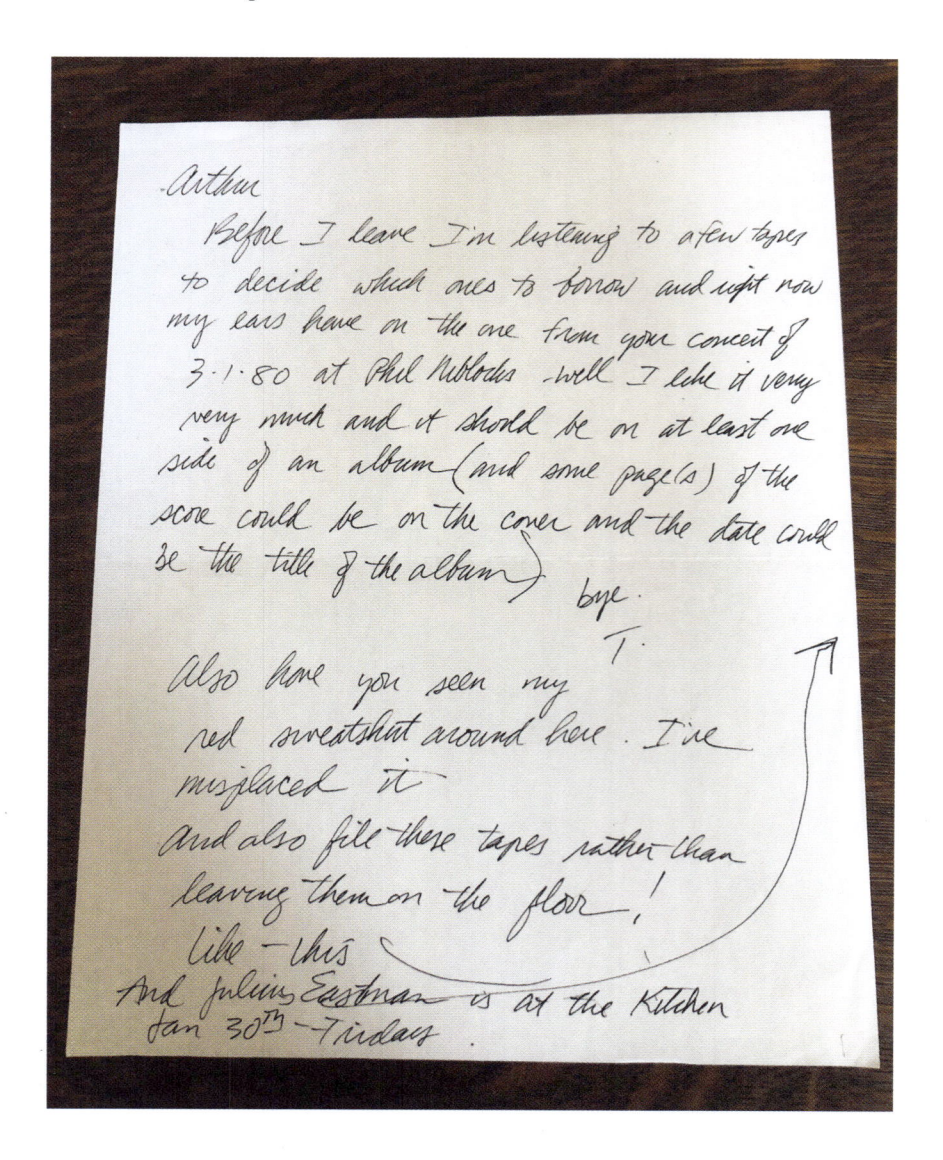

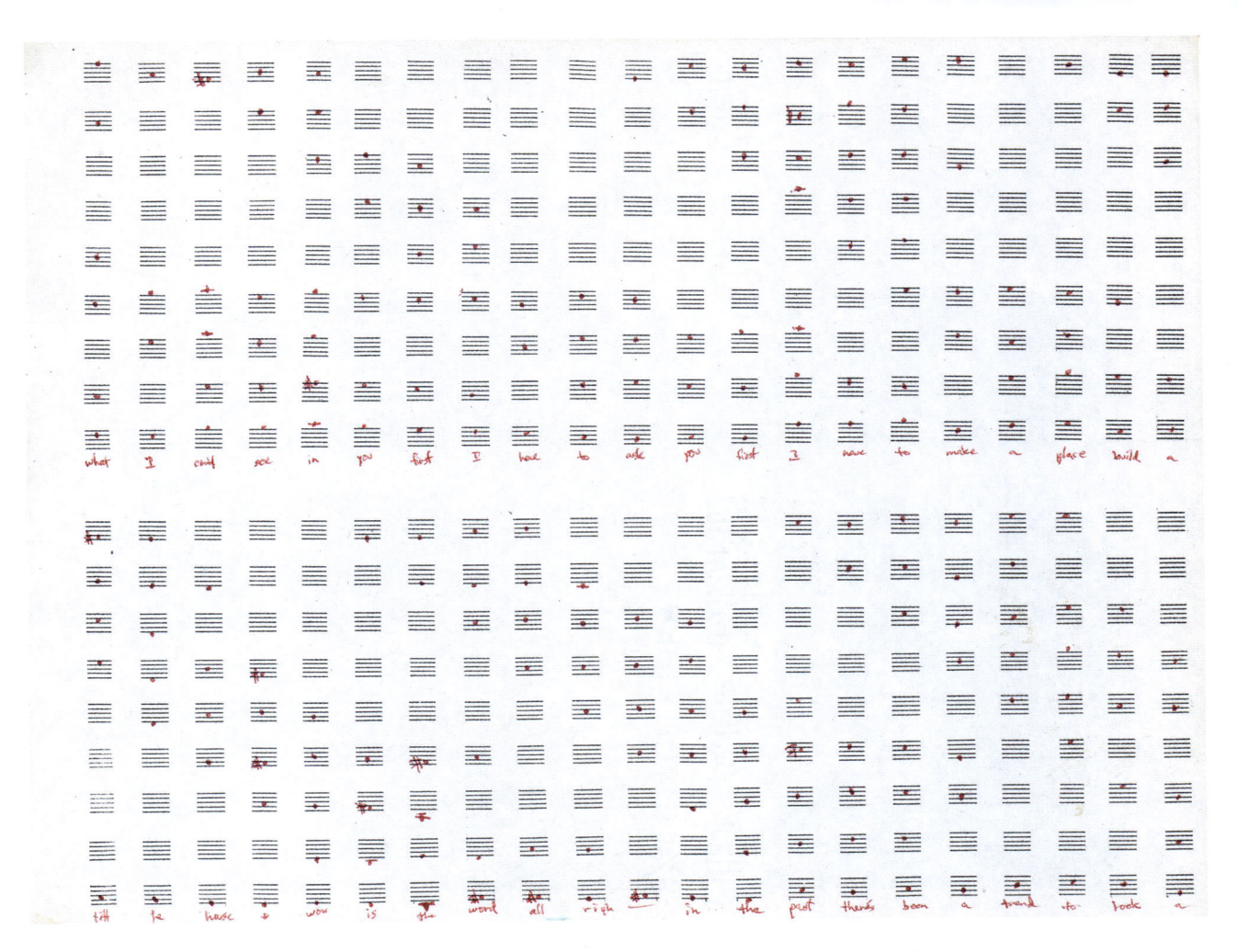

Arthur Russell's 'Tower of Meaning' score, 1981. A large section of the score has text, some of which reads like a love letter. The text also includes the names Tom and Tommy. The initials of the phrase 'Tower of Meaning' are TOM. There is also a suggestion in the text that Arthur may have considered giving the piece the titles 'Table of Meaning' and 'Temple of Meaning'.

Bill Ruyle: 'I think this was one stage of Arthur's composition process. There are no clef signs but I determined this was for treble clef. The other thing absent on this page is note duration. Did the text somehow have a relation to the duration of notes? The reason I wonder that is Arthur was interested in numerology. I'm curious if each of these words may have a numerical value according to Arthur's numerology system. It's just a thought. No one seems to know how he came up with those duration numbers.

'After Arthur and Bob Wilson had the falling out, what I understand is Arthur was desperate to get his hands back on the recordings, and he eventually did and then made some additions, I think he had Elodie Lauten do some overdubs on synthesizer. So the TOWER OF MEANING album is sort of like a suite from the MEDEA material.

'Some of the things on the TOWER OF MEANING LP were not used in the MEDEA production. Arthur made a mini architecture of the material, it has a certain kind of arc to it. He also varispeeded certain sections.'

Peter Zummo: 'For TOWER OF MEANING, Julius Eastman called me at 7 a.m. on Sunday morning to contract me for the session. I said, "Julius it's 7 a.m. on a Sunday morning." He said, "I'm contracting the session – I can call you whenever I want. Do you want to do it?" The original TOWER OF MEANING notation is not conventional music notation but whole notes with numbers. You can see how INSTRUMENTALS could be derived from that equally.'

Julius Eastman in rehearsal at the Kitchen, 1981.

The Kitchen Center for Video and Music
press release

JULIUS EASTMAN

January 30, 1981 8:30pm
$4.00/$2.50 members/TDF Music
The Kitchen, 484 Broome Street
Reservations: 925-3615

On January 30, The Kitchen's Contemporary Music Series will present <u>Humanity And Not Spiritual Beings</u>, two works by JULIUS EASTMAN.

"The first is a vocal solo, in which words and music are of equal importance. These words express my experience and thought as a human being. The melody colors, guides, and amplifies these words which do not diminish in importance without the music, just as the music is beautiful indeed without the words. I will sing about the concept of God and his conceptual substitutes.

The second work on the program is a written work for Pianos and Instruments, based on nothing else than Harmony and Melody. Harmonies and Melodies that build step by step, conclude, and then begin again.

I have sung, played, and written music for a very long time, and the end is not in sight. I sang as a boy soprano and I still sing as a boy soprano 30 years later. I have played the old masters on the pianoforte and have appreciated their help and guidance. But now music is only one of my attributes. I could be a Dancer, Choreographer, Painter or any other kind of artist if I so wished; but right thought, speech and action are now my main concerns. No other thing is as important or as useful. Right thought, Right speech, Right action, Right music."

(Julius Eastman)

484 Broome Street between West Broadway and Wooster, New York City

A MEMORIAL CONCERT OF THE MUSIC OF

CORNELIUS CARDEW
(1936-1981)
FOR THE BENEFIT OF HIS FAMILY

Tuesday, May 25, 1982, 8:00 P.M.

Symphony Space
New York

> Steven Hall: 'Steve D'Acquisto found out West End was making all these secret reprints of Arthur's songs and selling them on the black market directly to DJs, and Arthur realised that "Is It All Over My Face?" had made a huge amount of money for Mel Cheren, and then Arthur never got to see it. That's why he started his own record company, because he realised that's the only way he could get the money back.'

Arthur would visit record stores and see reprinted copies of his releases for sale of which he had not been informed. Although aware that he was working in an area of the music business that was rife with fly-by-night accounting and sharp practice, his frustration was such that he established his own label, Sleeping Bag Records, with co-founder Will Socolov, a process he would also ultimately find unfulfilling.

Arthur also needed to finance the completion of a set of recordings he had been working on with the intention of releasing either a Dinosaur L or Loose Joints album. Socolov set up a meeting between himself, his father, D'Acquisto and Arthur that resulted in Socolov's father investing $2,200 towards the completion of the recording – a sum of money D'Acquisto was apparently reluctant to pay back.

> Will Socolov: 'Arthur was always like, "We should do something for your father," because Arthur had a different mentality to Steve. I cannot tell you how many times Arthur would walk down the street, and there'd be a bum and they asked for money and Arthur, he would have like $5, he'd give the guy a dollar. And I didn't give the guy anything, I'm going like, "Arthur, you're broke, why are you giving ..." but that was part of Arthur's persona. Arthur was a really sweet guy. West End dropped them, and Arthur and I had become friends. We ran into each other and started talking, and after talking for about an hour Arthur said, "Would you like to start a label?" I said, "Sure."'

The first release on Sleeping Bag was 24>24 MUSIC by Dinosaur L, recorded in 1979 and released in 1981 in a run of around three hundred copies. .

Will Socolov: 'We called the company Sleeping Bag because we didn't want to be like a slick disco company; we wanted to be irreverent and ridiculous, and that's why we came with that jacket, the universal jacket with the flying saucer and a sleeping bag and like a camping scene. That's when guys had Nehru jackets and Jheri curls and they were looking supercool, and we were like, "Fuck it, we're not doing that." And it served us: I mean, people told me that specifically, they said, "It makes you different, it makes you stand out in a way, because you're not doing the same shit like all these street labels that had one or two good songs," but if they did jackets, they would be always gold and diamonds and watches, jewellery and shit like that. We were like, "We're not doing that."'

In 1982, 'Go Bang #5' by Dinosaur L was the first single to be released on Sleeping Bag Records. It was followed by the label's second single: 'Weekend' by Class Action, another track that became synonymous with the vibrancy of downtown nightlife during the era.

Peter Zummo: 'Part of the idea of being successful in whatever commercial-underground scene this was, was handing stuff over to people who would add to the lustre and add something different to it. Arthur would edit and select from what I was playing in real time. I think for the mix of "Go Bang!" that François Kevorkian made, Arthur took a solo I did at the end and put it at the beginning.'

Tom Lee: 'I printed up dozens and dozens of colours of this design for Arthur to approve, but he went with black-and-white. First thought, best thought.'

Peter Gordon: 'I'm sure Arthur didn't like the violence in this cover. For the track "Clean on Your Bean" I was working at the Big Apple Circus and there was an act from the circus school in Harlem with a couple of kids who rapped. I mentioned them to Arthur and he said, "Let's bring them into the studio," – and that was "Clean on Your Bean".'

Peter Zummo: 'I've heard unedited versions of 24 > 24 and I think I'm playing all the time. There was music on the stands for these sessions. Some of it was jamming, I don't remember which record it became, but I remember being in front of a mic outside the live room in the studio and Arthur saying to me, "Just do your chromatic thing," so that would have been improvised according to my schemes, but frequently there'd be pages and pages of music and I'd say to Arthur, "Where do you want me to start?" and he'd say, "Anywhere."'

Peter Gordon: 'There weren't filled-out arrangements but there were fragments of arrangements that were modular so they could be moved around.
    'The title 24 > 24 refers to having twenty-four tracks, then mixing down to another twenty-four tracks. It was a means of generating material: that's your raw material, your work, there are different iterations of it, but it's almost like the iterations are less important than the process itself.'

Rome Neal: 'It was no hassle in the studio with Arthur. He knew what he wanted, there was a free range to do what anyone needed to do to make it happen.'

Steven Hall: 'For 24 > 24 MUSIC, my idea was, when we were in the studio, it was like everyone was in love and everyone was in heaven and having a party and making these wonderful things and projecting that party, literally projecting the feeling of that party on to a dancefloor with the right DJ.'

A proposed full-colour picture sleeve for the album 24 > 24 MUSIC by Dinosaur L, printed by Tom Lee.

Will Socolov: 'When "Go Bang!" was mixed by François, I went to him and picked up an acetate and he said, "Bring it to David Mancuso at the Loft." Most nights, like everybody else, I would get on line at the Loft to get in. That night, when I came with the acetate, I got in line – there was a long line to get in – and all of a sudden, another side door opened, and someone who was working for David, said, "Will, come in." They knew I had this acetate, and they put it on, and the place didn't erupt: people were just grooving on it, whatever. But then – and I've never seen David Mancuso do this before – he lifted the needle off, during the party, and didn't mix it, put the same record back on. He only had one acetate, so he lifted it up at the end of the song and played it a second time. By the time he played it the second time, the place was erupting. They were going crazy.

'I had called Arthur and told him I had the acetate and was going to play it at the Loft. I got there at about one o'clock in the morning; Arthur took a nap and then came down, so it was like three in the morning. David had already played the record twice and then one more time before Arthur got there. So it had played three times in the club, so people were now getting used to it and listening to it, and they were familiar: they were at the party.

'He played it again, and Arthur came up to me, and people are now – I'm like pinned against the wall, staring. I'm not pinned by anybody pushing me: I was just pushed against the wall because I was watching the place go crazy and I was enjoying it so much. And Arthur walked up to me and said, "We're ruined." I said, "What?" He said, "Listen to the drums. François fucked up the EQ of the drums: we're ruined," he said. And I said, "Arthur," – and I said this to him: I mean, and I loved Arthur – I said, "You fucking asshole. Look at this place: that's the best you can say?" I said, "These fucking people, they're bouncing off the walls. I haven't seen any other song tonight that they're bouncing off the walls. People are loving this record."

'I mean, one guy just looked at me and goes, "Man, it's a fucking great record"; other record labels, people are coming up to me, saying, "It's genius." And François, I believe, said to Arthur, "This is one of my masterpieces." Arthur's original reaction was that, "We're ruined," because he said, "Compared to other songs, the drums ..." – I said, "You can't compare it. It's what it is. It's by itself. If you listen to it by itself, it's phenomenal."'

Tom Lee: 'The relationship between Arthur and Will Socolov was very difficult. On the one hand Arthur thought Will was ripping him off and refusing to release his music. On the other hand, Will probably expected his business partner to have a phone and be contactable and keep office hours every now and then. Towards the end of his life Arthur and Will reconciled and would go to clubs together. I was thankful for Will's kindness and support as the years went on.'

Steven Hall: 'I was about to sign my deal with Sleeping Bag Records, with Will Socolov at the desk, and literally when I was about to sign the contract, Arthur grabbed the pen and pulled me out into the corridor and said, "Don't sign it, because I'm going to lose you; you're going to become a big star and then you'll never want to work with me again." So I didn't sign it! He had this great ambivalence about him where he thought he had the ability to make someone a star but then they might turn around and take advantage of him.'

Dinosaur L, 'Go Bang! #5 / Clean on Your Bean #1' (Sleeping Bag Records, 12", 1982). The Sleeping Bag house sleeve was designed and drawn by Arthur's friend Joel Sokolov.

Will Socolov: 'Frankie Crocker, who was on the most important radio station in New York, which was WBLS at the time, played "Go Bang!" a couple of times, and when he did, the sales exploded. But he wouldn't play it a lot because it was too long and it was too weird, but he did play it, because Crocker went to the Garage a lot, he loved to play shit that Larry was playing that was hot. But that was a song that didn't translate as well to radio; it was really a club phenomenon. It was a peak song. Larry played "Weekend" and he played "Go Bang!", he had more than just two, he had many, but those two were what he called peak songs: the peak of the night.

'Numerous nights I was there and the place was going crazy to "Go Bang!" and he would shoot the confetti, and when he shot the confetti, that really was the peak, because those cannons can only get loaded once: once they get shot, they're empty, and that was his high point of the night. I also remember hearing "Go Bang!" on the beach at Coney Island. A lot of the kids that would go to clubs went down to Coney Island on a Sunday. They'd leave the clubs, hadn't slept, they'd go crash, dance, whatever. They went to Washington Square Park and Coney Island. And you could hear "Go Bang!" in those places solidly for a couple of years.'

WALKING ON SUNSHINE

Featuring
ROCKERS REVENGE
Special guest
**Soul Sonic Force
"PLANET ROCK"**

Also
Dinasour L "Go Bang"
T-Ski Valley "Catch The Beat"
Jazzy Five & Tina B "Jazzy Sensation"
Newyorican with Joe Bataan "Ritmo Suave"
Slvck "Beat The Bush"
Prince Charles "Fool For Love"

Thurs. July 15th

At The
FUN HOUSE
526 West 26 Street
New York City

Info: 691-0621

Master D.J.
Jelly Bean Benitez

ADM. $10.
Doors open at 10:00
Ladies Half Price Till 11:00PM

A SUNSHINE PARTY TIME PRODUCTION

Mustafa Khaliq Ahmed: 'The night that my son was born, we're in the hospital, in the private room, and in the middle of the night, like two or three o'clock in the morning, the black radio station that we listen to – because going back in those days, the music was very segregated – WBLS was the station, and in the middle of the night, "Go Bang!" plays. "Oh, bingo, are you kidding me?" I'm saying. "That's Arthur, that's Arthur!"

'And it was like, somebody decided to put that on the playlist, in the middle of the night! My son was born five hours later. That was 1982. So you would have heard this overnight on 16 October 1982. That is a true story. That's how I knew Arthur was a dude.'

Jeb Loy Nichols: 'Music felt like it was in the air, you turned on WBLS or you'd walk around town and that music was absolutely totally a part of the world.'

Tom Lee: 'Arthur and I heard "Go Bang!" on WBLS. There was also one momentous Sunday morning when we heard it coming up from the street to our apartment from a car. There was a little bit of that, of the song being in the air and that was exciting, but it was something that only happened in the New York area.'

Will Socolov: 'The amount of people that loved "Go Bang!", it crossed over, it really appealed to all different types of people.'

Rome Neal: 'Me and Arthur did a show at the [Paradise] Garage for "Go Bang!" People were hearing the song all over the place in New York and they were going crazy. They never met the group. So Arthur said, "We've got a gig to do the Garage and it's going to be on the Fourth of July and we're going to play 'Go Bang!'" I remember that one very, very well. The Garage was the Loft on steroids. They were really wild there. All different persuasions. All different sections of the LGBTQ+ community, all fun-loving folks just enjoying themselves and the music. And when they heard us play "Go Bang!" they went crazy; someone threw firecrackers up and security had to stop them. I was walking up the stairs to the stage and I turned round to someone and asked, "What's the first words of the song?" I was so hyped. But that was the spot and that was the song, and to be accepted by that audience at the Garage meant you were the king on the throne, because when we went out there they went off. They just loved it. The spirit in that place, some people were all high and everything, but in the Garage, I think that just took their spirit higher.'

Geoff Travis: 'Vince Aletti, the great authority on disco, took me to the Paradise Garage to see what was going. That was mind-blowing for me, a young suburban boy from Finchley. And Arthur took me, as well, and those were the two times that I went, and both times were magical, almost like I could hardly believe it was real.'

Jeb Loy Nichols: 'I went to the Garage regularly. It was not like Tier 3 which was a hang-out place but Paradise Garage you went there to dance. You paid to get in. Everyone paid, no one got in for free and you went in and you danced for five or six hours. It was an event, you didn't go every night. It was very black, very gay and very, very welcoming.'

Will Socolov: 'I remember being on Carmine Street, which is where Vinyl Mania, the record store, was, a block away from the Garage. Vinyl Mania was open on Sundays, because kids would leave the Garage at eleven, noon, whatever time Larry closed, and they would go in and buy a shitload of records. They knew what records Larry was playing, so they'd play it in the store, and people were like, "What's that record? Buy it."'

Jeb Loy Nichols: 'I did it myself. I used to go to Vinyl Mania, just beyond Tribeca, because they catered to people who'd come out of the Garage. You'd sing a bar of a song you'd heard and they'd sell you a copy.'

Will Socolov: 'One day, Arthur and I were walking on Carmine Street, because we were going to go see Charlie Grappone at Vinyl Mania and all of a sudden, there's an entourage coming down the street. Larry Levan is in the front with seven or eight other people, and then behind him, there's another seven or eight: it was like a huge moving crowd. And he saw Arthur and he just started screaming, "I love you, Arthur!" Larry played "Go Bang!" all the time, and Larry did love Arthur, but Arthur was sort of embarrassed or shy. He didn't dislike it, believe me, but he didn't know how to handle it. But I remember that I almost felt like the proud parent, like I wanted to push Arthur up front and say, "Yeah, he's the genius creator," and whatever.'

Alison Salzinger: 'Arthur was obsessed with making beats. He would spend hours and hours doing that; he was really into club music and that was part of his mystique for me. He had this art music world and this club music world. I never saw him dance, ever, but he knew that world and I thought that was ultracool.

'I would bump into him sometimes and he would have his headphones on and he would just be in a cloud of Arthurness. You'd have to knock on the side of his head and say, "Helloooo!" He was endlessly creative and always working on things.'

Lucy Sante: 'I'd pass Arthur in the building and he'd be wearing his headphones. I don't recall ever actually speaking with him, but he was very friendly!'

Alison Salzinger: 'I remember meeting him on St Mark's Place and thinking to myself, My God, this guy never stops working. He had just come from hours in the studio and was heading home to start working on his tapes again, which he'd been listening to on his way home. He never stopped working. He was lucky to have Tom taking care of him. I don't know how he would have survived physically, mentally, without him.'

Steven Hall: 'One quality the few people I think are geniuses have is that they literally cannot help themselves from constantly working. Even when we might be sitting talking about some boy we were looking at, Arthur might have been making notes about something about the boy or something, an idea about something he was going to say about what he saw, so it was constant.'

Tom Lee: 'Arthur was not able to get a part-time job to support his music. It just wasn't in his psyche. He worked briefly for a week or so as a messenger, but he had me and he had his parents so for whatever reasons – and it wasn't a brief time, it was twelve years with me – he was able to wing it along. He definitely had higher aspirations, maybe because of his success with dance music or his attraction to pop music. He had a huge collection of Tommy James and the Shondells records, I don't know if people in the downtown music world were interested in that.'

Kate Russell: 'My parents absolutely did not see or experience Arthur's work ethic. That was a tragic part of my father's business relationship with Arthur, which caused a huge amount of emotion. My father said after Arthur died, he regretted not giving Arthur more money.'

Peter Gordon: 'Because Arthur didn't engage in all the wider business stuff like agents, putting a band together, touring, all of that, that's why he could be so prolific. There wouldn't be that huge archive of tapes if he had been out there spending his time just hustling.'

Kate Russell: 'Arthur was so much in his own head during the day for so much of the time, which at the same time was the value of his work. But the hard edge of that was that he struggled to relate to the other world outside.'

Steven Hall: 'He didn't talk about his family very much; he didn't talk about the past very much. New York was absolutely where he wanted to be, but he pined sometimes for the Midwest and he enjoyed going there, and he pined even more for the West Coast. He was really maybe at his happiest when he was in California. Because if you think, a lot of his songs really have a sort of California feeling, sunny feeling.'

Ed Tomney (vocal, guitar synthesiser) and Ernie Brooks (bass and vocals) had formed The Necessaries in 1978 and were joined by Jesse Chamberlain (drums). By the time they released two albums on Sire Records, BIG SKY (1981) and EVENT HORIZON (1982), the line-up also included Arthur, who had become a member around 1980 and played guitar, cello, keyboards and sang. Arthur's membership of the band was somewhat short-lived and ended the year of EVENT HORIZON's release.

The Necessaries, L–R: Ernie Brooks, Jesse Chamberlain, Arthur Russell, Ed Tomney
— in the summer of 1981.

Arthur recorded the album CORN between spring 1982 and 1983. Although due for release by Sleeping Bag, the album was shelved. Musicians who played on the sessions included Mustafa Khaliq Ahmed (conga, percussion), Rik Albani (trumpet) and Peter Zummo (trombone). Among the songs recorded was 'This Is How We Walk on the Moon', later revised on the ANOTHER THOUGHT album (Point Music, 1993).

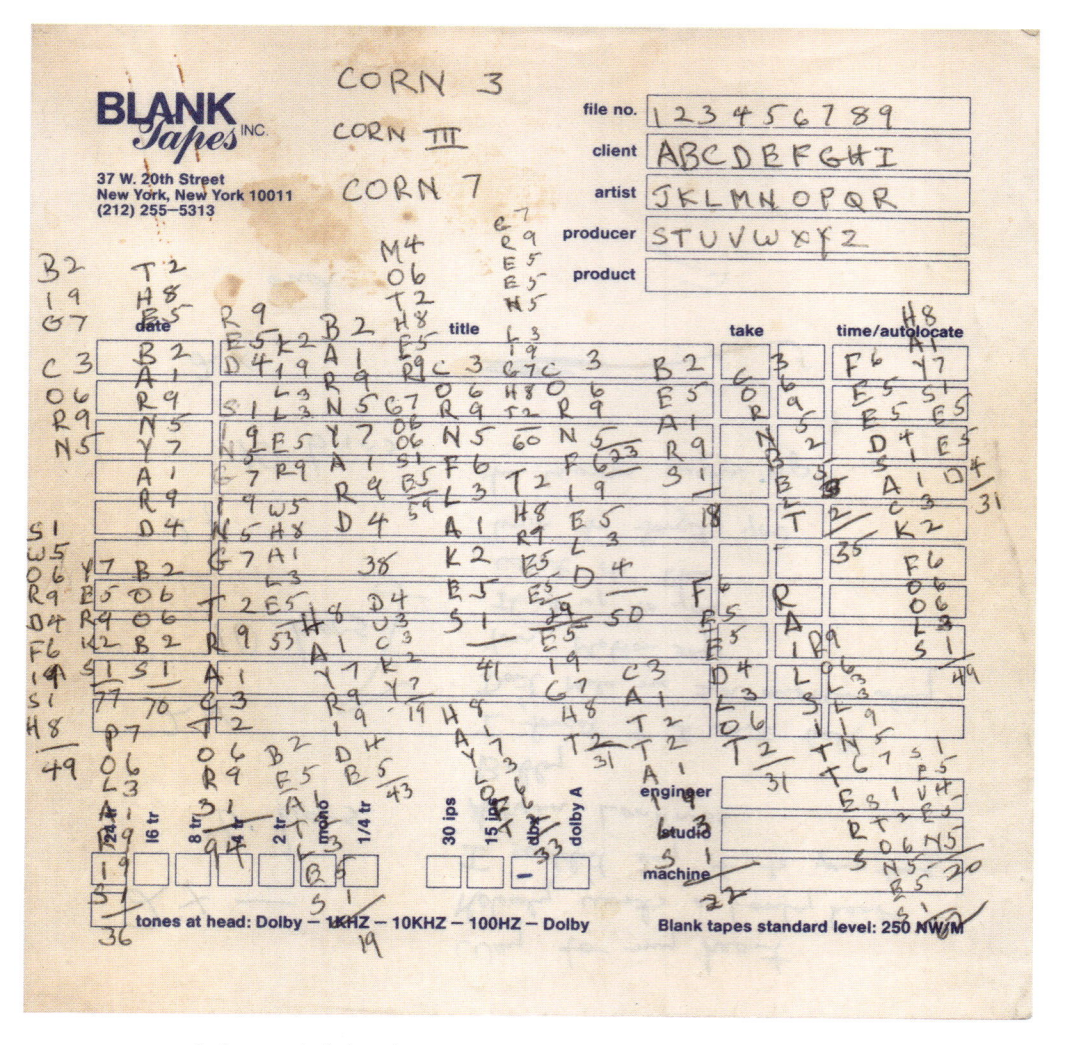

Arthur regularly bought numerology books from newsstands and enjoyed getting lost in the process of pairing numbers and words.

Tom Lee: 'I'm not sure there was anything too mystical about Arthur's love of numerology. I was amazed anyone had the spare time to do anything like that. Arthur's interest in numerology was something he shared with his friend Kirk Winslow, with whom he would consult. I was not aware of its interpretations but would see countless notes and papers that showed an alignment of numbers corresponding with song and album titles and possible band names.'

Peter Gordon: 'With numerology, it brings you to a certain space. There are certain practices, say chanting, which are its own form in various religions and processes but the result of each one of those is this unnameable space. Like in twelve-tone systems, there's a result but also a process, which puts one in a state and then you can make music with it.'

Ernie Brooks: 'It's so interesting how Iowa comes back in Arthur's work. The corn comes back.'

Mustafa Khaliq Ahmed: 'I'm a kid who grew up in a housing project in the Bronx, and even though I went to NYU and so on, and had a lot of exposure to white folk, I never experienced any personal racism or any of that. All of the teachers that I grew up with were white teachers; I didn't grow up in an all-black neighbourhood, I grew up in poor working communities. There was Italian, Jewish ... it was like everybody in the melting pot lived in the neighbourhood where I grew up, so some of these concepts of segregation and so forth were really more experienced by me through what was on the news.

'I'd see certain aspects of the Civil Rights on the news. My father worked for the Transit Authority. I knew guys who were bus drivers. There was no Rosa Parks experience up here: black people got on any seat that they wanted up here. However, once you got to your destination, the segregation began, so then we were talking about the black radio stations, the white radio stations, the black churches as opposed to the white churches.

'The thing about Arthur for me was, by my choice, and by Arthur's choice, it was the opportunity to join an integrated community of people with a goal to do the music. Arthur took me out of the ghetto of just doing R'n'B music with black cats. Now, that's not uncommon any more. But for me, personally, that was something that Arthur had, that kind of spiritual humanity. And today, Peter Zummo, Peter Gordon, we're all buddies and we do stuff with each other. Arthur knew the cats and he influenced the cats to be the men that we are today.'

Peter Zummo: 'In memory, recording "This Is How We Walk on the Moon" is very powerful. The studio had a new AKG mic that I assume was omnidirectional, and Arthur said, "Now play whatever I am singing." It's very mysterious or spiritual that without any latency I could do whatever he was doing, and I was singing also with him, and I think that's the part that sounds like a vocoder, a parallel harmony.'

Mustafa Khaliq Ahmed: 'I don't play rhythms: I play drum songs. They're singing rhythms. But that was something that conceptually I think I learned from Arthur, the value of the sound of the notes. And so, I stopped just playing congas; I started adding cow bells and chimes and all of these various different pitched instruments into my vocabulary.'

The Singing Tractors was a project orientated to a handful of live performances during 1982, consisting of Arthur, Peter Zummo, Elodie Lauten and occasional floating players. The red-and-white triangle on the poster mimics the road warning sign that agricultural machinery is in use. No Singing Tractors music was released in Arthur's lifetime. An eleven-minute track named "Singing Tractors" was included in the live recording THE DEER IN THE FOREST: MARCH 2, 1985 LIVE AT ROULETTE (Audika, 2020). The performance features Arthur, Peter Zummo and Elodie Lauten. An approximation of the musical style in which Arthur conceived Singing Tractors, which Ernie Brooks described as 'modular and muscular, like a tractor starting to groove', is audible in the piece.

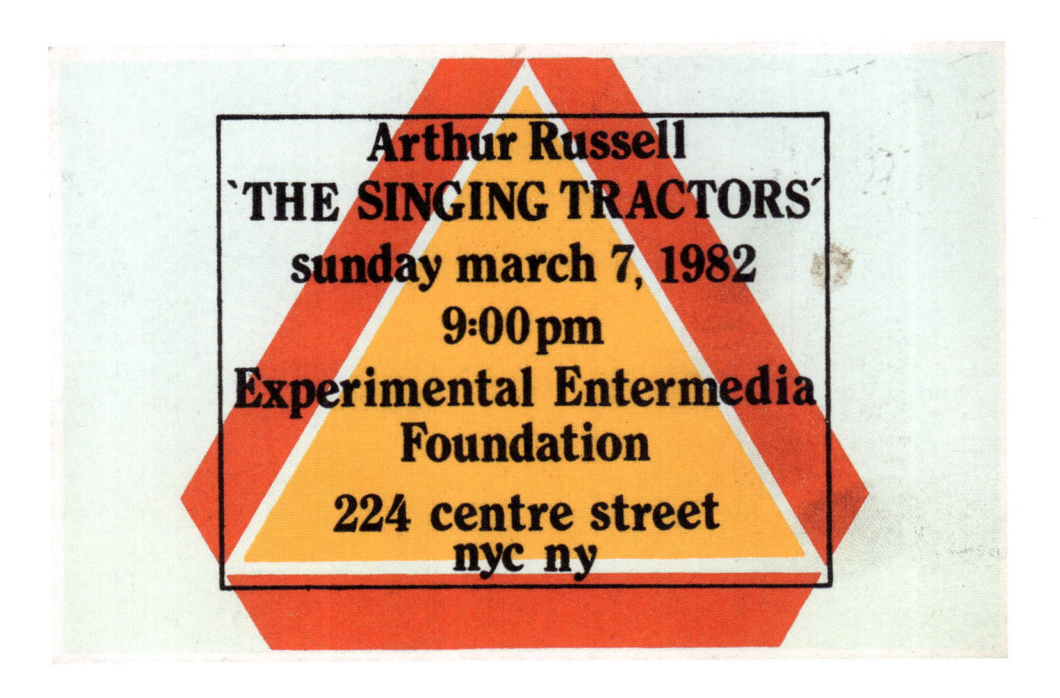

Kate Russell: 'When Arthur came home to visit, he and my father would take pictures as part of their business arrangement. They'd go out to the cornfields and find locations for photos.'

180

Tom Lee: 'Once I met Arthur's parents more solidly I was always selling Arthur and his music to them. They had various cassettes that Arthur would send them, but I felt it was my forcing the music on them that cemented it.'

Kate Russell: 'Arthur always had his notepaper and his sheaf of papers. I was blown away reading his lyrics, the way he put words together. The notebook that he was always working on would be in his pocket. He would send shirts to my sister and she would sew pockets on them so he could store manuscripts and paper and notebooks in there. When he was with us, he would be quiet and at the side and if we said something that wasn't quite right he would disappear into his work, get up and walk away and go back to his room and we would have to draw him out.'

Tom Lee: 'When Arthur wanted, say, a new keyboard for the home studio, I was a little more connected with his parents then; I would talk to them on the phone. His dad would ask me, "How are things going with Geoff Travis?" He would confer with me if he hadn't heard from Arthur.'

Kate Russell: 'Sometimes the only thing he'd want from us was our opinion of a song. He'd play these sounds to us and we didn't know what we were listening to. How could we respond? It would devastate him if we had nothing to say. I would see his face and say, "Arthur, that doesn't mean a thing, we don't know what you're doing. We have no grounding to compare it to anything." It would frustrate him terribly. He wanted us to give him some kind of validation and we just weren't capable. We'd listen to the whole song or the whole piece, but we couldn't give him what he asked for. We would listen in the car. But we were missing something. And I wonder how many musicians really understood it. I think he was in his own world.'

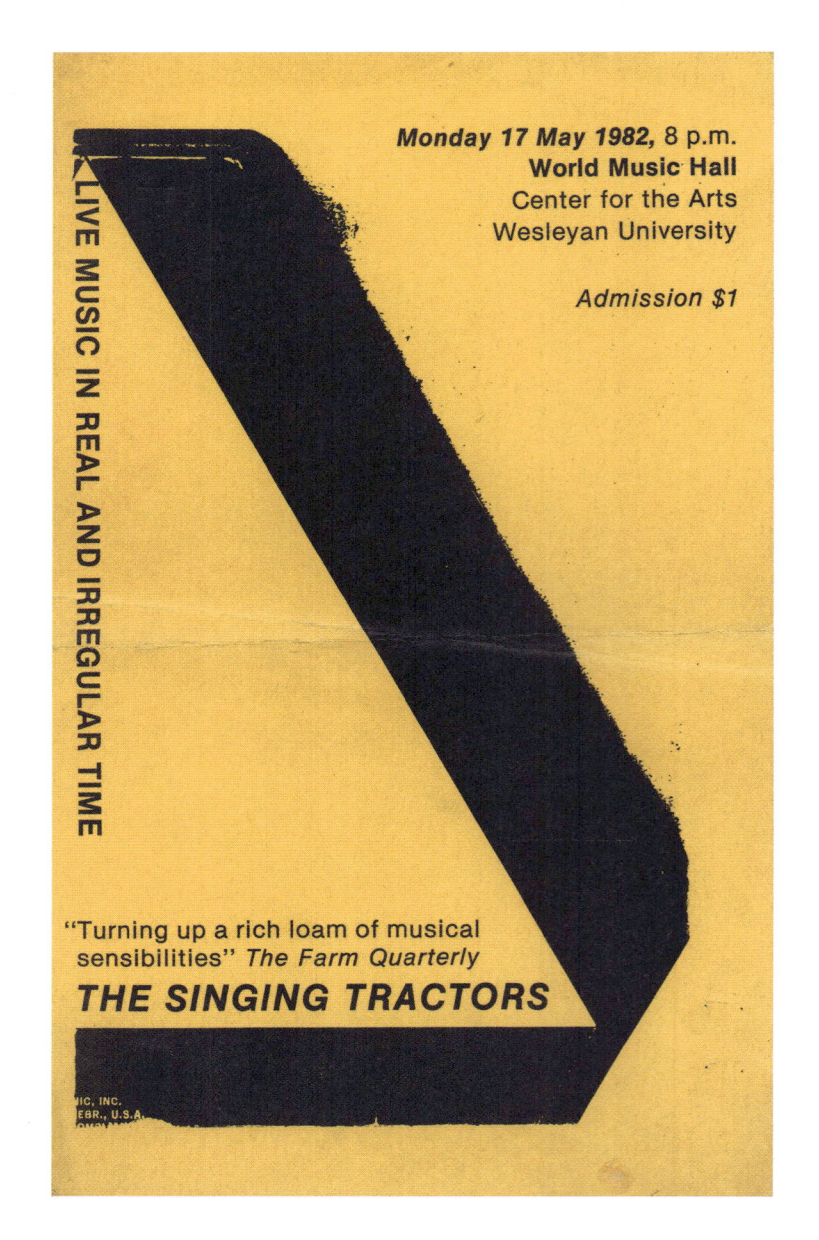

Monday 17 May 1982, 8 p.m.
World Music Hall
Center for the Arts
Wesleyan University

Admission $1

LIVE MUSIC IN REAL AND IRREGULAR TIME

"Turning up a rich loam of musical sensibilities" *The Farm Quarterly*
THE SINGING TRACTORS

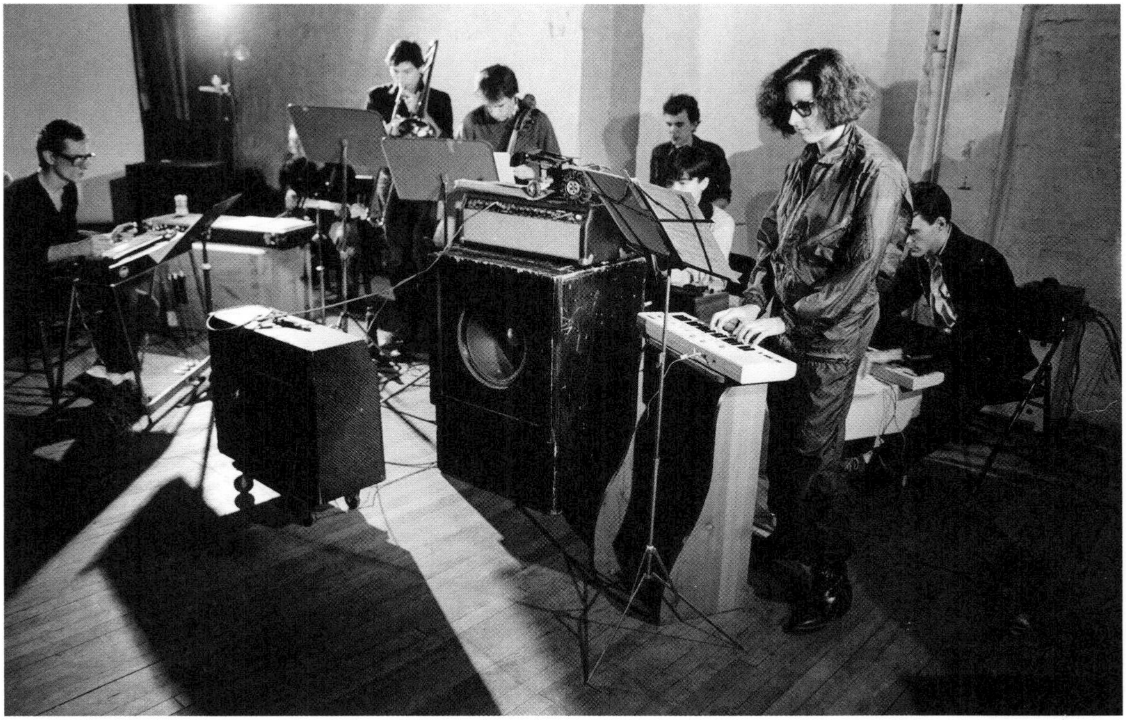

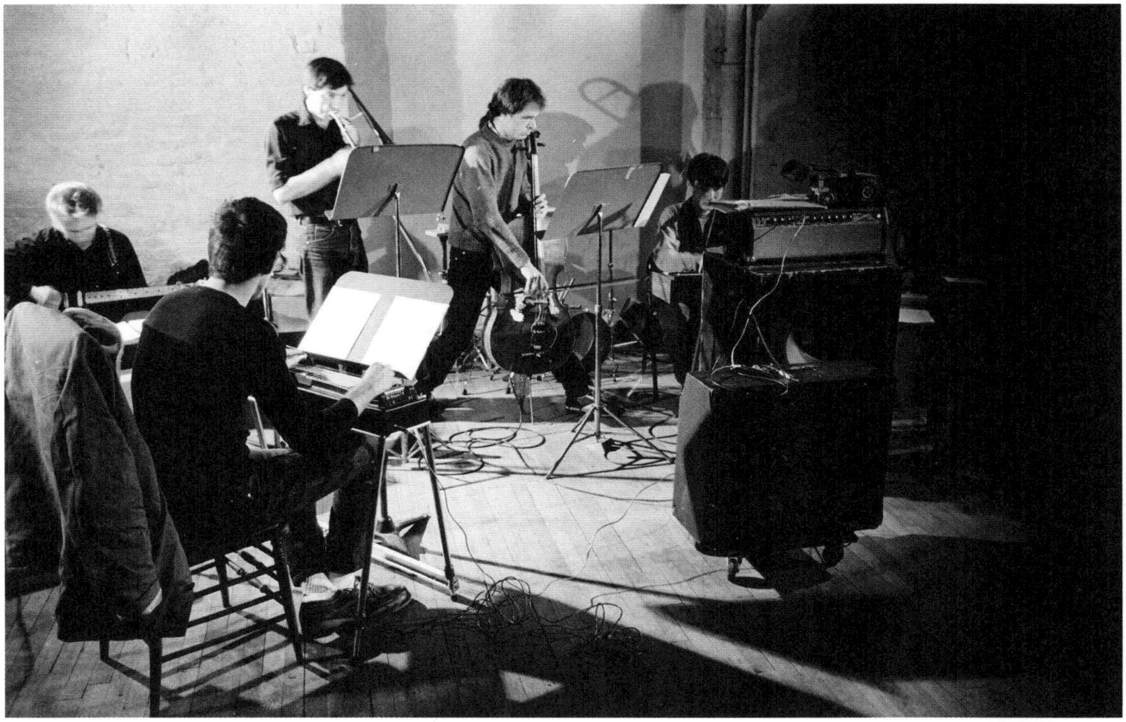

Moving Me Up

Each step is moving

moving me up

moving

moving me up

Each step is moving, moving me up

every step, moving me up

one tiny, tiny, tiny move

it's all I need and I jump over

one tiny, tiny, tiny move

every step is moving me up

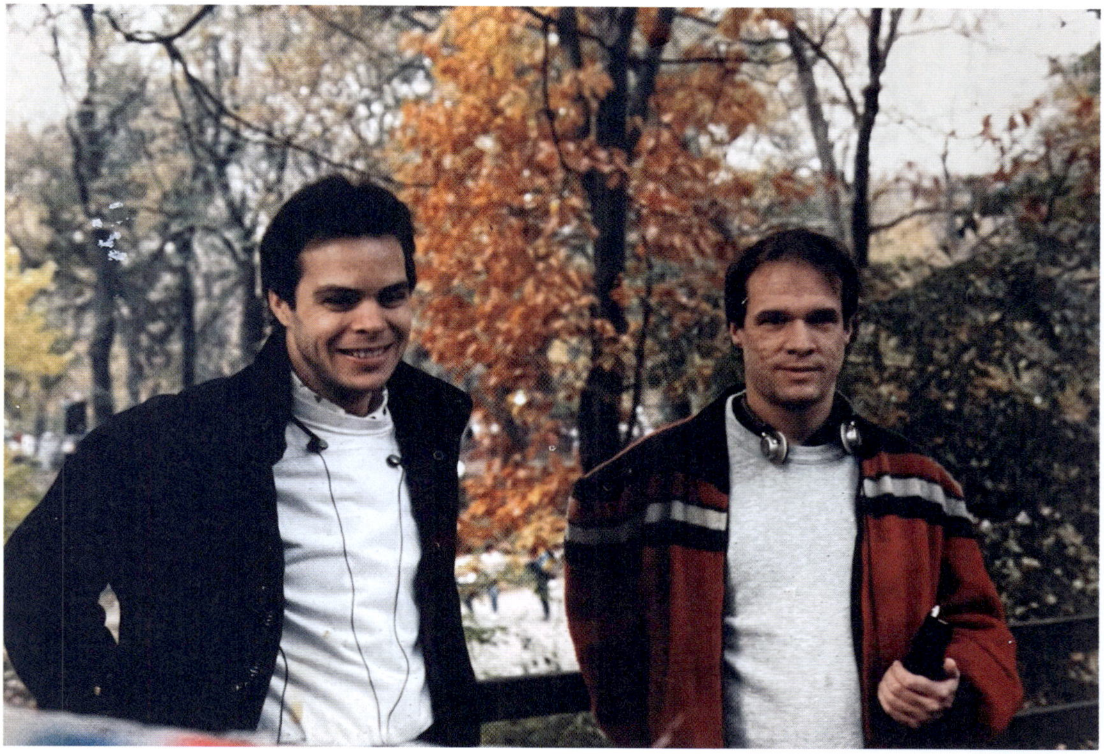

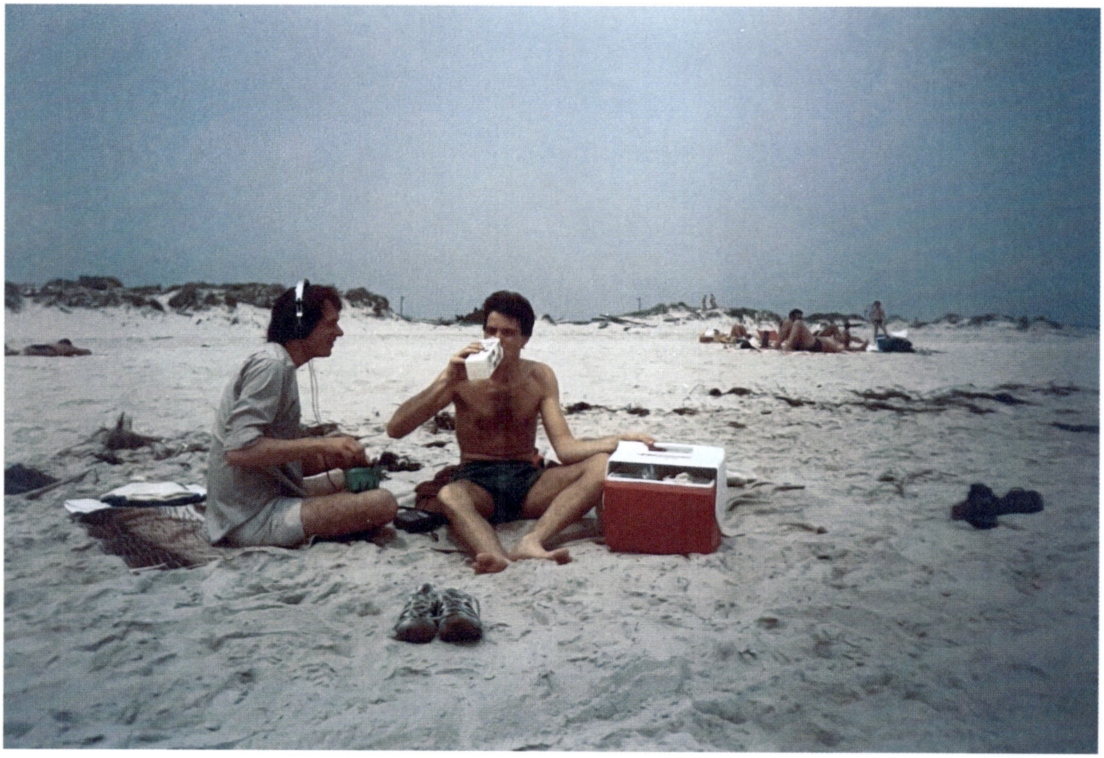

Kate Russell: 'Arthur could be very playful. It comes through all the time in his lyrics. I wonder if there was ever a contrast between the spiritual and the playful, or if the spiritual and the playful were one and the same for him. He could come out of his world and surface in the family and do a one-liner that was very specific, very appropriate and he couldn't do that all the time. But he could be very playful and I'm convinced that was the side of him Tom saw more.'

Ernie Brooks: 'Arthur could be incredibly funny. He would come out with the most incredible non-sequitur one-liners.'

Peter Gordon: 'Oh yeah. Arthur had a sense of the absurd.'

Tom Lee: 'We'd often be coming home from some place at God knows what hour and Arthur would fool around as we approached the apartment.'

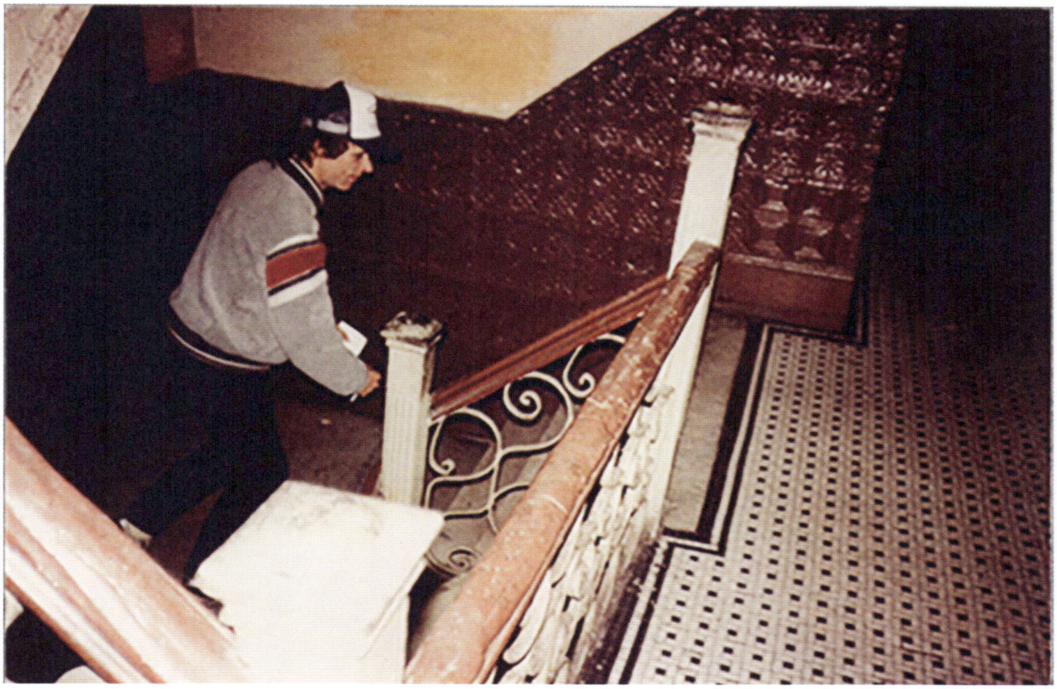

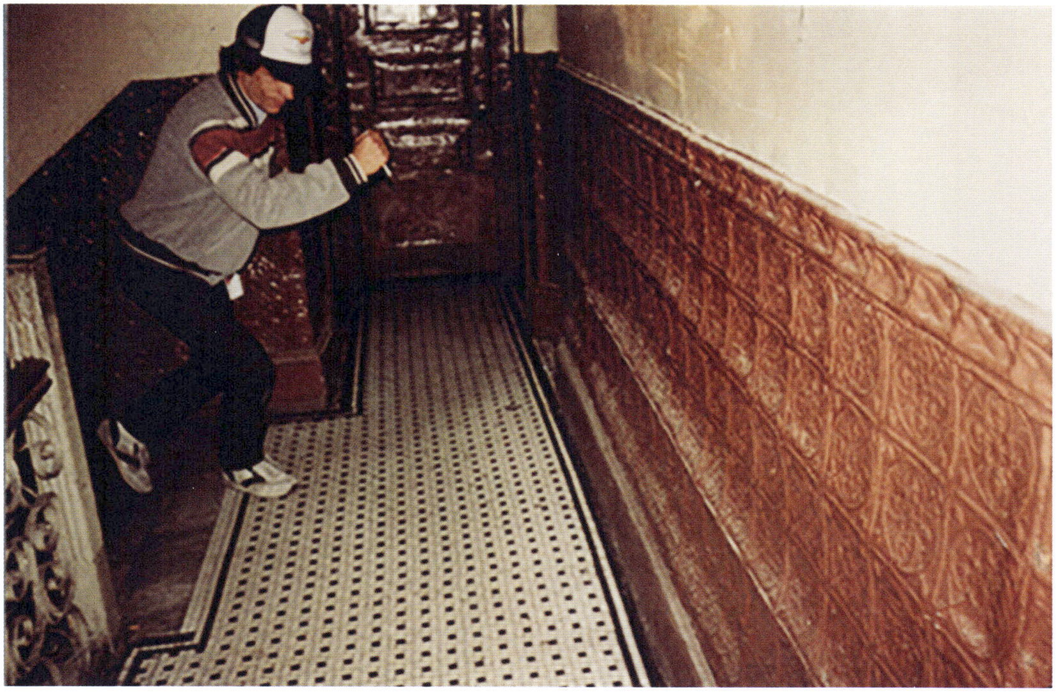

(Lower East Side / Summer)

Bricks will fall on us when you get home.

Darker wrecks will fill up in your ears.

Treasures from the lippy little gnome

jangle in your New York footpath-

        he twangs your legbone as he nears.

Verses:

Iain't got no car to take us home to the east side,

We will get there on our feet somehow.

Drink up our beer and in the summer we can wait;

Alley tails grown limp with sweaty brow.

We can't cut no corners cause ther's only corners here,
Drugstores take up every bit of room.
Delicatessen on our block is getting old
Bologna makes it smell just like a tomb.

Chorus

It's so hot in New York City laughing in my way,
leaving all my memories to bake.
Track down the flies that buzz around inside my head,
sitting still and try to stay awake.

Chorus

Twine around this thirsty town / my mustach has grown wet,
' think that I could lose my mind tonight.
Creep up behind a sleeping waiting working man,
In the subways same flourescent light.

Put your hand in my back pocket I'll put mine in yours,
You can trust my spare change to run out.
Put in the slug and let the turnstail let us in,
We will catch that train there is no doubt.
Chorus
Write my name on subway cars and I'll put yours by mine,
We could walk instead though if you want.
But step up your pace I think we've got to get away,
This old street has always been my haunt.

Chorus

DINOSAUR L

CBGB 315 Bowery

SUNDAY 4:30 December 26 1982

Dinosaur L, playing CBGB, Boxing Day 1982. According to people who have heard a recording of this concert, including Peter Zummo, it consisted of an hour of the same continuous beat and featured a dirge-like cello part.

Tom Lee: 'I would head to Danceteria and Hurrah's – we often had friends in bands playing there. Arthur was more the Loft and the Garage. Although when I was with him, he would stand against the wall and listen. We would go out and he'd say, "They're playing my song between twelve and two," – it was very specific.'

T·H·E K·I·T·C·H·E·N
1982-1983 SEASON
484 BROOME STREET   RES: 925-3615

MUSIC

BANDS AT THE KITCHEN

Dec. 27 BILL'S FRIENDS
         SONIC YOUTH
         SWANS

Dec. 28 ELEPHANT DANCE
         MON TON SON
         THE MOB

Dec. 29 INTERFERENCE
         TOY KILLERS
         V-EFFECT

Dec. 30 BEASTIE BOYS
         MOFUNGO
         ORDINAIRES

$5.00 per night; $14 series ticket (4 nights). 8:30pm

VIDEO

VIDEO VIEWING ROOM
(Tues-Sat, 1-6pm)
FROM SWEDEN BROADCAST SAMPLER Excerpts from Sveriges Television T.V.2 (1-2pm)
FROM FRANCE BROADCAST SAMPLER Excerpts from I.N.A Antenne (2-3pm)
TAPES BY REQUEST (3-4pm)
IMAGE/PROCESS Including tapes by Sara Hornbacher, Mimi Marton, Matt Schlanger, Joe Tripician/Merrill Aldighieri, etc. Curated by Shalom Gorewitz (4-5pm)
ROBERT WILSON
Video 50, Deafman Glance (5-6pm)

GALLERY

(Tues-Sat, 1-6pm)

JON RUBIN *Undercover Amusement*
December 4-31
Opening Reception
Saturday, December 4, 5-7pm

Arthur performing at the Kitchen as a member of Bill's Friends, 27 December 1982,
L–R: Tim Schellenbaum (guitar, violin), Craig Kafton (drums), Jill Kroesen (percussion, vocals),
Arthur Russell (cello).

Allen Ginsberg with the Gluons, 'Birdbrain' (Alekos Records, 7", 1981).
Inscribed to Arthur from Allen Ginsberg.

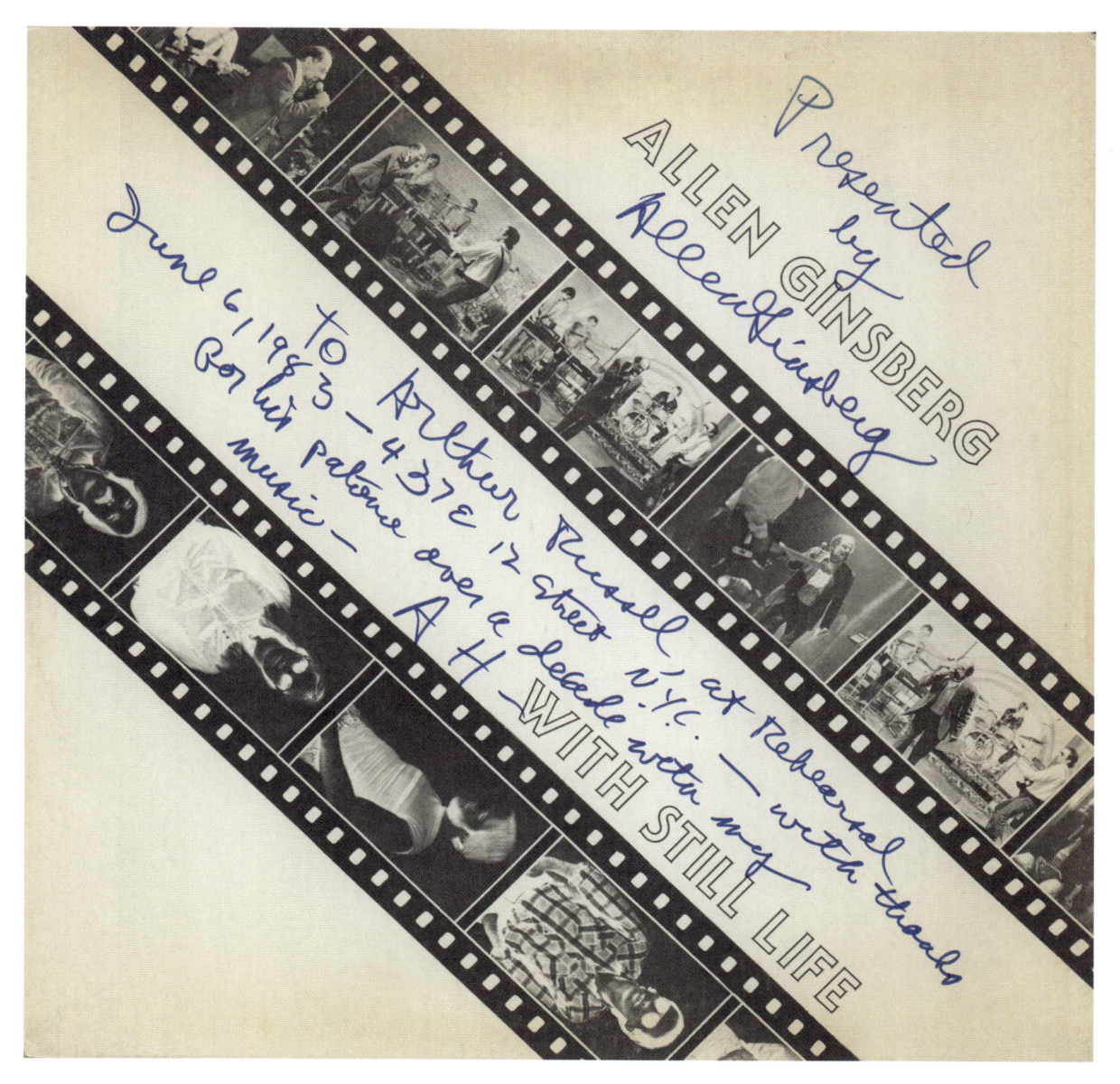

Allen Ginsberg, WITH STILL LIFE (Self-titled Local Anesthetic Records LP, 1983).
Inscribed to Arthur from Allen Ginsberg.

Danceteria
30 W 21st NYC 10010 TEL 212-620-0515

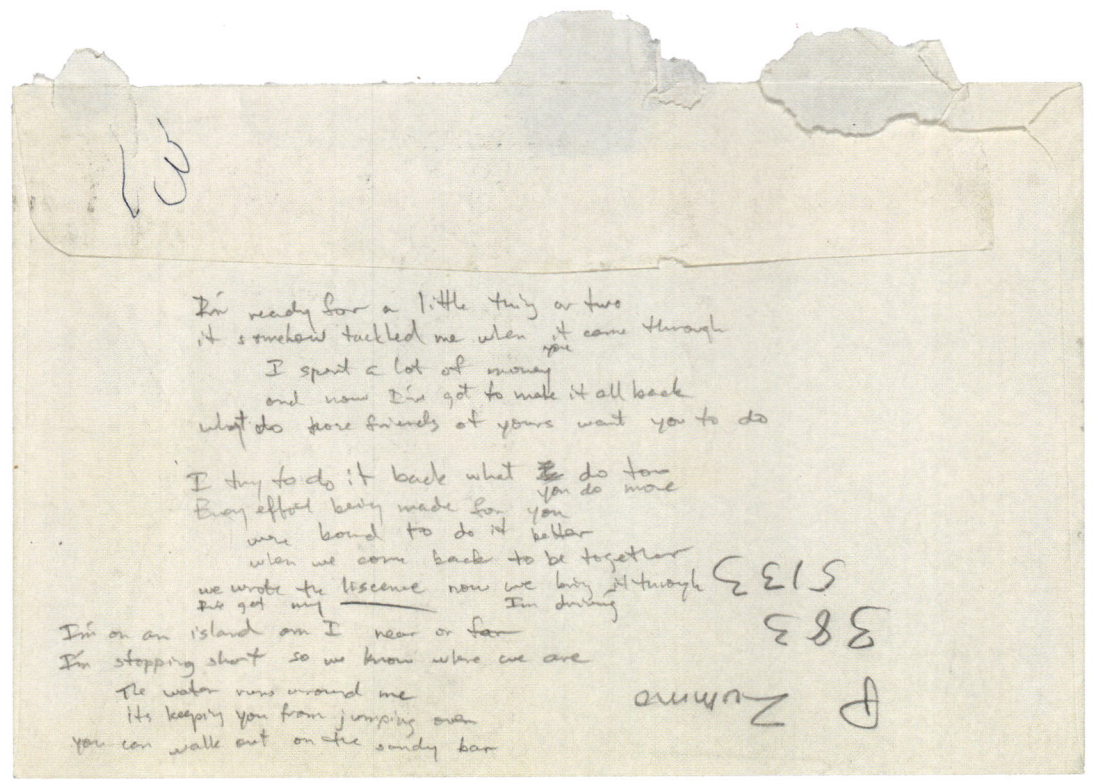

NEW YORK, NY
-PM-
MAR 2
1983

USA 20c

Tom Lee
437 E. 12th St. #38
N.Y. N.Y. 10009

I'm ready for a little thing or two
it somehow tackled me when it come through
    I spent a lot of money
      and now I've got to make it all back
what do those friends of yours want you to do

I try to do it back what I do too
              you do more
Every effort being made for you
    were bound to do it better
    when we come back to be together
  we wrote the liscence now we buy it though
  I've got my   I'm driving
I'm on an island am I near or far
I'm stopping short so we know where we are
    The water runs around me
    its keeping you from jumping over
you can walk out on the sandy bar

Kate Russell: 'Arthur would often come home for a reason. He was a family member who came home for reunions and summer gatherings and that kind of thing. And he brought himself to us, but he stood apart from us. We would have to pull him out of himself to be with us in our own way. I didn't always get him. He was gone before I knew him is the tragic part for me, but the world is giving him back to me.

'My father would always have these big tanks of cars and they would have sound systems and tape decks and Arthur would love to listen to tapes of his music in these closed spaces. He would bring home his music on cassette and go driving and listen to them. I used to laugh to myself, thinking he wouldn't come home unless he could listen to his music, driving these floaty cars, out in the cornfields. He would drive the gravel roads listening to his music.'

> Arthur:
>
> Here is your tape back. Found in the front seat of the car.
>
> How is your 'Sale' going to the record company?
>
> Dad.
>
> 10-7-83

Tell You (Today)
(New Shoes)

Part I -
Part II -
(Russell)

Free Form Dancing (Mix) Attorney Street
by ~~Killer Whale Bathhouse~~
Prod. by ~~Killer~~ Whale
and Steve D'Aquisto

TL* Music Ascap

Tell You (Today)
(Russell)

Mixed by Larry Levan
Prod. Arthur Russell
& S. D'A.

Tell You (Today)
Instrumental

284 —   Arnold
394,   388-2596
244,
3800

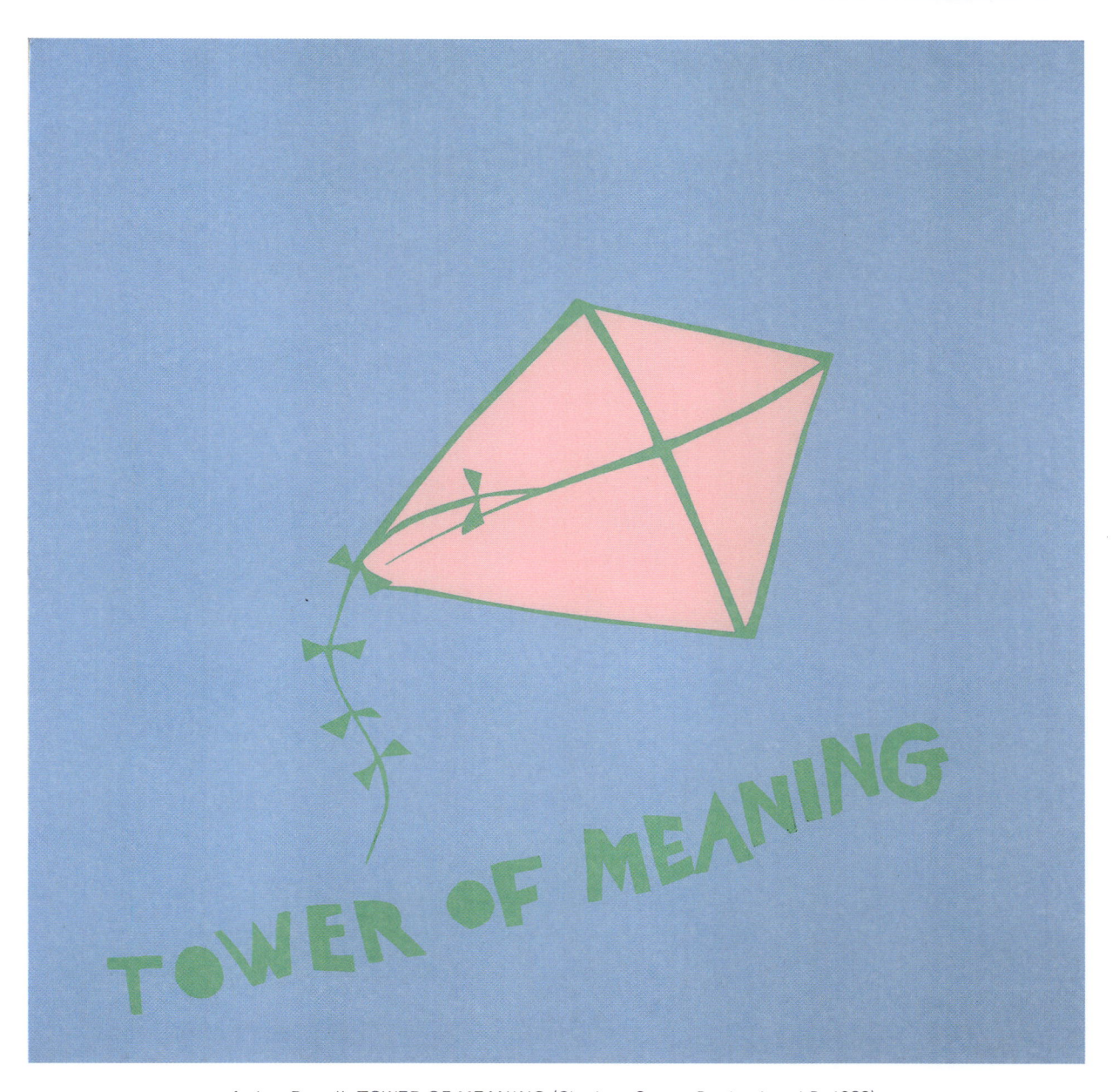

Arthur Russell, TOWER OF MEANING (Chatham Square Productions LP, 1983).

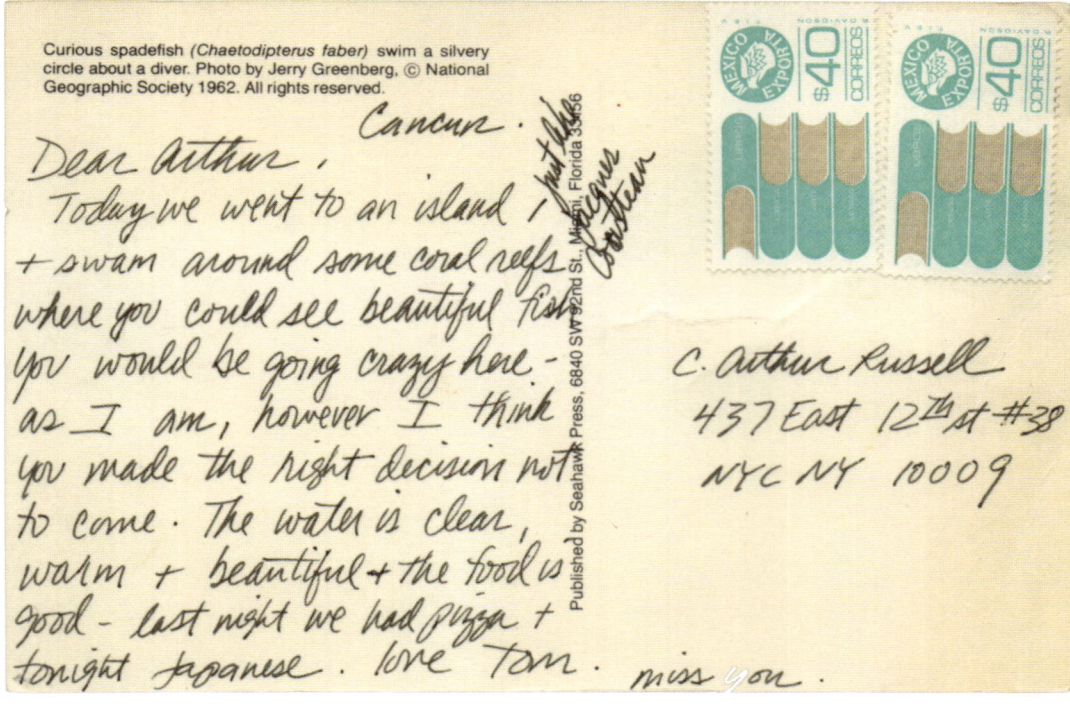

Curious spadefish (*Chaetodipterus faber*) swim a silvery circle about a diver. Photo by Jerry Greenberg, © National Geographic Society 1962. All rights reserved.

Cancun. *Jacques Cousteau*

Dear Arthur,
Today we went to an island + swam around some coral reefs where you could see beautiful fish. You would be going crazy here — as I am, however I think you made the right decision not to come. The water is clear, warm + beautiful + the food is good — last night we had pizza + tonight Japanese. love Tom.

C. Arthur Russell
437 East 12th st #38
NYC NY 10009

miss you.

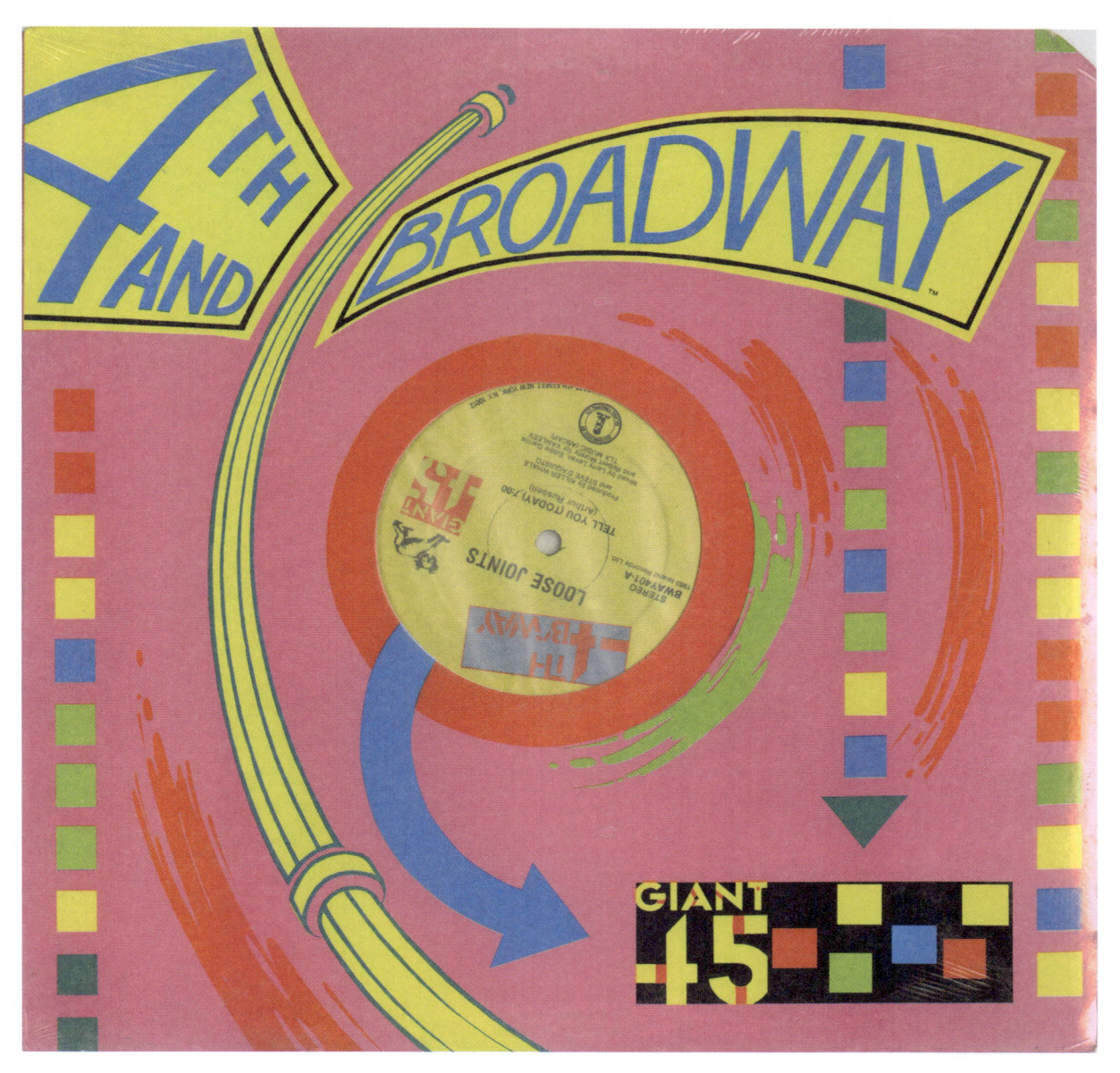

Loose Joints, 'Tell You (Today)' (4th & Broadway, 12", 1983).

STERLING
SOUND

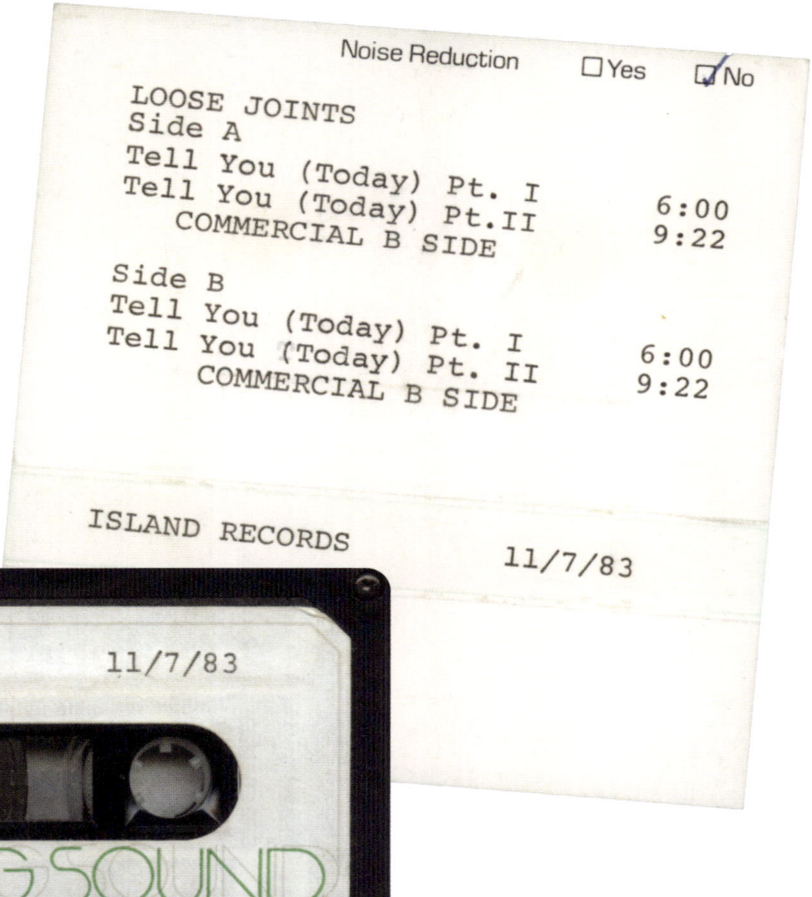
Noise Reduction ☐ Yes ☑ No
LOOSE JOINTS
Side A
Tell You (Today) Pt. I 6:00
Tell You (Today) Pt.II 9:22
COMMERCIAL B SIDE
Side B
Tell You (Today) Pt. I 6:00
Tell You (Today) Pt. II 9:22
COMMERCIAL B SIDE
ISLAND RECORDS 11/7/83

LOOSE JOINTS 11/7/83
STERLING SOUND

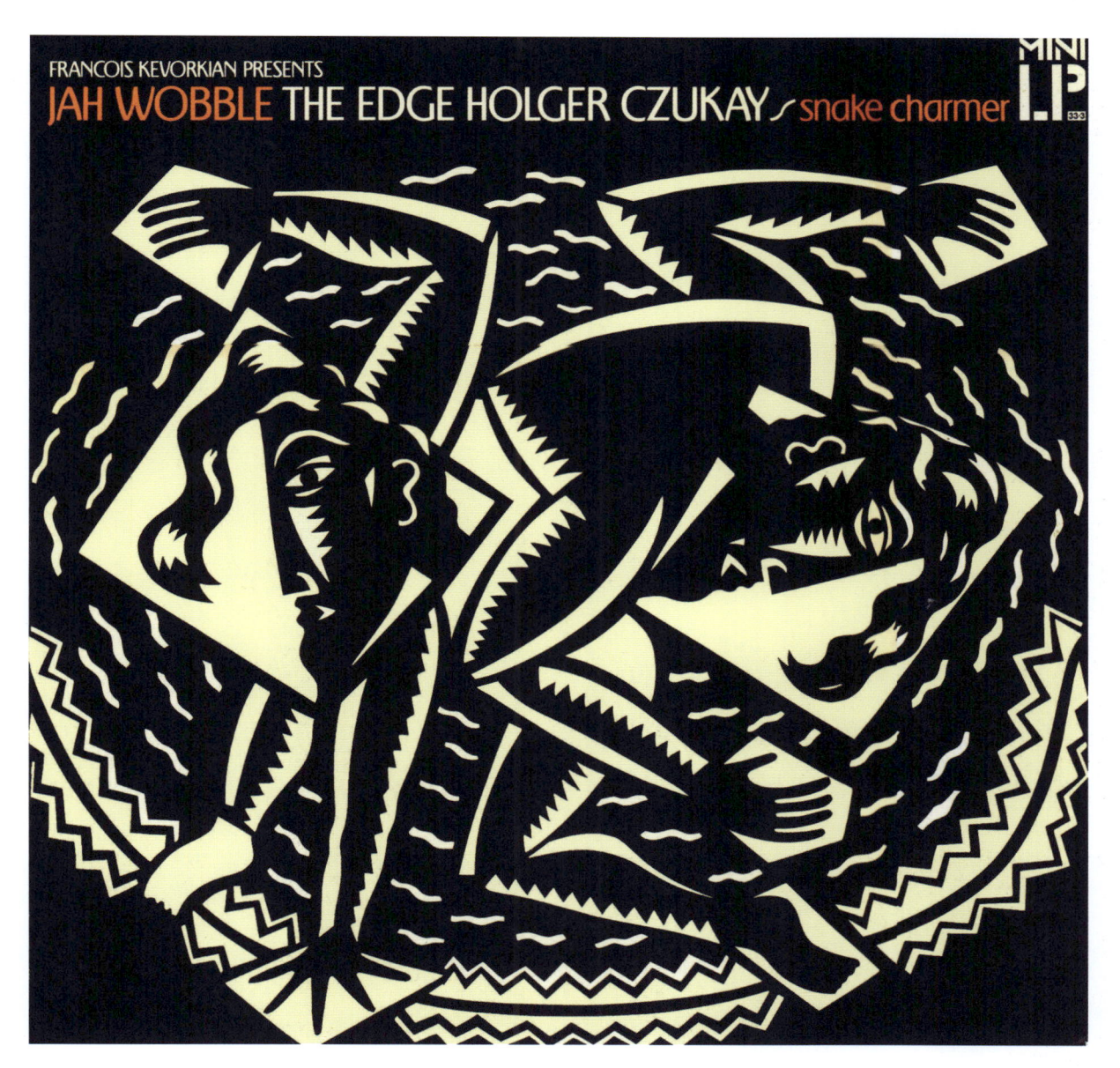

Jah Wobble, The Edge, Holger Czukay, SNAKE CHARMER (Island Records, Mini-album, 1983)
(Arthur wrote lyrics for the track 'Hold On to Your Dreams').

202

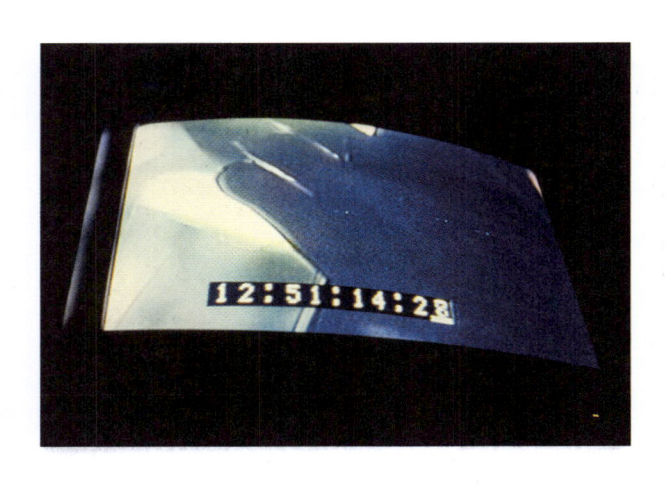

Phill Niblock: 'At one of the concerts Arthur played at our place in the mid-1980s, I suggested to Arthur that we do a video project together, where I shot what he was doing very differently than I would normally shoot anything else. And he also came up with this music that was quite different from his other stuff, which he became very well known for, but it came from that video shoot.'

Peter Zummo: 'You'd arrive at Experimental Media Foundation four thirty and load in and there'd be food cooking in the kitchen. It was a casual atmosphere.'

Bill Ruyle: 'I think it was always a spaghetti dinner, which was fine.'

Peter Zummo: 'There were speakers all over the place, capable of making a surround-sound environment and increasingly video spaces as that became more of an element. Admission included a glass of wine. At one point there was a fire and he had to get rid of his wood-burning stove. The landlord tried to evict him. I think this night was the night Phill made the video that led to the WORLD OF ECHO material that was released on record.'

Phill Niblock: 'That's the stuff where WORLD OF ECHO came from, it came directly from that tape that we recorded that night.'

Arthur Russell
437 East 12th St
New York 10009

EXPERIMENTAL INTERMEDIA FOUNDATION

JUNE 1984

DEAN DRUMMOND — TUE 19
ZOOMOOZOPHONE PLUS, FEATURING NEW BAND

PETER GORDON — WED 20
RECENT TAPES AND CLARINET

PHILL NIBLOCK — THU 21
AH, THE LONGEST DAY AGAIN, BUT A SHORT CONCERT, MORE OR LESS

MARY JANE LEACH — FRI 22
AN INTERMEDIA EVENT: PIECES FOR SLIDES, VOICES AND FLUTE

PAUL WILLIAM SIMONS — SUN 24
SONG-POEMS FOR VOICE AND CELLO/GUITAR

ARTHUR RUSSELL — MON 25
SKETCHES FOR WORLD OF ECHO

WITH SUPPORT FROM THE NEW YORK STATE COUNCIL ON THE ARTS AND THE NATIONAL ENDOWMENT FOR THE ARTS

224 CENTRE STREET AT GRAND, NEW YORK 212 431 5127 9PM $2.50

World of
Rabbits Bar
Home Away from Home
name of next song
Happy Ending

I'm just Born
very reason
Although you
keeping up
I'm not checking up
boy + the dog
losing my taste for the nightlife
telling no one

As I considered to echo in various meanings, as acoustic reverberation or electronically as a single delay, it seemed that in its concepts of time and space were expressed sonically, and in the latter case projected dynamically into a theatrical "world", with a more practical application: using currently available echo/delay guitar boxes to provide an independently generated world of time to move through, like a PA system that can process any input, introducing a concept of interchangability of materials.

However, the idiomatic style I ended up using is not immediately referenceable, and use of any echo matrix, whether simple delay or layered computer devices, bears only incident reflection on the idiomatic sensibilities of listeners, apparently the ultimate focus of attention.

After listening to tapes of World of Echo as well as foreign language singing, I've enjoyed the musical effect of words as sounds, but where the meaning is not totally withdrawn. As the intention is not determined by genre, nor meaning by dialect, thresholds of musical understanding can occupy any threshold defined within a style and musical structure, or outside it. Breakthroughs can occur at any point in the chain.

When I have written songs, the functions of verse and chorus seem to be reversed for some unknown reason. It was my hope, through the various possibilities of a World of Echo P.A. system, to redefine "songs" from the point of view of instrumental music, in the hopes of liquefying a raw material where concert music and popular song can criss cross.

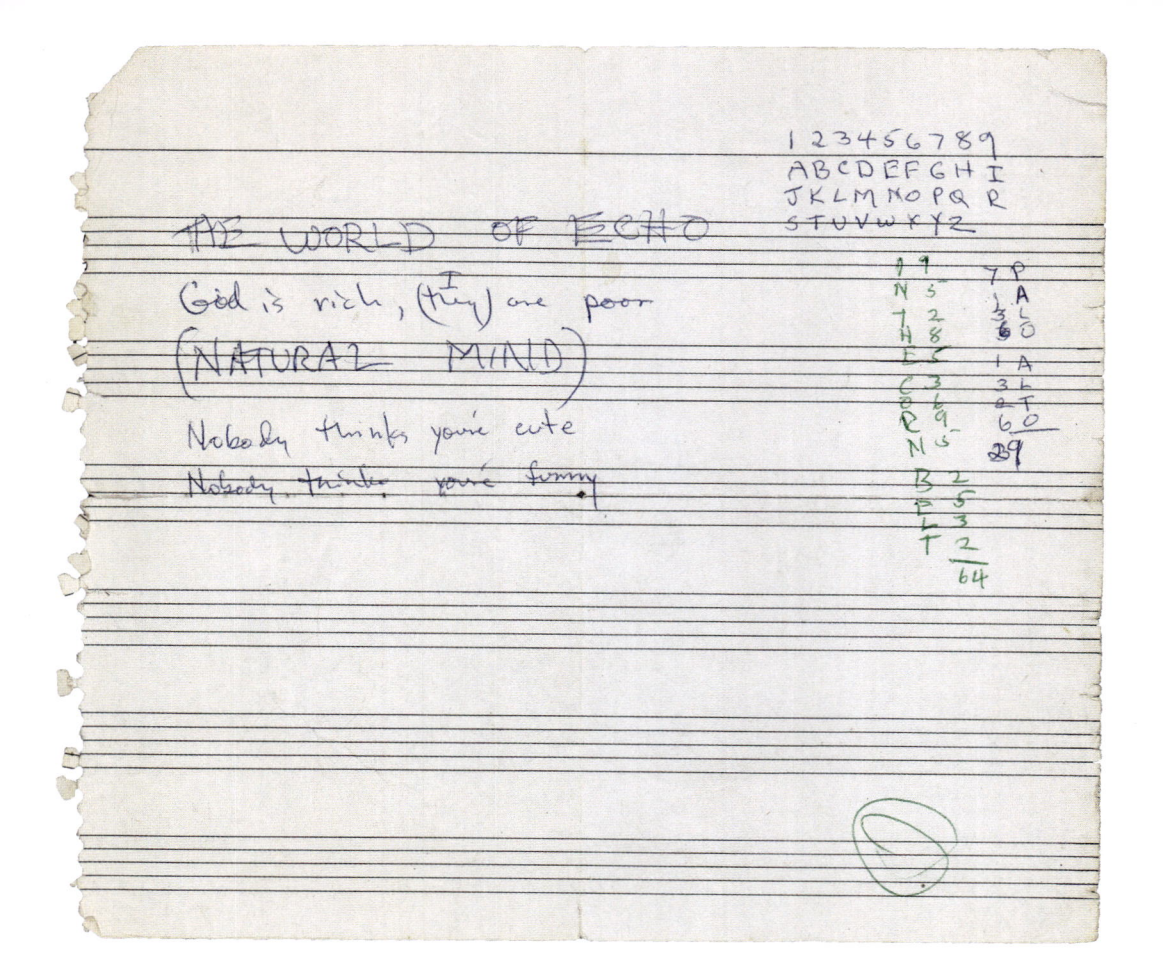

THE WORLD OF ECHO

God is rich, (they) are poor

(NATURAL MIND)

Nobody thinks you're cute
Nobody thinks you're funny

Arthur Russell, INSTRUMENTALS, 1974 – Vol. 2 (Another Side, LP, 1984).

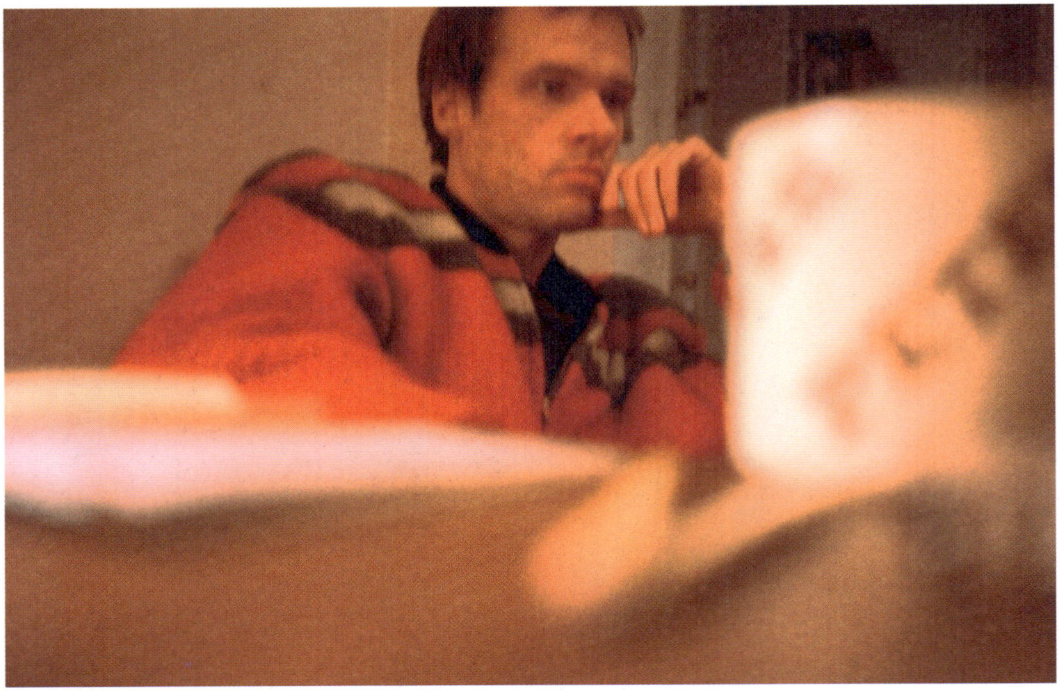

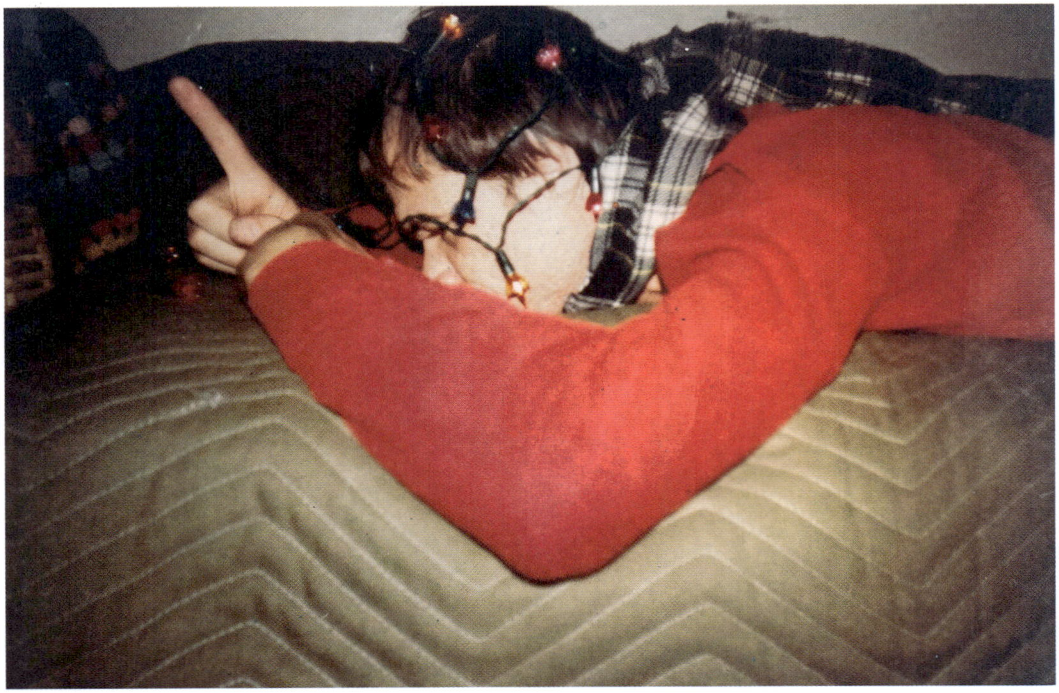

Alison Salzinger: 'I met Arthur through Peter Zummo's wife Stephanie, who was my teacher at Oberlin College. Arthur came to play there in a student production, then after I graduated Tom saw a show of mine and introduced me to Arthur and suggested we collaborate. Arthur was very, very shy and sometimes thought everyone hated him. This was a class I taught at Oberlin after I graduated. Arthur worked with me there. He had been rejected by Oberlin as a student, which was probably a good thing because it would have squelched his creativity, but he was salty about that while we were there.'

Peter Gordon: 'This is the cello and pedals set-up Arthur used for the WORLD OF ECHO material.'

Alison Salzinger: 'We didn't have much of a method when we worked together. We were both pretty intuitive. My approach was to have two separate streams running at the same time. I worked on the dancing and Arthur worked on the music and then we tried to mash things together. Most of the material I used was songs he had already written, some of which were included on WORLD OF ECHO, but there was definitely some improvisation in the playing as well. They weren't the same every time he played them.

'We did a performance at Performance Space 122, where I wanted to have him sitting on stage but he insisted on placing himself behind the audience. Some people didn't even know he was playing live at the show, but people just loved his music. PS122 was my favourite place to perform. It felt like a home base. It was funkier than Dance Theater Workshop. It was really dance and performance art oriented. They had something on Tuesday nights called Open Movement that really shaped me where people just came and danced. There was no music, which I really liked, there was no talking, just absolutely dance as a language. You would go there, warm up in the corner and just join in. There was a lot of contact improvisation. No meetings or discussions, people just jumped in and danced together.'

press release
THE KITCHEN
video • music • dance • performance

CONTACT:

MaryAnne McGowan
(212) 925-3615

MONDAY SERIES IV:
ARTHUR RUSSELL
DAVID LINTON

March 19, 1984; 8:30 P.M.
The Kitchen
Reservations: 925-3615
$5.00/$3.50 members/TDF + $.50

On March 19, 1984 The Kitchen will present ARTHUR RUSSELL and DAVID LINTON.

ARTHUR RUSSELL will present music performed with violincello, harmonica, and vocals, as well as premiere portions of a new composition-in-progress entitled WORLD OF ECHO. Mr. Russell was born in Oskaloosa, Iowa and has lived in New York since 1973. He began playing amplified cello in 1972 and acoustic guitar in 1971, and has played in bands in collaboration with his friends. In 1977 he began working as a record producer. He has presented work including The Tower of Meaning, The Deer in the Forest, 24 → 24 Music, Fuzzbusters, The Singing Tractorz, and Instrumentals Volume 2, as well as live recordings of his composition Instrumentals. Instrumentals is expected to be released on Crepescule Records this year, and Tower of Meaning on Chatham Square Records. As a cellist, Arthur Rusell has premiered works by Christian Wolff, Jon Gibson, Philip Glass, Peter Zummo, and Jackson MacLow.

DAVID LINTON will premiere N.O.M.D.(The Narcissism of Minor Differences), a new live performance musical unit, with the assistance of choreographer Tamar Kotoske. Live drumming will act as a trigger to gate multiple a-synchronous pre-recorded tape tracks and other signal processes toward the shaping of songs normally associated with the band context. "I first performed in New York in September 1979 at the now-defunct Max's Kansas City with a band called 'The Fluks' from Binghampton, New York, which was co-founded with Sonic Youth's Lee Renaldo. Subsequently, over the last four years, performing in New York, throughout the U.S. and Europe, I have worked with...Rhys Chatham, Robert Longo, Eric Bogosian, Red Decade, Karole Armitage, Charles Atlas, Jeffrey Lohn, Glenn Branca, Plus Instruments, Off Beach, I/S/M, Elliot Sharp, The Din, Interference, Jim Self, Kinematic, Carbon,

(OVER)

59 Wooster Street, New York, New York 10012   (212) 925-3615

MONDAY · MARCH 19

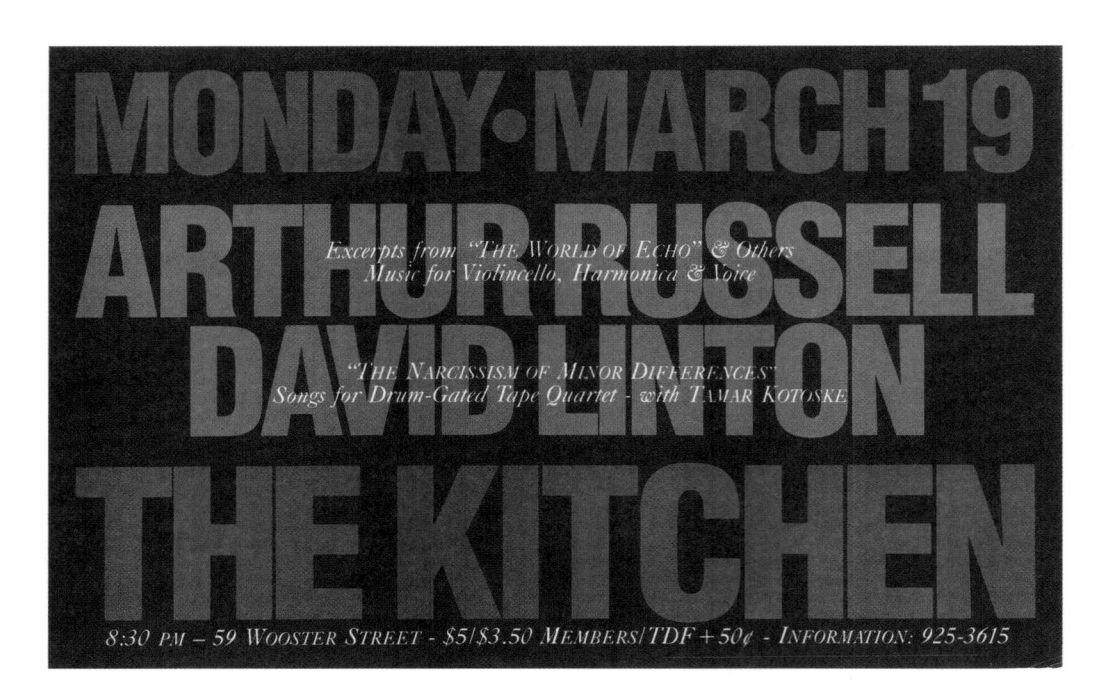

ARTHUR RUSSELL
Excerpts from "The World of Echo" & Others
Music for Violincello, Harmonica & Voice

DAVID LINTON
"The Narcissism of Minor Differences"
Songs for Drum-Gated Tape Quartet - with Tamar Kotoske

THE KITCHEN

8:30 PM – 59 Wooster Street – $5/$3.50 Members/TDF +50¢ - Information: 925-3615

VIDEO, MUSIC, DANCE, PERFORMANCE & FILM

THE KITCHEN

MARCH 19, 1984

MONDAY SERIES IV:
ARTHUR RUSSELL
DAVID LINTON

ARTHUR RUSSELL

1. World   Let's   Tower
2. of   Go   of
3. Echo   Swimming   Meaning

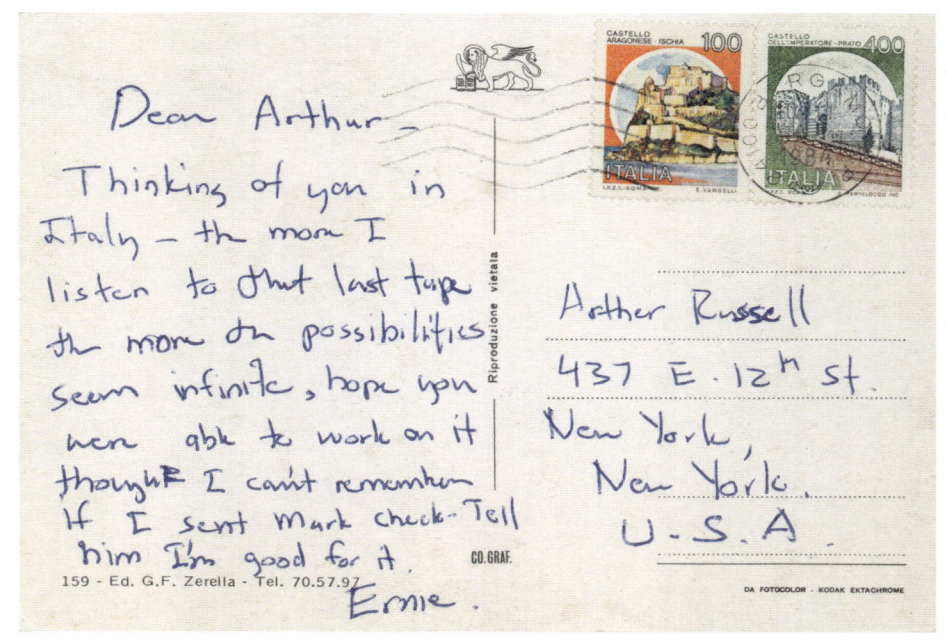

Ernie Brooks: 'The Mark mentioned on the postcard was Mark Freedman at Battery Sound studios. Arthur had a deal with him and kept some of master tapes at the studio. It was located very near the World Trade Center; Mark's father owned the building. I was touring a lot in Europe at this time. These would have been songs Arthur sent me, this is after The Necessaries. We were still trading songs and Arthur got me to go and play with him.'

Peter Zummo: 'Arthur had access to Battery Sound and would go and record things there on his own. It was around this time working there with Arthur and by myself that I came to appreciate edits. Arthur was doing a lot of them. I appreciated how they had to work and also that they can be a sublime, good thing, on their own.

'Mark Freedman built the studio all by himself, all the carpentry. It was a good studio but there was a problem with the plumbing vent stacks, so it smelled like shit especially in the hallways and elevator area. There was a lot of recording equipment lying around; Arthur used to wheedle equipment out of people. He managed to find a Nagra [a portable tape recorder]. At another point he had a Sony F1 which was an early digital recorder, and we used VHS hi-fi.'

Arthur Russell and Sydney Murray, who was introduced to Tom by Arthur as one of his former girlfriends, East Twelfth Street, mid-1980s.

ARTHUR.
this is for the Amp.
I can't reach you
and I need it for my
recording, I'll leave the
check, and I'm using
it, if for any reason
you have changed your
mind leave me a note
and I'll return it to
you here, otherwise
we have a deal -- call
me at 243-3700 or at
RCA Recording Studios -#©
10AM-6PM MON-FRI   Tom

Letter from Tom Waits, then recording his album RAIN DOGS at RCA Studios in Midtown, to Arthur Russell regarding the sale of an amp, 1985.

During Arthur's visit this summer (Aug, 85) In Rockefeller gardens in Seal Harbor, Arther paused for a moment of study.

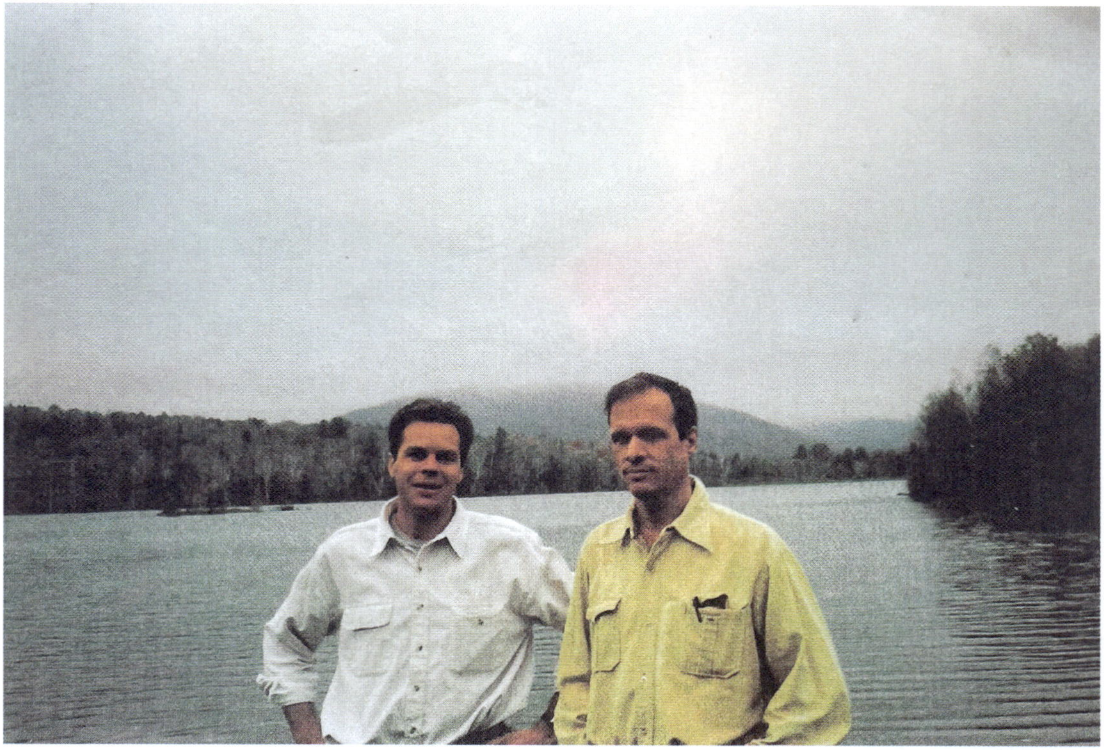

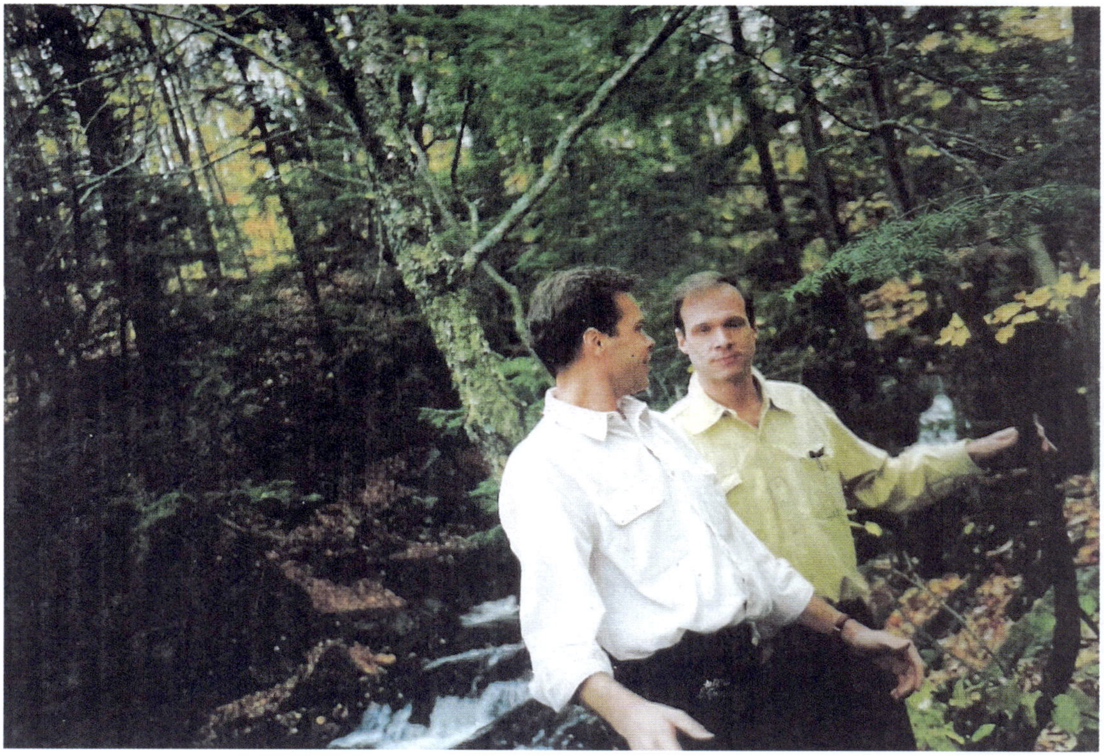

Peter Zummo: 'I worked with Trisha on LATERAL PASS for about a year and then in September 1985 we workshopped this with the group, in Minneapolis and we were there for a week, the band playing with the dance company. In LATERAL PASS, piece IV ('Quintet'), the long groove with the tabla with Arthur humming and singing was a response to the dance performance, but music is music. They put us in some motel in the backside of town. There was a lot of stuff going on in this hotel.'

Mustafa Khaliq Ahmed: 'Prior to starting this project, Arthur and I were working on "Let's Go Swimming". Hours, days after days, going back and forth to this piece. And then this project comes up, and during the rehearsals that Peter was having, Arthur is appearing more lethargic, there's a couple more cancellations he makes.'

Walker Art Center

Trisha Brown Company

Residency
12 August–7 September 1985
Hamline University Theater, St. Paul

Programme for LATERAL PASS presented by Walker Art Center, Hamline University Theater, St Paul. The piece featured accompaniment by The Peter Zummo Orchestra. Mustafa Khaliq Ahmed (percussion), Guy Klucevsek (accordion), Arthur Russell (cello), Bill Ruyle (marimba), Peter Zummo (trombone).

Mustafa Khaliq Ahmed: 'So then we get to Minneapolis, and I'm like all over the place, because I'm thinking, Ah, finally, we're out of the city, Arthur has no distractions: when we're not rehearsing, he and I can go back to talking about how we're going to finish "Let's Go Swimming". And so at some point, Peter Zummo comes up to me and he says, "Yo, Mustafa, Arthur's with that dancer," and he basically tells me that Arthur's gay, but he thought that I knew that Arthur was gay. And after all of this time that I was with Arthur, I had no idea that he was gay.

'Also at this time, after we finished LATERAL PASS, that's when I find out that Arthur might have AIDS, then we go through that. So, working on this project, it was not just about the music, but my awareness of how naïve I was, of what I had learned about the fact that all men who might be gay are not effeminate. This is the first person that I had ever had a relationship with that's just two guys doing our thing – it wasn't about our sexuality, we weren't going out hitting on chicks, we were working on something that was pure, the music. My God, I'm like, "Oh, man, I didn't know that Arthur was gay," and it was like a little joke for everybody else, because everybody else knew that part of his life, and it was like, I was naïve.'

Lucy Sante: 'Crack seemed to arrive all at once, even though it's not quite true, but that's the impression it gave. AIDS was more like a snowball rolling downhill. The first AIDS death in the building happened in '83, right at the beginning, and the second one a few months later, and it was the lead singer and manager of a band called The Stimulators, who sometimes backed up Allen Ginsberg – most of the members lived in the building. The third person who died of AIDS was Klaus Nomi, and it was like that for a while, like somebody would die every six months or so, and then it reached its peak around '88, '89, '90.'

Part IV

1986–92

1986 was arguably the most momentous year of Arthur's life, one in which he received a positive diagnosis for HIV or what was then often colloquially referred to as AIDS or 'the AIDS virus' and released a series of extraordinary recordings that demonstrated both an artist at the height of their creativity and the possibility of further unexplored musical directions. WORLD OF ECHO, the first and only solo album Arthur released in his lifetime, was issued on Upside Records in the United States in the second half of the year. (It was followed by a version on Rough Trade Records available in the UK and Europe in the spring of 1997.)

WORLD OF ECHO had been preceded by the twelve-inch single 'School Bell/ Treehouse', which Arthur released under the alias of Indian Ocean on his former record label, Sleeping Bag. In contrast to the mediative personal space of WORLD OF ECHO, the release saw Arthur further experiment in music that could function in the context of the dancefloor, while also refusing to repeat himself. The record was raw, minimal and showcased Arthur's vocals at their most immediate and confident. Another twelve-inch, 'Let's Go Swimming', was released on Rough Trade Records under Arthur's own name before the end of the year. Both singles were unclassifiable, almost mystical in their grasp of dynamics and sound design and unlike any other contemporary records in the dance idiom.

Arthur's final years were filled with a renewed commitment to creativity and unceasing live and recording work. He regularly performed the WORLD OF ECHO material and incorporated several of its compositions in collaborations with choreographers active in New York's innovative dance community. Arthur worked closely with Diane Madden, Alison Salzinger, Stephanie Woodard and John Bernd, continuing to play his cello and effects boxes hidden behind a curtain, or off-stage, as the choreographers' pieces were performed.

Arthur Russell during a family holiday in Minnesota, 1986.

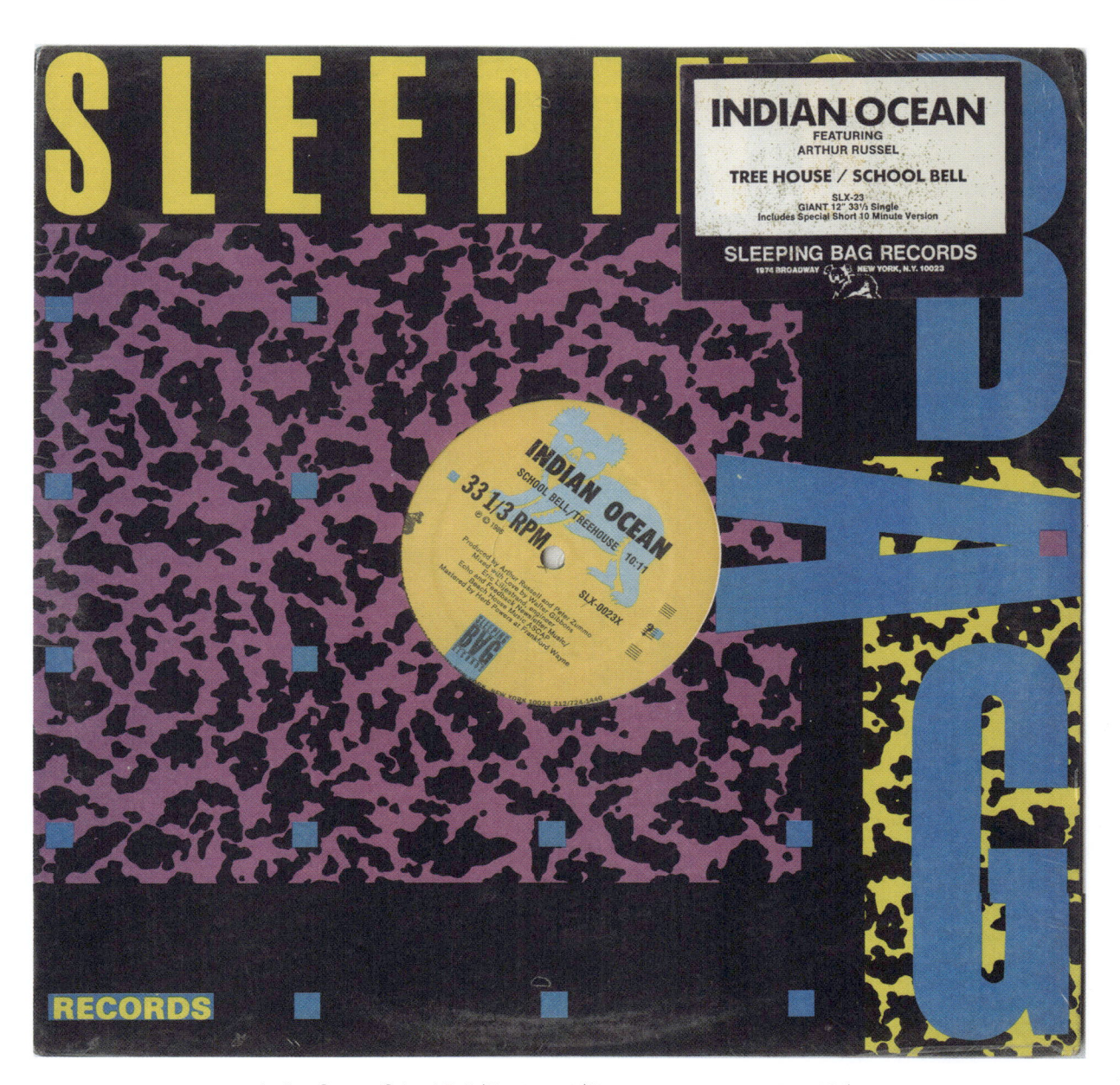

Indian Ocean, 'School Bell / Treehouse' (Sleeping Bag Records, 12", 1986).

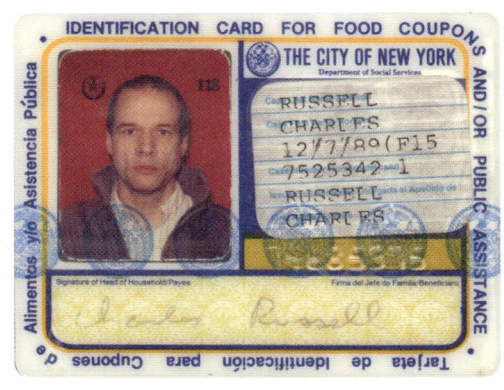

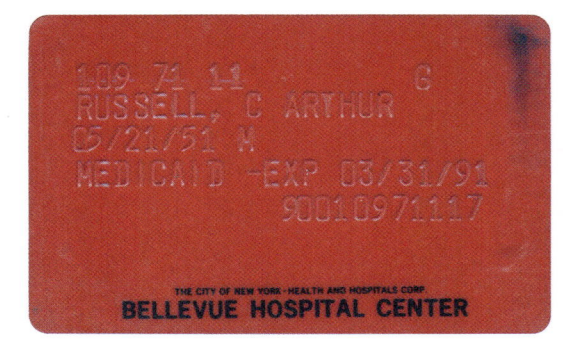

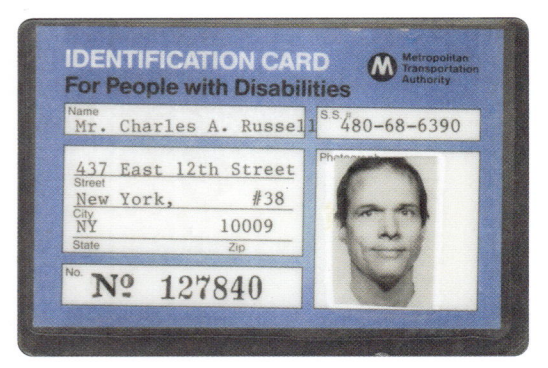

Tom Lee: 'We were concerned, from rashes, and he had symptoms before he got tested. I remember the day we received the paper that confirmed the AIDS test and that he was sick with HIV, and I recall going from work and we just sat on the couch in tears. Then there was a big thing about what to do? One of the places Arthur went to was the Community Health Project. He needed to go someplace that was free health care. There was a woman at the Community Health Project who guided us through right to the very end. She was a great, great support.'

Kate Russell: 'Julie and I had worked out he was gay in the 1980s. My parents hadn't talked to each other about the fact Arthur was gay until Arthur told them so, and this was after Tom and Arthur were together, and they kind of went, "Oh." But neither of them – Mom and Dad – had talked with each other. Mom said, "Oh, I didn't want to talk to your dad, I thought it would just devastate him." My dad said he didn't want to talk to my mom for the same reasons. And when he had to tell them, because he had AIDS, that's when it all came down, and both Julie and I knew a year before they knew.'

Tom Lee: 'I met his parents once before he was sick, or around the time of the diagnosis, when he wasn't sick sick. There was the odd lesion but he seemed okay. His parents had come to New York, to the frame shop I had. They didn't know Arthur was sick. He wasn't that open about it. He didn't talk about how they had to know. I think it became more apparent on the telephone. He and I didn't talk about whether to tell his parents. Everything was pretty discreet for a long time. I think it was just the nature of things. People were not out there about AIDS.'

Kate Russell: 'I did not meet Tom until one summer before Arthur was sick and that was in Maine.'

Will Socolov: 'Arthur and I had a falling out, and when we split Sleeping Bag up, it was on bad terms. What happened with Sleeping Bag is that I wanted to make money and I wanted to do a lot of commercial records, and Arthur had – and I think there was a lot of validity in this – he had his own sense of what his path was, and he never thought or wanted to go on a commercial path. I did records with Larry Levan, I did the Jamaica Girls, Class Action, "Weekend", records like that, but Arthur knew that, as an artist, that wasn't the way he was going to go. But he could be so insecure. I remember him talking to me about Leroy Burgess, and he said, "Leroy Burgess sings like a beautiful bird – I can't do that." And I said to him, "Arthur, first thing, your voice is not as bad you keep making it out to be, and yes, you're right, you shouldn't sing a gospel song, it's not appropriate for your voice, but there's a million things you can sing that are appropriate." So we had those kind of arguments.

'He put himself down all the time. I would have very frank conversations about good-looking men and he would just go, "Well, nobody like that would be interested in me," and I'm like, "What the fuck are you talking about? In your own way, you're very handsome." He was very self-deprecating in his voice, in his abilities, in many things, and yet there was also an arrogance. Arthur was extreme in many ways: he knew what was good, he knew what was bad, but he would fight Ernie [Brooks], and other people.

'I once ran into Seymour Stein, who had Sire Records, and I was with someone else that knew him, and the guy said, "Hey, this is Will Socolov, he's partner with Arthur Russell," and Seymour looked at me and he said, "That kid is fucking talented but meshuggeneh, oy!" Seymour liked to use his Yiddish expressions – meshuggeneh is Yiddish for like crazy, a little crazy – and that was his only comment about Arthur.'

Peter Gordon: 'I'm not sure how far along Arthur was when he told me he had AIDS. He said "Whenever I tell someone I have AIDS the first thing they ask me is, 'How long have you known?'" I think of the people I know who were dying round then: Willi Smith '87, Arnie Zane '88, Keith Haring at the start of 1990. For much of Arthur's and my music, it was a largely gay audience. The scene was shifting, clubs were dying, people were dying.'

Will Socolov: 'When we split up the company, it was a little rough, and then when Arthur knew that he was sick, he came back and we not only patched up, he blew my mind. We were driving in a car when he told me: "Will, I have AIDS." I had a very close friend that had died of AIDS already, and I just said to him, "Arthur, whatever you want, whatever you need from me, I'll do whatever you want." I was devastated.'

As HIV and AIDS spread through the communities in which Arthur and his friends and collaborators lived and worked, the predominant emotional response to the virus and its effects was fear. During the mid-1980s the difference between HIV and AIDS was not clearly differentiated in public consciousness, nor were the routes by which the virus was transmitted fully understood.

> Peter Zummo: 'Arthur didn't want to admit that he had it. There was a harmonica that I'd lent him and he'd had it for a year. And when he gave it back to me I said, "Is this okay to use?" and Arthur said, "There's a virus." It was uncomfortable.'

Having received a positive diagnosis, Arthur dedicated himself to his work with a renewed vigour and sense of purpose. He would continue to record new songs and rework older material and continue to play live, either in solo performance or joining friends and colleagues in their various ensembles.

> Peter Zummo: 'Arthur was comfortable enough with his artistry and sensitivity to write this way. To put down his ideas this way, and then he sought to push it out into our little world of rehearsals and local gigs and recordings. Arthur told me, "If you're intending or thinking that you're doing serious music, then you put a beat behind it that's good enough to move the body, the serious music establishment will absolutely dismiss you."'

> Ernie Brooks: 'I remember Mark Freedman at Battery Sound got furious with Arthur a couple of times, thinking he was never going to get his money back because Arthur was never going to release anything. Arthur was flexible about format and songs.'

Arthur and Steven Hall at Battery Sound Studios c.1986.

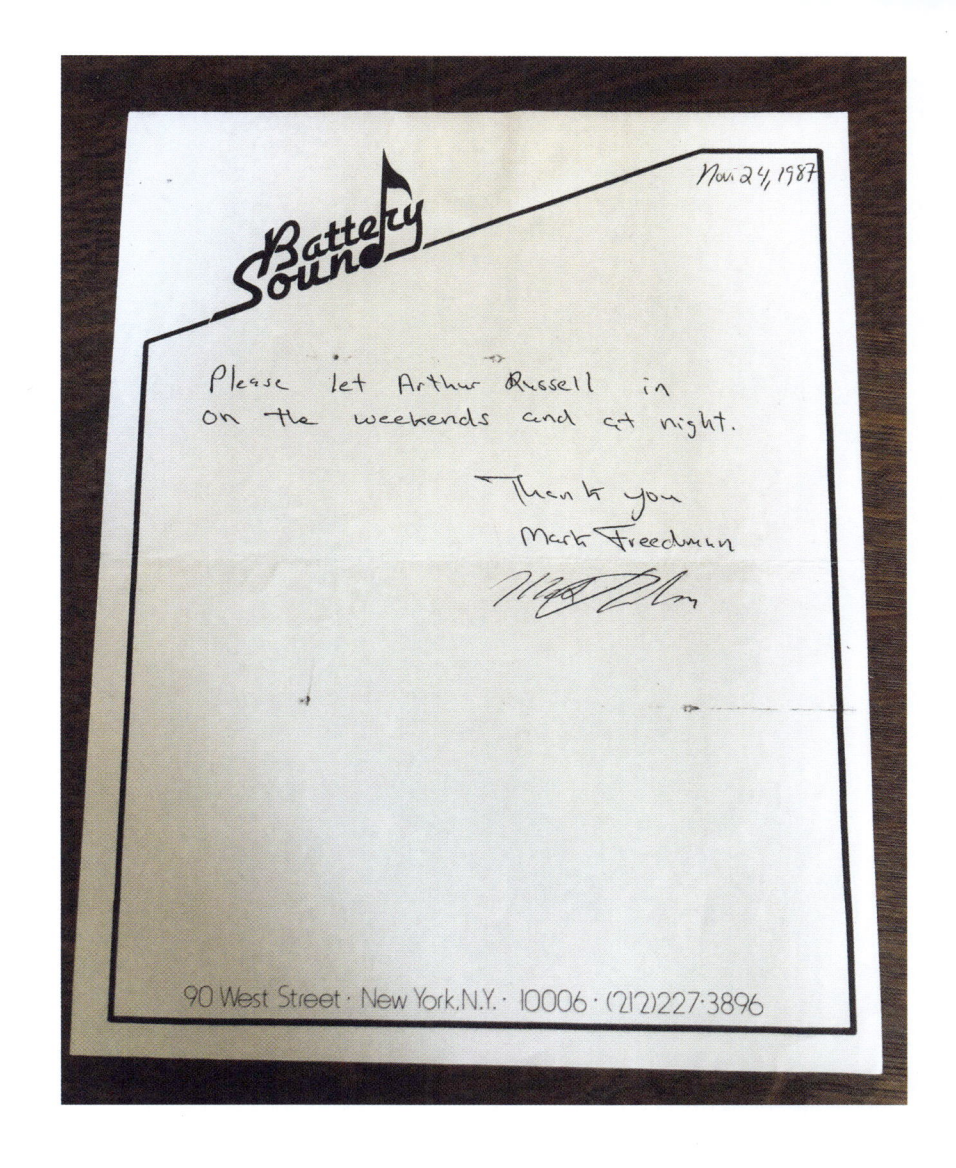

> Nov 24, 1987
>
> Please let Arthur Russell in on the weekends and at night.
>
> Thank you
> Mark Freedman

Steven Hall: 'Mark at Battery Sound would say, "Here's the keys to the studio, knock yourself out," and that was him in heaven, and if Tom was there, that would be even more heaven.'

Tom Lee: 'Some of the work he did with Ernie in The Flying Hearts on some of the more pop songs – there seemed to be a goal: "We're getting this band together, we're going to get a record contract." That was the only time I could remember that sort of straightforward ambition. With his other projects, it was, "I'm going to bring all these elements together and Geoff is going to do something with it."'

Geoff Travis: 'I saw Arthur as being completely singular. Completely in his own world.'

Battery Sound

1·19·86

School Bell/Treehouse Mix

ARTHUR RUSSELL
---

11 HRS 24 tr	$605 —
1/18 2 HRS 24 tr	110 —
1/6 .75 HRS 24 tr	41.25

TOTAL   756.25

9 HRS BETA ($45)   801.25

PAID CK #383   581.25
CASH   220.00
   801.25

90 West Street · New York, N.Y. · 10006 · (212) 227·3896

Treehouse is my idea of where commerceial music ~~is going~~ could be going

My idea of a treehouse is a platform — or a house with fewer walls. Yet ideas or concepts close or identified with ourselves seem to manifest in tangible form only ~~outside~~ on the other side of a partition from an immediate vision. Echo delays the onset of a sound in air long enough to engender perceptibility, however short a time

ROUGH TRADE RECORDS LIMITED
61 COLLIER ST, LONDON N1 9BE
PHONE: 01-833 2133
TELEX: 299579

ARTHUR RUSSELL - "LET'S GO SWIMMING" (RTT 184 - 12" only)

  side 1 - Coastal Dub
  side 2 - Gulf Stream Dub and Puppy Surf Dub

A skinny kid from Oskaloosa, Iowa comes to New York in 1973 to join the burgeoning New Music scene after studying Indian Music at the Ali Akbar Khan school in San Francisco. A skilled cello player, vocalist, and keyboardist, he studies at the Manhattan School of Music and within 2 years delivers a landmark concert of modern music at Soho's famed Kitchen. Philip Glass was in the audience and later composed music for the play "Cascando" specifically for him to perform.

Simultaneously Arthur has a vision of fusing ALL music - serious, pop, dance etc. and brings his avant - compositional chops to bear on what the serious music mavens consider to be the highest form of art : Dance Music.

With two definitive cult jams under his belt, on the radio and on the charts (Dinosaur L's "Go Bang" on Sleeping Bag and Loose Joints "Is It All Over My Face?" on West End) our man decides to apply the same principles to rock. He records "Kiss Me Again" under the name Dinosaur on Sire (David Byrne appears on the record) and joins the seminal new wave group The Necessaries (with former Modern Lover Ernie Brooks) delivering one classic album on Sire. Hating the rigorous touring grind, he suddenly quits The Necessaries by bolting out the door of their van, cello in hand, en route to a gig somewhere in New Jersey. 4th and Broadway releases "Tell You Today", an out-take from the original Loose Joints sessions, as their first release, and he withdraws to further concentrate on neo-classical music ("Instrumentals" on Crepescule and "Tower Of Meaning" on Chatham Square). Simultaneously, he perfects his self-contained cello/vocal performance, which he takes on the road as a virtual one man band, combining complex structures, feedback harmonies, and interlacing them with sumptuous, almost devotional vocals.

Now, on September 22 1986, Rough Trade Records is proud to bring Arthur Russell out from the aegis of pseudonymous dance productions and into the spotlight under his own name with a new 12" dance release "Let's Go Swimming". With a remix by legendary Walter Gibbons (Strafe's "Set It Off"), this record is just a taste of the musical brilliance which Arthur posesses in abundance. "Let's Go Swimming" isn't Hip Hop House or any easily categorised offshoot, but rocks like crazy.

Arthur Russell - a true unsung pioneer of the New York underground music scene - the twilight world where rock, dance, and experimental music overlap has been a best kept secret... but not any longer.

Dance Crazy - Chris (Radio) and Karen (Press) on 01-833 2133.

Arthur Russell, 'Let's Go Swimming' (Rough Trade, 12", 1986).

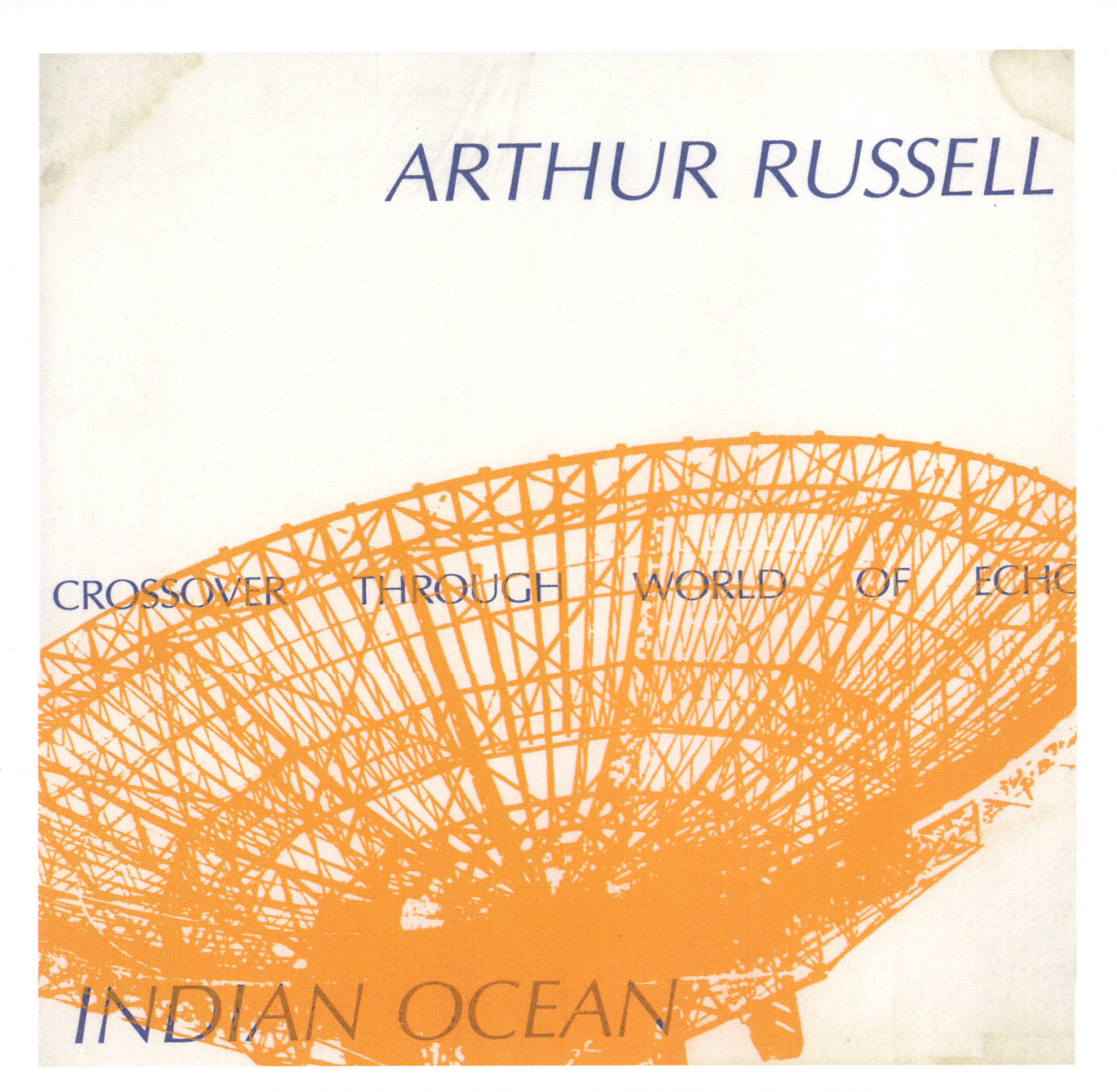

Mock-up of visual ideas for what became the WORLD OF ECHO album, c.1986.

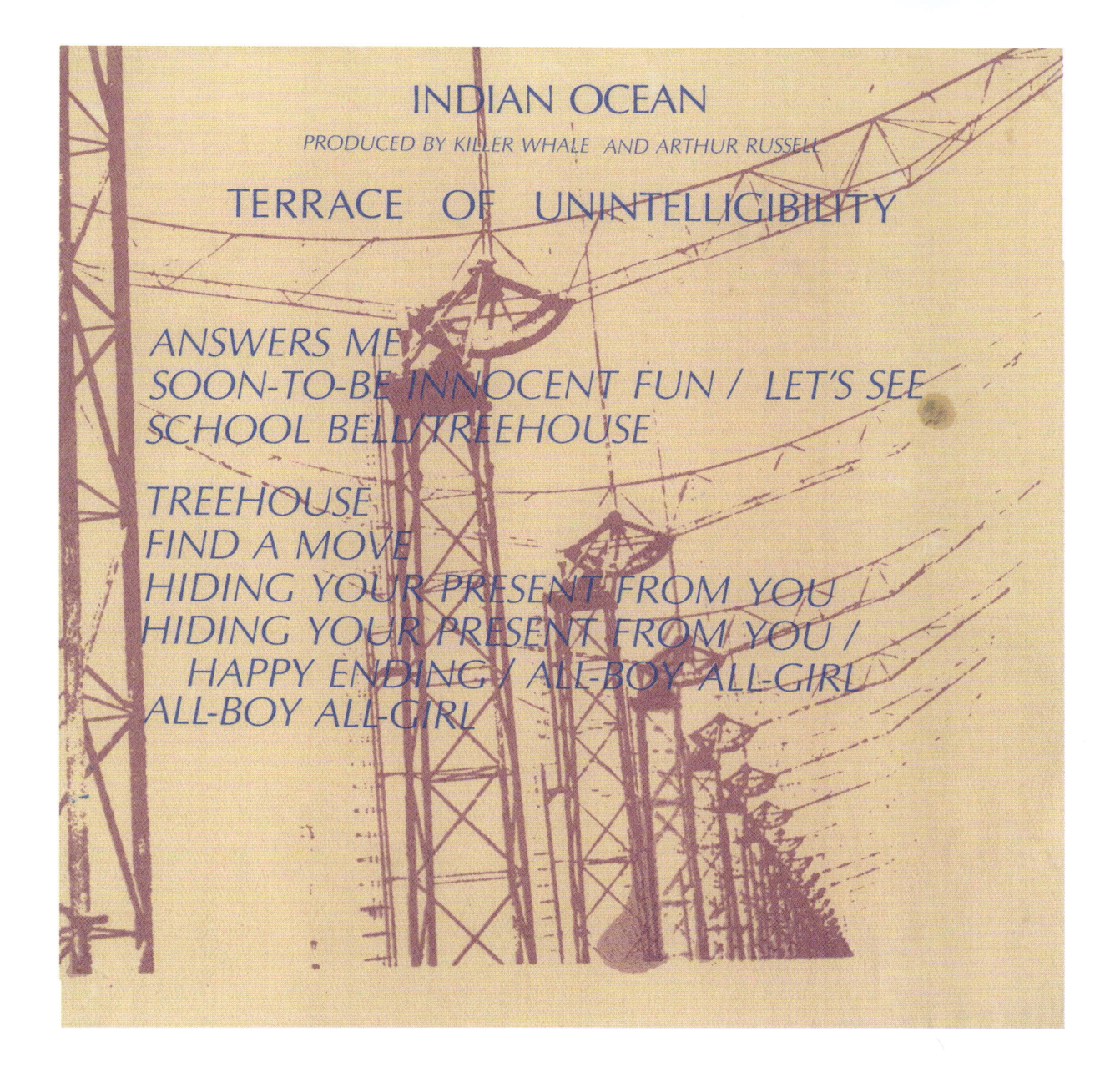

INDIAN OCEAN
PRODUCED BY KILLER WHALE AND ARTHUR RUSSELL

TERRACE OF UNINTELLIGIBILITY

ANSWERS ME
SOON-TO-BE INNOCENT FUN / LET'S SEE
SCHOOL BELL/TREEHOUSE

TREEHOUSE
FIND A MOVE
HIDING YOUR PRESENT FROM YOU
HIDING YOUR PRESENT FROM YOU /
   HAPPY ENDING / ALL-BOY ALL-GIRL
ALL-BOY ALL-GIRL

Throughout his career a series of influential producers and executives had championed Arthur and his music: John Hammond, Karin Berg (who oversaw the careers of The B-52s, The Cars, Hüsker Dü and REM) and Jerry Wexler (who recorded DUSTY IN MEMPHIS, Aretha Franklin and Wilson Pickett) had all shown interest in working with Russell. Arthur's career as a musician, composer, songwriter and recording artist was one rich in opportunity. Although he only released two records on the label, his relationship with Geoff Travis of Rough Trade Records was among the most fruitful. Having released 'Let's Go Swimming' and WORLD OF ECHO, Travis continued to finance Arthur, in fairly generous terms, until the final months of his life. The majority of the material Arthur was working on from 1986 onwards was intended for release on Rough Trade. Travis had first encountered Arthur's music through Upside Records, the label that released WORLD OF ECHO domestically in the US and from whom Travis licensed the recording for the UK.

Arthur Russell at the family home with his sister Julie, mid-1980s.

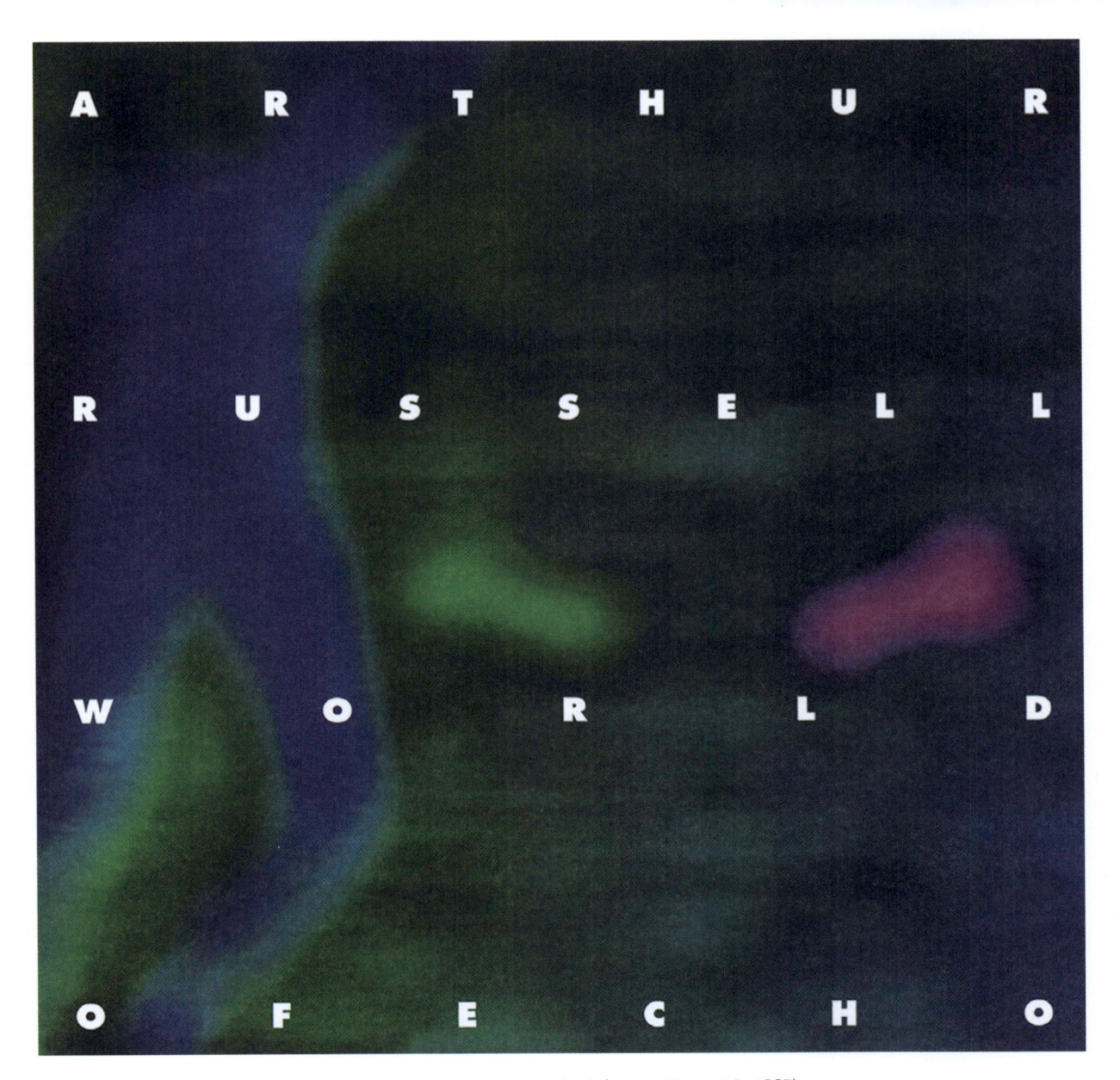

Arthur Russell, WORLD OF ECHO (Rough Trade, LP, 1987).

Geoff Travis: 'I don't know where I first met Arthur, I think he might have started coming around to our New York office. You'd always see him walking around, round about St Mark's Place with his headphones on. I didn't really spend that much time with Arthur in real time, but I spent quite a lot of time with him on the phone from New York, he would ring. He was always really, really nice to me. I suppose the only thing was, it was not probably the best thing to call really late at night! I was too naïve to say, "Look, Arthur, this is outside work time, call me in the morning."'

Tom Lee: 'Those pictures in the cornfield were taken once Arthur had started working with Geoff Travis with a release in mind. I think that firmed things up between Arthur and his parents: he'd gotten money for his music and things felt very positive. Prior to that my memory is that there was very little connection with his parents. Then after I moved in there wasn't much talk about his family. He would go back to Iowa for Christmas. If his parents were going from Iowa to Maine, he would somehow get up to Maine, but intermittently. They would have to give him some money to travel and it's vague in my mind how often that was. He would take keyboards or his cello with him; he wasn't sitting around the kitchen table talking.'

Geoff Travis: 'I suppose I never really got to know him that well. What is odd is that I supported him for so many years and spent such a huge amount of money on him, and I can't really quite rationalise that. It's not that I thought, Here's Albert Einstein, this is the greatest artist I've ever encountered, he's a genius, and one day he'll be ... I didn't really think that. I don't know what it was. I probably didn't even appreciate how brilliant WORLD OF ECHO was.'

Mustafa Khaliq Ahmed: 'When Arthur came to me, he wanted to do dance music, he wanted to do my percussion with dance music. "In the Light of the Miracle", "Platform on the Ocean", I can go on and on. That's where Arthur was, this is where he ended up. He was a white soul brother. And yet he was very quirky. This was the beginning of this kind of fusion music between dance and pop and the world beat type of stuff. Nobody ever played an agogô bell out front like I did on "In the Light of the Miracle" and blew up like that. Now, thirty years later, you hear a lot of little agogô bells in popular television commercials, bingo.'

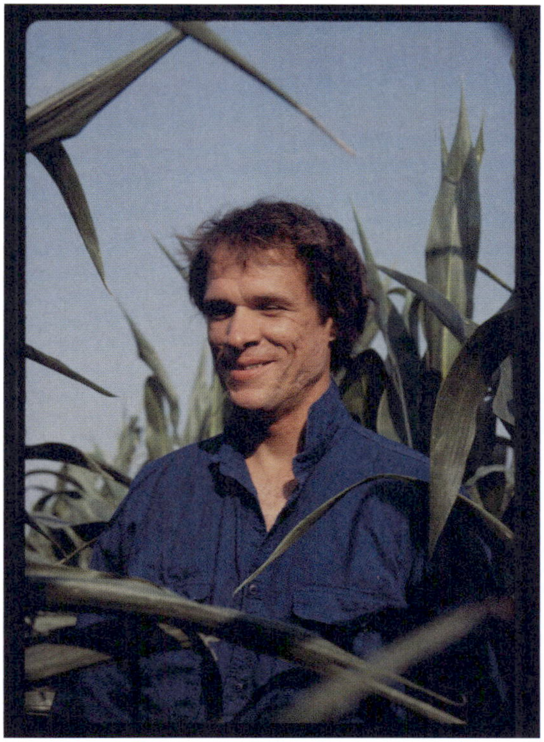
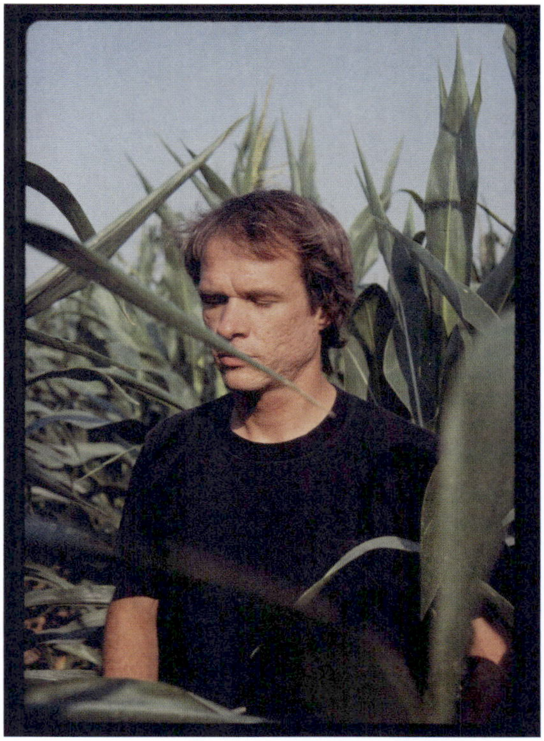
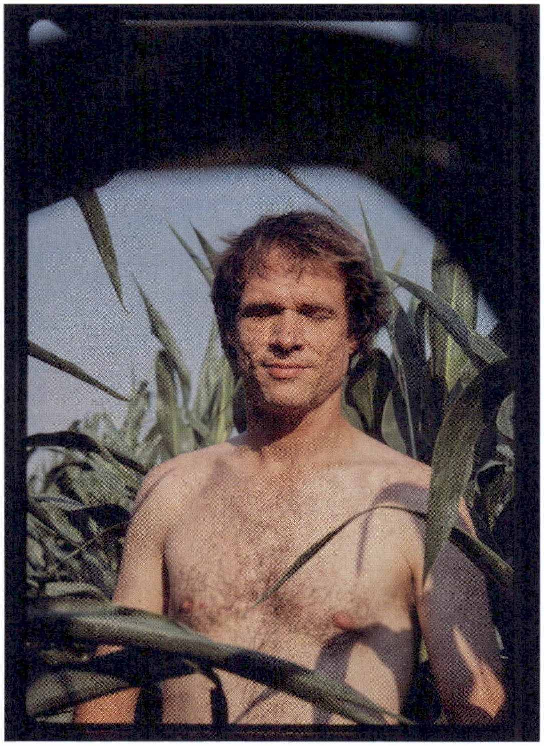
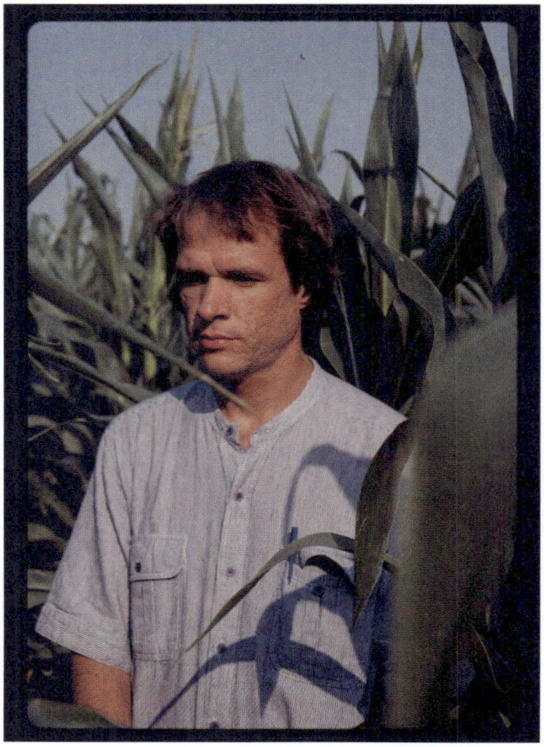

Steven Hall: 'Arthur would get bored when he mastered something. He would get bored, or when he became successful, then he would say, "Okay, I got that," and then he would move on. And that would be very frustrating to some of us, because we were like, "Hey, you're doing well here, why don't you stick with it?" which is the American method of defining success: to find something you're good at and keep doing it until you become, until you prevail. But his way of doing it was not that way. He had a self-sabotaging quality.'

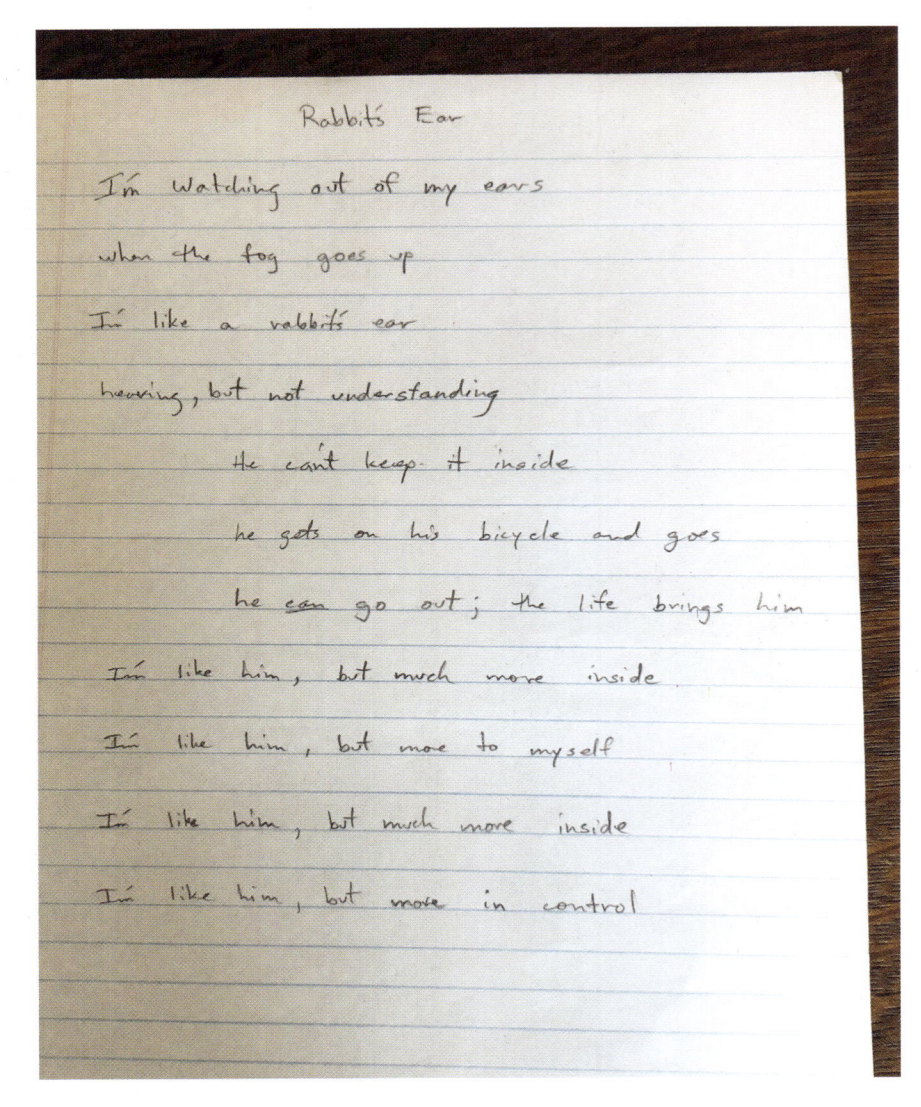

> Rabbit's Ear
>
> I'm watching out of my ears
>
> when the fog goes up
>
> I'm like a rabbit's ear
>
> hearing, but not understanding
>
> He can't keep it inside
>
> he gets on his bicycle and goes
>
> he can go out; the life brings him
>
> I'm like him, but much more inside
>
> I'm like him, but more to myself
>
> I'm like him, but much more inside
>
> I'm like him, but more in control

Handwritten lyrics to 'Rabbit's Ear', recorded during the sessions from which the material of WORLD OF ECHO was drawn and included in the original release of the album on Upside Records (1986) and Rough Trade Records (1987).

Tom Lee: 'Arthur had a rationale for always working on songs like "Let's Go Swimming", or "School Bell/Treehouse"; he reworked them thinking someone else could take the mix to another level. He didn't have the means to make it happen himself. That's why he was reliant first on Will and then with Geoff, he thought, There was someone who can get my music mixed. At the same time, I don't know of any artist on Rough Trade that Arthur raved about. Arthur never really talked about wanting to go to Europe to play live. Arthur always felt he wasn't finished with the work yet.'

Geoff Travis: 'Arthur hid himself away. He never made any great claims for his music to me. He never said, "This is a masterpiece, what are you going to do with it?" He really enjoyed the Paradise Garage and hearing his music being played there. Maybe he was thinking, I've done this track, "Hop on Down to Petland", I'll get someone to make it more contemporary, commercial in a way that I don't know how to. He inhabited a space that was so original, it took the world a long time to catch up with it. He wanted to be successful. That's the paradox. And I suppose when I say he could be difficult, that's what I'm talking about, really. He was always wanting me to get someone to remix things, for it to do better commercially, and he was semi-ironic and then semi-not. I feel a little bit guilty that I didn't give him more time. If it was today, I think I would probably go to New York and spend a couple of days with him and just try to get to know him a bit more. Back then I didn't really have time, or the kind of knowledge that that was the right thing to do.'

Ernie Brooks: 'For all his focus on his work, he really did want recognition, he did want fame. I'm not sure about money. I think he wanted enough to get himself a cheese sandwich and a roof over his head. He didn't seem to want material objects. He didn't want fancy clothes, any of that.'

Alison Salzinger: 'I think Arthur did want attention, he wanted to be cool and have reactions from the audience beyond the kind of shows he usually did.'

Steven Hall: 'I think what Arthur realised when things were in the later stage were that he could do it on his own, and he got a taste of that with the disco hits that he had, but then very quickly moved on to other things, never staying very long in one genre, even when he was becoming successful. But in terms of ambition, he wanted to be more successful than Philip Glass, who he considered a kind of uncle.'

May 17, 1987

SPRING FIELD is a work-in-progress basing itself on interacting monophonies and their accompanying time continuities, and also further explores the use of word sequences, as well as phrases, in a musical or nonverbal way.
"Interacting monophonies" means single note melodies or note sequences.
"Accompanying time continuities" refers to the support system (and its by-products) used to conceive or perform these note sequences whether mechanical, human or other.
It is my desire to include within the established scope of this project the widest range of these systems, in concept at least, as well as the local melodic performance, to be loosely considered "percussion". This could be where the melodic monophonies composition performance is considered in its basic structural capacity and other events produced as a result of its articulation, (such as perfunctory demarcation of its meter, vocal response, creaking of keyboard keys, etc.) are categorized with it. This leaves open the possibility of unrelated events being arbitrarily assigned to a monophony's domain, and reassibned at will, useful for the purposes fo organization for further composition.
"Interacting" refers to points at which a melodic content will (a.) affect another support system, (b.) combine with it, or (c.) remain neutral in relationship to it.
Of the three, (c.) I consider, naturally, to be the broadest category, including materials being performed or those not being performed. It also includes therefore all melodies or monophonies which would be performed. Again, it is my desire to devise a method which makes use of this vast category without inhibiting the specific performances of a musical idea or score. While improvisation is the most natural form of this, other forms can and do exist; probably on an infinite scale with our personal limitation affecting our awareness of them.
To these ends I hope to find usable methods which could be effective as a soul ful quiet music as well as dense rhytmic activity. A key component in these

methods will surely be time and space. Perhaps by creating contrasts within the timing of events (as above) and displacing space with the interaction of these monophonies through the use of multi channel playback. Various loudspeakers of very different sizes could be located through the room, some very small and high-sounding, others medium to large, being driven by different channels of the sound system. Signal processing could be then applied to alternating channels or locations in the room.

The vocals in SPRING FIELD are to be considered both in the light of text/sound as is WORLD OF ECHO and literal meaning. I hope to time their delivery according to the structures set out above and available technology presents exciting possibilities od sampled words being used as afterthought (percussion as above), forethought (sung as part of a monophony), or both (!). The relationship between various phrases of these intentions as well as the various shades of literal and graphic meanings inherent, could be underscored by using a computer-keyboard driven alpha-numeric display, the kind that are in department stores

Programme for the spring series at Dance Theater Workshop, Chelsea, 1987, featuring Alison Salzinger's piece 'Like You'. Arthur provided the music for the production. The programme lists the songs 'Hop on Down to Petland', 'Anti-Gravity Soap', 'Hiding Your Present', 'It's a Good Sign', 'Waterfall'. The performance was one of several collaborations with contemporary choreographers Arthur undertook during the period. As well as with Alison Salzinger, Arthur performed WORLD OF ECHO and related material with Diane Madden, Stephanie Woodard and John Bernd, usually playing his cello and effects boxes off stage as the choreographers' pieces were performed.

Alison Salzinger: 'I had that photograph taken on Avenue B or C where they had backdrops of nature scenes. Dance Theater Workshop was the place you wanted to get produced if you were a downtown performer. It was a small venue but had an amazing lighting designer. DTW was a very professional, tightly run space. Everybody wanted to perform there.

'Arthur won a Bessie Award with the choreographer Diane Madden, it was like the Oscar for dance. That was a big deal in the dance world. Whenever I performed with him people would say, "My God, I loved that music so much," but most of them hadn't heard of Arthur before.'

David R. White is the series producer of DTW Presents.

* * * * * *

This presentation of ALISON SALZINGER is a full production project of Dance Theater Workshop, Inc., and is supported in part with public funds from the National Endowment for the Arts (a federal agency); the New York State Council on the Arts; the New York City Department of Cultural Affairs; and Materials for the Arts, New York City Department of Cultural Affairs.

DTW also acknowledges, with heartfelt appreciation, the private assistance and commitment to these programs of Art Matters Inc.; AT&T; The Bankers Trust Company Group; Ballet Makers Dance Foundation Inc.; The Birsh Foundation; Booth Ferris Foundation; Mary Flagler Cary Charitable Trust; The Chase Manhattan Bank, N.A.; Chemical Bank; Robert Sterling Clark Foundation; The Coca-Cola Foundation; Consolidated Edison; Exxon Corporation; The Ford Foundation; Foundation for Contemporary Performance Arts, Inc.; Fund for the City of New York; Grace Foundation; Harkness Ballet Foundation, Inc.; Home Box Office, Inc.; JCT Foundation; Jerome Foundation; Manufacturers Hanover Trust Company; Joyce Mertz-Gilmore Foundation; Metropolitan Life Foundation; Mobil Foundation; Morgan Guaranty Trust Company; National Broadcasting Company, Inc.; New York Telephone Company; The New York Times Company Foundation, Inc.; Philip Morris Companies Inc.; The Reed Foundation, Inc.; Jerome Robbins Foundation; The Rockefeller Foundation; Billy Rose Foundation; The Peg Santvoord Foundation, Inc.; The Scherman Foundation, Inc.; Emma A. Sheafer Charitable Trust; The Shubert Foundation; Time Inc.; the Wallace Funds; and "Friends of DTW". DTW receives additional corporate support from Avon Products Foundation, Inc.; Chemical Bank; IBM; Morgan Guaranty Trust Company, Inc.; Philip Morris; and Time Inc., through employee matching contributions programs.

* * * * * *

These performances are being documented on videotape for the permanent archives of Dance Theater Workshop and the Dance Collection of the New York Public Library with support from the New York State Council on the Arts. This documentation also provides formal notice of copyright protection, as determined solely by the artist(s).

ALISON SALZINGER

Like You

Choreography: Alison Salzinger
Music: Arthur Russell
Songs including: "Hop on Down to Petland"
"Anti-gravity Soap"
"Hiding Your Present"
"It's a Good Sign"
"Waterfall"
Dancers: Rahil Abdullah, Nelson Figueroa, Cynthia Fraley-P., Irving Gregory, William Liebeskind, Daniel McIntosh, Michael O'Rourke, Alison Salzinger, Chloe Waldman
Scene Paintings: Robert Raphael
Video: Daniel McIntosh
Lighting Design: Phil Sandström
Technical Assistant: Lori E. Seid
Costume and Set Design: Alison Salzinger
Card Design and Printing: Tom Lee

* * * * * *

Jewelweed
Dancer: Alison Salzinger

* pause *

Pokeweed
Dancers: (in order of appearance) Daniel McIntosh, Chloe Waldman, Nelson Figueroa, Irving Gregory, William Liebeskind, Cynthia Fraley-P., Michael O'Rourke, Rahil Abdullah, Alison Salzinger

* pause *

Tumbleweed
Dancers: The Company

** THERE WILL BE NO INTERMISSION **

This piece is dedicated to Betty Jackson.

Special thanks to Carl and Molly Waldman, Durriyya and Ali Rashid Abdullah, Pat Finn, Suzy Salzinger, John Antrobus, Robert Raphael, Tom Lee, and all the performers.

* * * * * *

ALISON SALZINGER was born in New York City in 1960 and began studying dance in 1966. Alison graduated from Oberlin College in 1982. Her work has been presented at P.S. 122, BACA Downtown, Ethnic Folk Arts Center and on DTW's Fresh Tracks Series. Ms. Salzinger has taught dance at the 92nd Street Y, P.S. 122's Morning Moving, and will be in residence at Oberlin College in January and February of 1988. Salzinger has also performed in the work of Sally Silvers, Cydney Wilkes, Stephanie Woodard and others. She has been working with Arthur Russell since 1986.

RAHIL ABDULLAH is a seven year old student at P.S. 41, the Greenwich Village School. Rahil has a wide range of interests and abilities and is currently studying tap dancing with Kate Jacobs at the Visual Arts Center at the Children's Aid Society. This presentation of *Like You* will be her first public performance.

NELSON FIGUEROA was born in Puerto Rice in 1976. He moved to New York City in 1980 where he lives with his four brothers and four sisters. Nelson attends P.S. 61; he likes math, baseball and wrestling. He might like to become a policeman. This is Nelson's first dance performance.

CYNTHIA FRALEY-P. attended Ohio University where she received a B.F.A. in Studio Arts. Since arriving in New York she has worked with Jo Andres, The Alien Comic, The Full Moon Shows and Jennifer Monson. She has performed solo works at P.S. 122, Darinka and WOW Cafe. She is currently painting, hanging out and looking for the perfect job.

IRVING GREGORY is a performer with many years of experience.

WILLIAM LIEBESKIND is a painter. His works are in private collections in the United States and in Europe. This is his first dance performance.

DANIEL MCINTOSH is a dancer and a video artist. In September he will present a new dance and video performance at Performance Space 122. He has performed in Salzinger's work since 1985 and they have collaborated on numerous improvisations. Daniel has been a member of Elizabeth Streb Ringside Inc. since 1984 and will be performing with her at The Kitchen tonight after this show. He has performed in the works of Ishmael Houston-Jones, Sally Silvers, Brian Moran, Jennifer Monson, and on Channel 13 in Mary Lucier's "New Television" video. Daniel has been experimenting with video since 1981. His subjects include flora and fauna, and dancing with a camera. He has also developed a vocabulary of kinetic video paintings.

MICHAEL O'ROURKE, Principal Skater with the Ice Capades, soloist in Ice Spectacular Los Angeles, appeared in the television special, Tom Jones Live. Mr. O'Rourke attended Carnegie Mellon University and Oberlin College. He has danced with Andy DeGroat in New York and throughout Europe, and with Wendy Perron, most recently at Marymount Manhattan College. O'Rourke designed decors for the Opera de Paris and La Scala di Milano. He has choreographed commercials for French television. Mr. O'Rourke has presented his own work in New York, France, Belgium, Spain, Italy, Switzerland, Holland and Denmark. He currently resides in Paris.

ROBERT RAPHAEL is a college art teacher and a painter. He has done puppet shows and is now looking forward to doing more scenery for the theater. He lives with his wife and two sons in Princeton, New Jersey.

ARTHUR RUSSELL was born in Oskaloosa, Iowa and came to New York in 1973. As a cellist Russell has premiered music by Christian Woolf, Philip Glass and Peter Zummo and also has two definitive cult jams under his belt (Dinosaur L's Go Bang on Sleeping Bag Records and Loose Joints' Is it All Over My Face? on West End Records). Russell continues to work in diverse areas in the music world, turning out a 12 inch record every day. Arthur Russell's record World of Echo, recently issued on Upside and Rough Trade Records uses solo vocal and cello performances with a variety of echo/delay methods; and, in concept, the maximally widest range of echos. Other projects exploring the interrelationship of performance and recording events include 24 to 24 Music (Sleeping Bag), Instrumentals (Crepuscule), and Indian Ocean (Sleeping Bag). As planning continues, outdoor acoustic performances of World of Echo with no reverb could happen. In the future, Arthur Russell will be recording for Rough Trade.

DANCE THEATER WORKSHOP presents
THE SPRING EVENTS 1987

FRESH Tracks

The 11 O'Clock New(s)
"Tapnology"
Charles Moulton
May 29 & 30 at 11 p.m.

CHARLES MOULTON's choreography, combining games, sports, dance and elements of pop culture, has earned him wide critical acclaim as a leading figure of the post-modern dance movement. "Moulton can make crackerjack dancing, can make your eyes sizzle," wrote Deborah Jowitt in The Village Voice. At DTW, Moulton will premiere Tapnology, a suite of dances which will feature electronically amplified tap shoes designed in collaboration with DAVE MESCHTER, sound consultant to the Merce Cunningham Dance Company, that transmit signals to trigger a specially prepared synthesizer, replacing the acoustics and rhythms of regular tap dancing with a battery of percussive and found sounds around which new dances will be created.
$7 or TDF +$2

FRESH TRACKS, an ongoing series of new dance by new choreographers, selected by a special DTW audition panel.

CAROL CLEMENTS
"So Low"

MEG EGINTON
"Cézanne's Doubt"

RUTH FÜGLISTALLER
"Wild Patience"

BETSY HULTON
"Hekyll and Shy"

CAROL KUEFFER
"Fad"

ASPASSIA YAGA
"Mikph Eikona (Small Picture)"

"The Crowd... Action and Mass Emotion"
Stephan Koplowitz

June 4-6 at 8 p.m.
June 7 at 8 p.m.

STEPHAN KOPLOWITZ is a choreographer, composer and visual artist who creates dance works that are resolutely humane, infused with a knowing intelligence of human foibles, concerns and expectations. At DTW Koplowitz will offer the world premiere of The Crowd... Action and Mass Emotion, featuring the fifteen performers of the IRONDALE ENSEMBLE, text by Irondale's resident playwright JONATHON WARD, as well as Koplowitz's own song-cycle composed especially for this piece. The Crowd... Action and Mass Emotion, a movement-theater work, is about crowding, being a part of, escaping into, going with and getting lost in a crowd.

DTW's Bessie Schönberg Theater 219 West 19th Street, New York City
$8 or TDF (Weekdays) TDF + $2 (Fri, Sat, Sun) except where noted
Reservations: (212) 924-0077 Voice/TDD

CHLOE WALDMAN is ten years old. She has studied modern dance, tap dance, ballet, gymnastics, karate, and piano. She attends P.S. 3 in New York City where she recently choreographed and performed a dance piece "Walk Like an Egyptian", with a friend. Chloe has also participated in a number of tap recitals at the Children's Aid Society. She wants to be a dancer, writer, illustrator, farmer or veterinarian when she grows up.

* * * * * *

ALISON SALZINGER is a member artist of Dance Theater Workshop, Inc., a non-profit tax-exempt organization. Contributions in support of Alison Salzinger's work are greatly appreciated and may be made payable to "Dance Theater Workshop, Inc." earmarked for "the DTW member project of Alison Salzinger." All contributions are fully deductible to the extent allowed by law. (Note: A copy of DTW's latest annual financial report filed with the New York State Department of State may be obtained by writing to the N.Y.S. Dept. of State, Charities Registration, 162 Washington Avenue, Albany, NY 12231, or to Dance Theater Workshop, 219 West 19th Street, New York, NY 10011.)

Donations to Alison Salzinger Dance Company to help defray production costs are tax-deductible and should be made payable to Dance Theater Workshop, but mailed to:

   Alison Salzinger Dance Company
   P.O. Box 20914
   New York, NY 10009

* * * * * *

Production Electrician: Ain Gordon

Cover Photo: J.C. Photo Studio

Arthur Russell on a family holiday, Maine, 1987.

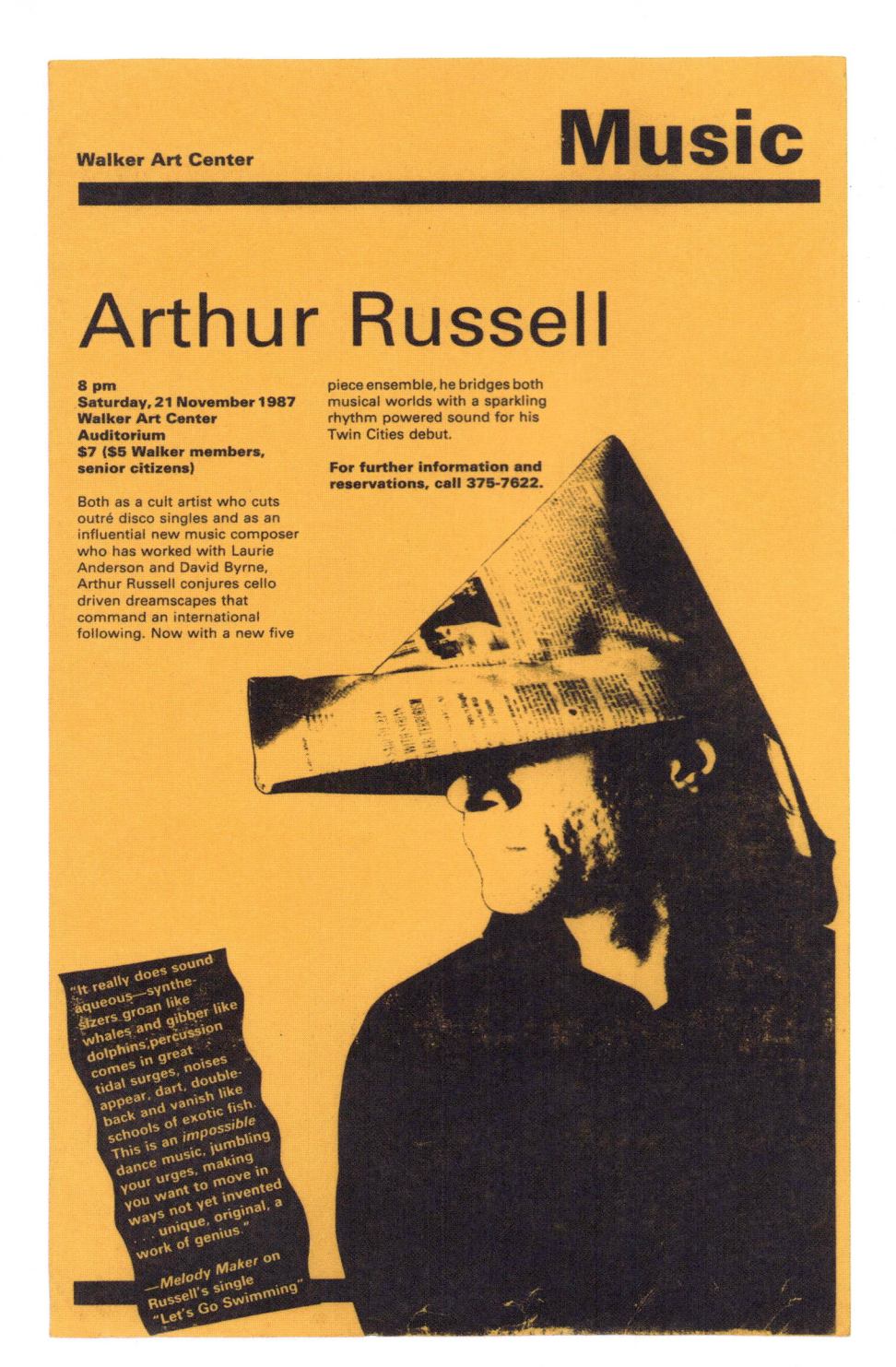

Flyer for Arthur Russell's performance at Walker Art Center Auditorium, Minneapolis, thought to be one of the scant handful of headline concerts Arthur played outside New York City, November 1987. According to Chuck Helm, the Center's musical curator and producer, the concert was one of the most difficult he arranged, as contacting Arthur and then agreeing to commit to a date was a convoluted and erratic process. Attendance at the 350-capacity venue was around eighty people, four times the number of people who might attend a concert by Arthur in New York.

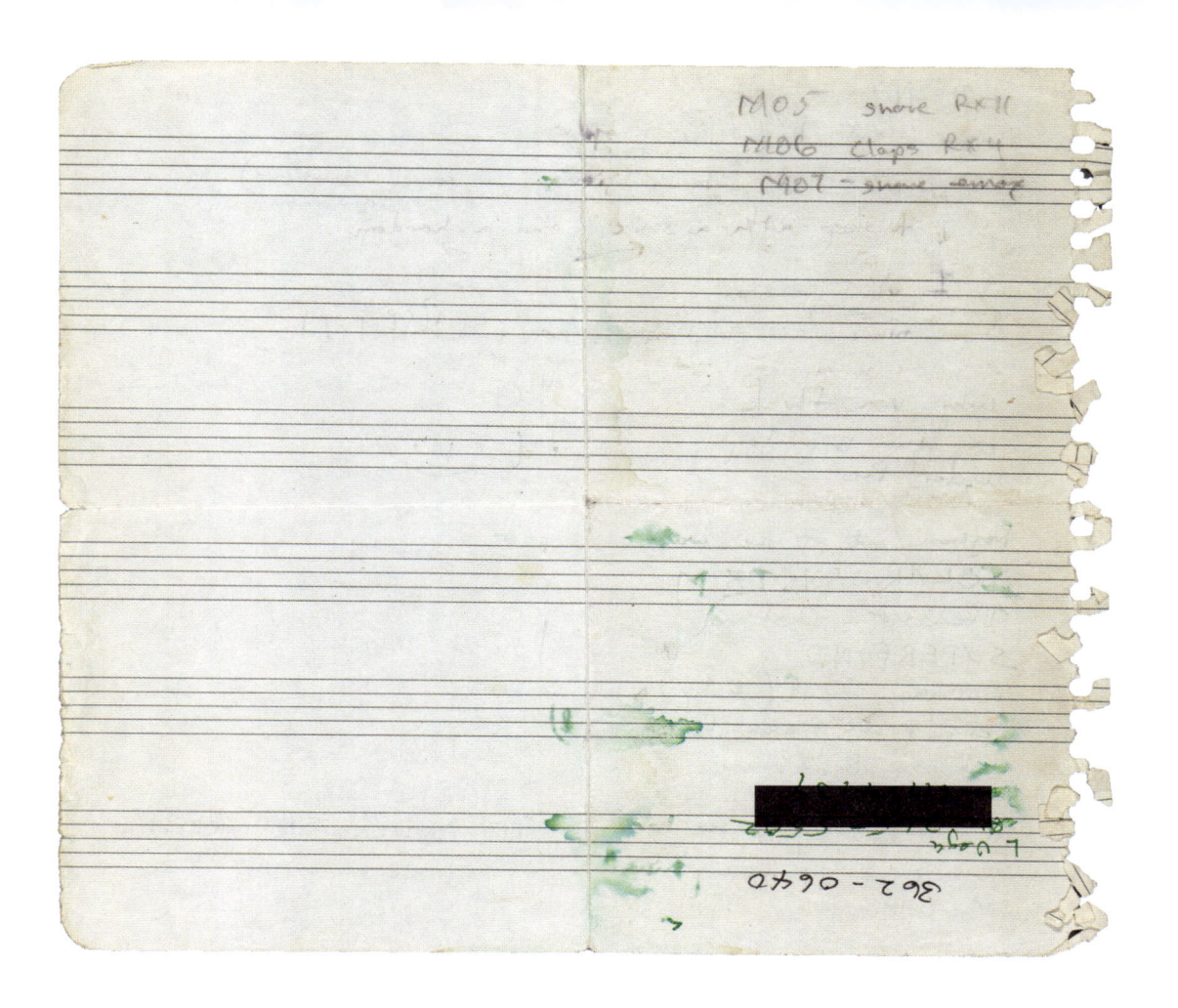

Alison Salzinger: 'I remember he was really obsessed with the handclap sound in the beats and tracks he was making. Maybe it was a Buddhist thing but he talked about it so much. It was so minimal, but he absolutely obsessed about it.'

Tom Lee: 'The problem with Arthur's Buddhism was that he wouldn't kill any roaches or mice. We lived in a sixth-floor walk-up and if we caught any mice in the trap we had to walk downstairs with them and release them into a lot across the way.'

KEEPING UP

(referenced to male vocal)

YOU LIKE IT ,,

WHEN THEY LOOK AT YOU ,,

YOU LIKE IT ,,

~~THAT I~~ ~~WHEN THEY~~ CAN'T CATCH YOU

KEEPING UP //// won't

KEEPING UP (YEAH ~~~)

WITH A FEELING (OH YEAH)

<u>GETTING TO KNOW</u>

<u>WHAT YOU LIKE</u>

<u>AND WHAT YOU LOVE</u>

chorus)
(I'M) KEEPING UP, I'M KEEPING UP

I'M TRYIN TO KEEP UP } 2x or More

Moving Up Here Closer to Me

Moving Me Up / Wax the Van

Wild Combination

Rabbits Bar / Anti Gravity

Keeping Up

A Sudden Chill

Let's See

Kate Russell: 'Once Arthur was sick, Julie and I visited him and Tom every Christmas and took Arthur to the studio, we have wonderful memories of those times. It was late at night that we went. I think the only time he could get studio time was after hours, so it was like at ten o'clock we took a taxi to this place, Battery Sound.'

255

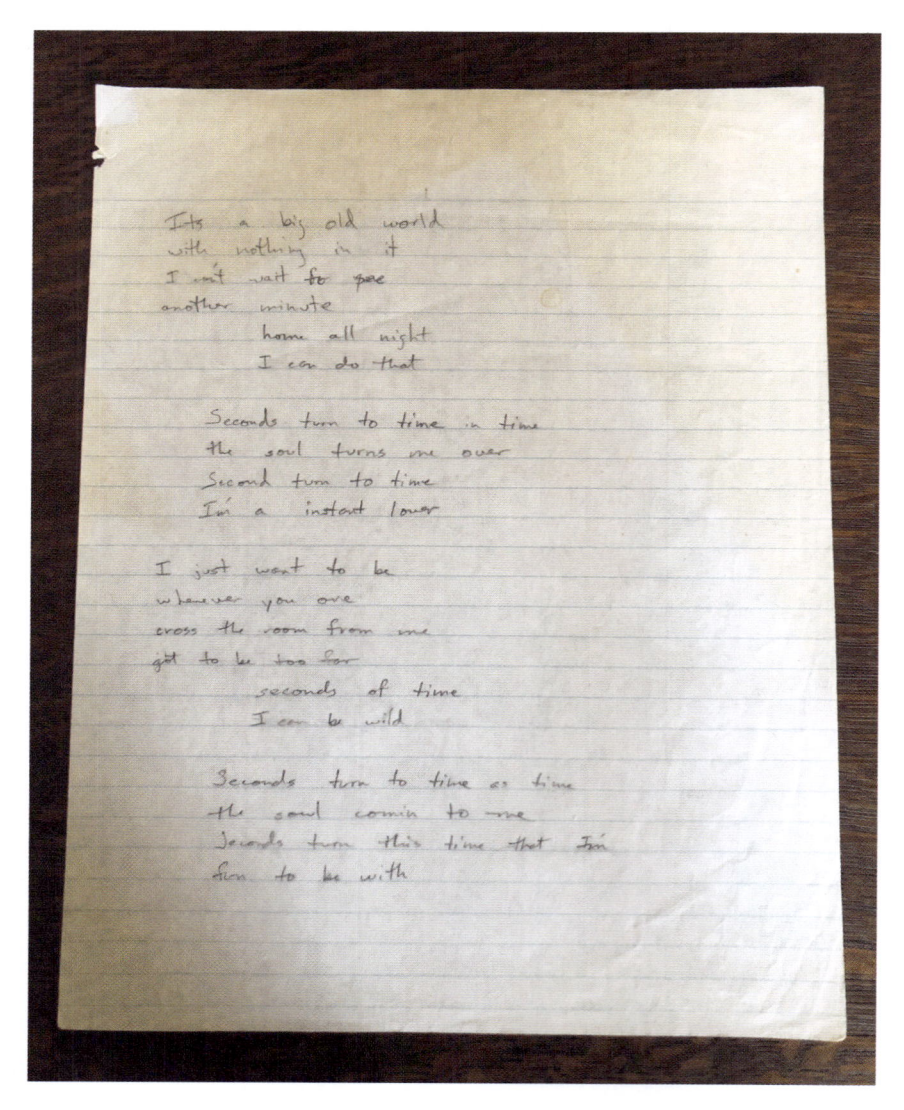

'Wild Combination', which features the voices of both Joyce Bowden and Jennifer Warnes, was a song recorded during this period to which Arthur Russell gave a relentless attention to detail.

Ernie Brooks: 'Arthur was able to keep track of everything he was doing. To me sometimes the difference between two drum sounds was so slight I'd say, "Come on, they're both great." He never went over old tape. That's why there are so many of them. He'd make up cassettes for comparison to walk around with on his Walkman. I remember "Wild Combination" really well, because it was this magnum opus that just went on and on. I played on some rough versions of it and thought this is incredible. Some of the lines: "That's us before we got there," just by itself that's remarkable. I must have heard a hundred versions of it, some of them just fragments, just to hear the sound of the drums, different combinations of the voice tracks, some with Jennifer Warnes on them, some with Joyce, and by then I don't think that was a song he'd ever do live. He had a couple of DAT machines at home at that point, so he could bounce back and off, he could still go to Battery Sound, but he worked and worked and worked on that song.'

Joyce Bowden: 'Jennifer's voice on "Wild Combination" is extremely wonderful. Arthur tried to have me sing it first, but it wasn't exactly what he wanted.
The way it was presented to me was as a spontaneous thing, we walk into a studio and we sing over the track, but with Jennifer he sent the sound bed and the lyrics weeks ahead of time and booked the studio and she had time to work on it. And then they went into the studio to capture all that beautiful and wonderful work. And when Arthur came back he had me add a couple of things.'

Tom Lee: 'Arthur and Jennifer were in touch a lot with "Wild Combination" and Arthur was traveling out there to California to see her. He'd also asked her to pass some of his songs around to see if it could generate any interest.'

Ernie Brooks: 'I once slipped on a tape of Arthur's songs when Geoff was visiting, because Arthur had insisted on playing [him] different bass drum treatments for "Wild Combination". Forty different bass drum levels, how much echo on the snare should there be? That kind of thing. Arthur went to get a sandwich and Geoff turned to me and said, "Wow, we could put out those songs and sell some records." And then Arthur accused me of betraying him.'

It's a wild, combination
It's a wild — combination
It's a wild
It's a lovin you baby
It's a talk in the dark
It's a walk in the morning

I just wanna be
wherever you are
cross the room from me
it's always too far
seconds of time
I can do that

It's a big old world
with nothin in it
I can't wait to see you
another minute
seconds of time
I can do that

Peter Zummo: 'Arthur wasn't about being a businessman first, but he was about being first in terms of what could be accomplished – "let's get this record out". He thought it really important that you date your work, to demonstrate it was your innovation first.'

Geoff Travis: 'I remember hearing, I think, "Calling All Kids". I heard "Hop On Down to Petland". I don't think I heard "Wild Combination" at the time, because I would have said, "Let's do that as a single," immediately. It was just so outside what anyone else was doing, it was hard to really put it into a context. I suppose I didn't really understand quite what the roots were of what he was doing. But that's what I liked about it: that's what really caught my attention. Because when you can hear all the influences clearly, unless they're transcended, it's not interesting, is it?'

Beginning

Intro | / / / / | / / / / | / / / / | / / / / |

Am / / / | / / / / | Bm / / / | Em Am / / | 3x
Am / Bm / | Em Am / / | 2x   Am / Bm / | Rest / / / |

Am / / / | / / / / | Bm / / / | Em Am / / }
                                             4x

Am / Bm / | Em Am / / | Am / Bm / | Em Am / / |
Am / Bm / | Rest / / / |

♩

Make 12

Jennifer —

Thanks for everything — I'm really just beginning the vocals on some of these — most of these songs. Some I have few tapes of them with any vocals at all and in some cases its hard to make out vocals over the music, home musical reference tapes, keyboard practice tapes etc.

1. Oh Fernanda Why —
has some backups by my friend Ernie Brookes, this tape from session where he recorded them, will keep many of them especially where he sings "Oh Fernanda Why", which is doubled, I believe, on the two inch.

2. Keeping Up
has some backups also, but needs harmonies where its underlined or bracketed on lyric sheet (or anywhere else, on the Keeping Up part), existing backups may need to be redone. probably augmented

3. Arm Around You (Really Ready)
reference vocal, kind of out of tune, but gives you an Idea. very out of tune, really, but the only tape I have at this point.

4   Forgive + Forget
    this tape of it is the existing backup
    part, the chorus, repeated, track will be
    muted part of the time in a mix
    situation, could use a harmony. I plan
    to add answering parts

5   Wild Combination
    practice vocal — needs harmony
    body of song not represented here,
    this is the chorus, I think. practice tape,
    first segment is reference vocal on 2", second is
    approximation of part on lyric sheet.

6   My Tiger
    I thought you would sound good for
    some reason on this, in a setting
    I don't remember hearing you.
    practice vocal, very hard to hear, may
    be difficult to think it's good, but I
    think has a lot of potential.

Again, sorry for the mixes — really messy, on
second listening almost unlistenable
I haven't gotten through to The Music Box yet,
just got an answering machine —

                                Arthur

                        in L.A., 213 654-0415

LA MAMA E.T.C. TO PRESENT SECOND ANNUAL NEW MUSIC FESTIVAL

Ten days of Musical Mayhem at The Club @ La MaMa

La MaMa is proud to announce it's second annual **MUSIC FESTIVAL**, May 18th through May 29th. Filling "**THE CLUB**" with altered sounds of strings the Festival opens with two nights of "Avant-disco cult jam" by **ARTHUR RUSSELL and FRIENDS**, Thursday, May 18th and Friday, May 19th at 10 P.M. **JOSHUA FRIED** kicks in with *SHOE MUSIC II* on Saturday, May 20th and Sunday, May 21st at 10 P.M. **PETER ZUMMO** will wind up the first week of performances on Monday, May 22nd at 9 P.M. The second week begins with the innovative wit of **BRIAN WOODBURY** and his 15 (fifteen) piece **VARIETY ORCHESTRA** on Thursday, May 25th and Friday May 26th at 10 P.M. **DAVID LINTON'S** *Drum Midi-Evil* rolls in on Saturday, May 27th and Sunday, May 28th at 10 P.M. and the festival winds up with a Memorial Day Bash to the "Rock Rhythms of **FACULTY PARTY** on Monday, May 29th at 9 P.M.

ARTHUR RUSSELL AND FRIENDS will preview "drastically altered" work from his forthcoming album *1-800-Dinosaur* on Rough Trade Records. He will expand his usual solo format to include vocalists, electronic percussion and horns in addition to his signiture "Amplified Cello" His music is a merge of art and rock proving that minimalism and progressive pop can fuse into an exciting experience. "music that jumbles your urges, making you want to move in ways not yet invented...this is unique, original music, a work of genius." (Simon Rynolds, MelodyMaker)

JOSHUA FRIED will present *SHOE MUSIC II* furthur explorations into the use of the "Musical Shoe Tree" invented with a commision from La MaMa for the 1988 Music Festival. Along with special guest artist LINDA FISHER, JOE MARDIN and ALAN BEZOZI, Fried will present a collection of recent work including two world premieres. The "Musical Shoe tree" has been described as "a funny looking yet versitile drum kit; stark and theatrical." Of **SHOE MUSIC**, Kyle Gann of the Villige Voice has said "Fried has the good sense to know that music must entertain before it can do something more"

***(Zummo section is fine)

La MaMa E.T.C. Presents

MUSIC FESTIVAL '89

Arthur Russel & Friends

May 18-19, 1989

La MaMa E.T.C. Presents

Arthur Russel & Friends

portions of the following will be performed:

Calling All Kids
Home Away From Home
Wild Combination
You and Me Both
My Timing My Tiger
Spring Field
See Through
Last Night the Movie
Corky
Set Up
Love is Back
I'll be Outside

Arthur Russel is a classically trained composer who makes dance records. His LPs include *Tower of Meaning, World of Echo, Dinosaur L,* and the forthcoming *1-800-Dinosaur.*

Mustapha Ahmed was born in New York and now lives in the Bronx. He plays all variety of percussion and works regularly with Peter gordon, Peter Zummo and Charles Lompo. He will be providing the music for Risa Jaroslow & Dancers on June 3 & 4.

Steven Hall was born in Scotland and lives in Little Italy. He has been making music with Arthur for ten years. He is also editorial director of Shiny Magazine.

Joyce Bowden lives in Harlem and she is the only Northerner in her family. She has been singing with Arthur off and on since 1981. Currently, she's collaborating with Jerry Harrison on his next Casual Gods album and will tour with him in the Fall.

Douglas Rice has been in the audio industry since 1980. He currently enjoys working as a freelance engineer at recording studios and live concerts. He also installs recording studios and finds time to teach each week at the Institute of Audio Research. "I just love working with sound and people," he recently said. He has worked in all styles of music with literally hundreds of artists, including Billy Basinski, Dem Vackra, Helen Hooke, Ornette Coleman, Adrian Belew, The Persuasions, Buster Poindexter, and The World Saxophone Quartet.

Bill Ruyle: 'Julius [Eastman] had become homeless. I guess he'd been kicked out of his apartment, and he was living in Tompkins Square Park. At that time there were a lot of homeless people living there, it was almost like an encampment. I was living very close to there and I know Arthur had mentioned to me that he had seen Julius over by the East River of Manhattan. At a particular spot below Houston Street, there were abandoned piers. There was a piling of a pier there, that had caught fire. And Arthur was there and concerned that someone should put this fire out. And apparently Julius was nearby. I don't know whether he had recognised Arthur, but he started calling to him saying, "Young man, young man, don't put that fire out. That's incense!" Arthur told me about it and was very concerned about Julius.'

Will Socolov: 'I think Julius also spent time in the baths, Saint Mark's Baths, and places like that where he could stay for three days, sleep there and have sex, sleep and someone would feed him.'

Peter Gordon: 'I'm not sure what really happened to Julius at the end, what did for him, at one point there was speculation it was syphilis. He lived in Tompkins Square Park and then he was in Bellevue Hospital. He had personal demons. He was really drinking a lot, even when he and I were working together earlier on, at places like the Kitchen he would come by and talk and put away bottles of wine I'd set aside for cooking. Lenny Pickett would visit him in hospital toward the end and he said at that time, Julius was writing chorales and hymns and he had a notebook and I always wondered what happened to that; it disappeared. Julius was a unique case, he was turned out as a homeless person and lost his possessions and scores.'

Bill Ruyle: 'I think it could have been in 1989, I saw Julius in front of the apartment I lived in on Avenue B, he was just hanging out, and I talked to him and said, "Hi, Julius." I said, "I don't know if you remember me, we worked together a long time ago," and so on. "I've done some work with Arthur Russell and his music is starting to get heard and that's a really good thing," and Julius said: "Oh yes, oh yes, I remember him; he's a very talented young man." Julius was pretty spacey and told me, "I live in Tompkins Square Park. I don't do music any more, I just chant the names of the saints." I gave him all the money I had in my pocket, which was only $40.'

Ernie Brooks: 'Arthur called me when I was back in France and he said, "Ernie, I have AIDS." I'm not sure whether he told me if he was dying, he still had energy and he still had vitality, but he was tired. I regretted that I didn't come back to see him more. I came back to New York for something, I think it was the second, CASUAL GODS album. I sensed something was up with Arthur and I kept saying, "You look tired, you look tired," and then the last time I came over I gave Arthur a motorcycle jacket I bought in Paris and I gave it to him and he looked so emaciated, it just hung off of him. But he was still fearless and committed. We were working on a session for that record and Arthur went up to Bernie Worrell, one of the funkiest keyboards players of all time, and explained to him that he hadn't got the phrasing right. He was insistent, showing Bernie how he should be doing it differently. Arthur still had that incredible musical focus.'

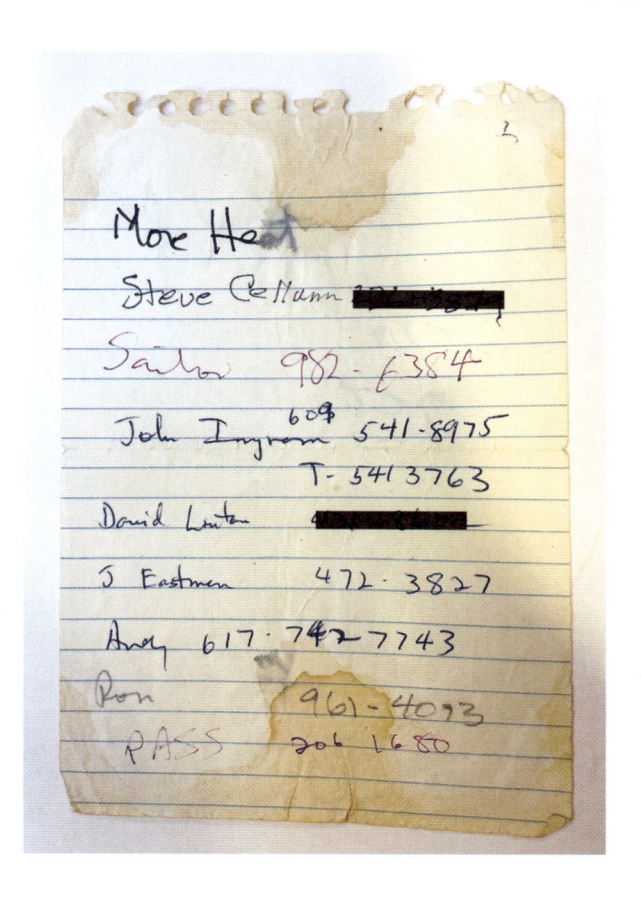

Bill Ruyle: 'I don't think I knew that Arthur was sick until 1989 or 1990 or so. Peter Zummo told me. I had two performances of my own work at Dance Theater Workshop around that time. One of the pieces was called DROP LIFT and I dedicated it to Arthur at the performances, at that time I didn't know he was sick. Once I knew about his condition it became obvious he was unwell. I'd go and see his solo performances and he'd be in a somewhat weakened state.'

Geoff Travis: 'He kept it from me, really, for a long, long time. He didn't tell me anything. I think he was scared to tell me because he felt responsible that he owed me a record: he didn't want to say anything; he didn't make any excuses about why it was taking years to deliver the record, but then people like Arthur don't really see time in the same way, that's the point.'

Joyce Bowden: 'He never came and said it to me, that he had AIDS. I had to bring it up, that mortality, that living, wasn't all it's cracked up to be and the bridge between the two worlds is nothing to be afraid of. And I was beginning to talk to him in that way so he could unload, because I thought his chances of survival would be better if he spoke it. And right after that he wrote "Love Comes Back" and brought me to the apartment to listen to it. It was the most beautiful thing I'd ever heard 'til I reached Everest one day at a time, emotion wasn't to be there in my chest again, "love comes back, put your little hand in mine". It's like "all is forgiven, we're all going to die."

Ernie Brooks: '"Intelligence in the air, it's winning me again", from "Love Comes Back", is a line that I always thought described Arthur very well.

'As Arthur's voice was getting more subtle and expressive but never crossing the line to be more artificial – it was sounding more and more like his voice – he got sick. The later songs, "Love Comes Back" and "Time to Go Home Now", it's easy to cry listening to that song, there's no question those songs are among his most powerful.'

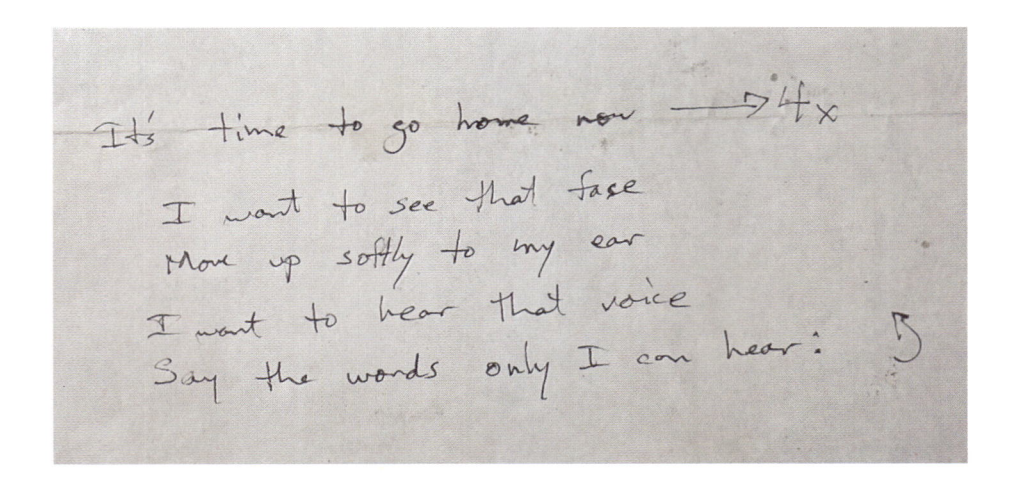

It's time to go home now ⟶ 4x

I want to see that face
Move up softly to my ear
I want to hear that voice
Say the words only I can hear:

Arthur Russell in Maine, 1990.

Geoff Travis: 'I went to visit him a couple of times, and it was always really nice. There were tapes on all the walls, twenty-four-track masters, reel-to-reels. And then I went to see him when he had AIDS, and it was a real shock to see him. I'd never really been that close to someone that was in the state that he was in. We went into a café and you could feel everybody in the room visibly recoiling. And then we went on a boat trip round Staten Island, and he gave me his headphones and played me loads of things: it was a pretty amazing trip. That was really incredible. It was really moving. We didn't really address the issue. I think I might have said, "Are you okay?" but I didn't say, "Obviously you're dying, what have you got, what can we do?" But it was a pretty tragic day. He didn't give me any warning. So that must have been going on for a long time. I don't think it could have been that much longer before he died.'

Tom Lee: 'I think Arthur referenced part of his illness in his lyrics:
That's you and that's me and that's me and you, in a rocket ship.
I need to be told what to do.
I'm in a world of my own;
I need to be told what to do.
It needs to be told what to do;
It's in a world of its own.
('Arm Around You')
    'I always interpreted this as his confronting his loss of sexuality. He used to pine for these cute people he'd pass on the street and now he's mourning the loss of that and experiencing the confusion of early dementia.'

Ernie Brooks: 'I remember walking around the Village with him listening to stuff. "Wild Combination", "Love Comes Back", "Time to Go Home Now". The material he pretty much did on two-track at his apartment. I always wonder what he would have done had he had the digital multitrack possibilities that came along not so long after. That might have made him crazy, because he went crazy enough doing analogue mixes and cutting and editing them into multiple variations. He wanted something in his apartment that meant any time, day or night, he could get up and record, because he was always thinking of ideas.
By then he was so much more confident in what he was doing and he had done WORLD OF ECHO which had a great sound. He went to keyboards as well because of all the sounds he could use.'

Geoff Travis: 'He wasn't really using any of the contemporary studio tricks, the sounds of his drums were just really unique and also, it's his sensibility, Buddhist, coming from Iowa, the whole Corn Belt thing, is really unusual. It's definitely all there in the music. I always thought his voice verges on being Brazilian, in that beauty, the ease of it, the kind of virtual talking but not talking, it's just so beautiful to listen to. He just had the most beautiful voice.'

Ernie Brooks: 'He worked so hard on his voice, especially later on, his voice is really in tune and that's not easy. He was obsessed with tuning: he studied with Joan La Barbara for a while; she was a vocal coach and sang in Philip Glass's early operas. She had this whole thing of getting the nose bones to vibrate and finding the resonance of those bones in your forehead. It was sort of mysterious, but it clearly worked, because his singing got better and better and more and more fluid. ANOTHER THOUGHT sounds so gentle and at the time you didn't hear a lot of gentle music.'

Peter Gordon: 'Arthur died right before the entry into digital technology. What he could have done with a home studio with that technology would have been pretty amazing. I think Arthur was really treating the studio as a composer of electronic music. Not as a place to record a set of songs.'

In 1991 Arthur made a final visit to California, to spend time by the ocean and also to meet with Yuko Nonomura, his Buddhist teacher from San Francisco, with whom he had remained in contact in the intervening years. While in California he stayed with Stephanie McGuire, a friend and colleague of Tom's.

Tom Lee: 'Arthur would visit my friend Stephanie, who was someone I worked with and was close with. The purpose was to see Yuko, but that relationship had grown a little strained. He had kept in touch with him all the while. I think Yuko was maybe a little rejecting of him because Arthur was gay and then he had AIDS.'

Stephanie McGuire: 'I had moved to San Francisco from NYC, living with my surfer boyfriend in a big one-room loft, when Tom sent him out to stay with us for a week. We were twenty-five at the time. Arthur wasn't smiling too much during that visit. He was very sick and the old friend/spiritual leader he came out to see refused to see him. This made him very sad.'

Stephanie McGuire: 'This photo of Arthur with the football team hat on – he borrowed it from a friend who drove us up to Muir Woods and Dillon Beach, just north of San Francisco, for the day.

'It was a long day and he was ready to go home. He switched his smile to that face right when I took the photo, so it was more of an annoyed, get me out of here face than a sad one.'

'Arthur was sitting there on the noisy beach recording the ocean. As I was taking the photo, I quietly said, "Smile," then he turned around towards me with that beautiful smile. He knew I didn't think he could hear me and I would be surprised.'

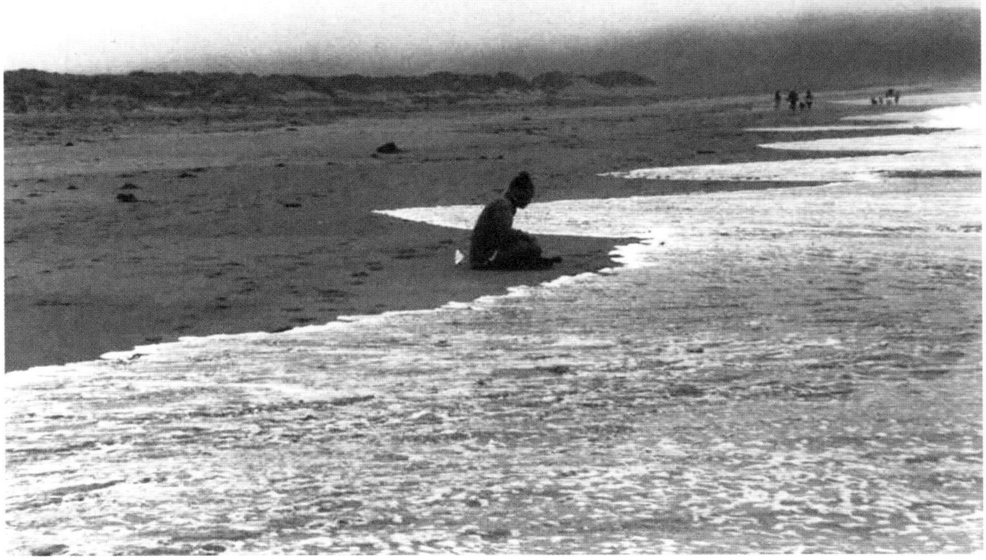

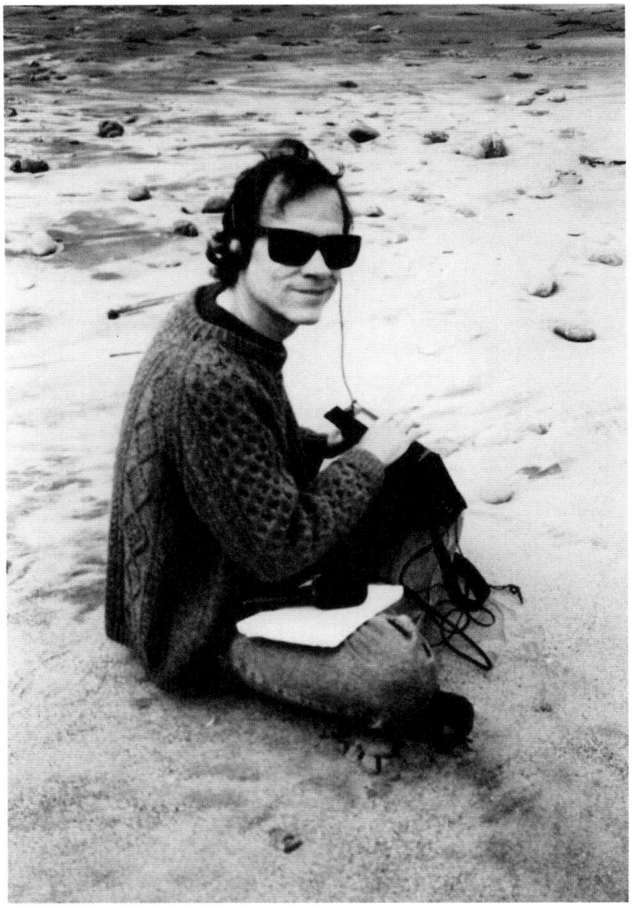

Steven Hall: 'I've never met anyone who was more convinced of their own ability to be successful, ultimately, and also I've never met anyone who was more resourceful in terms of finding opportunities, because he really impressed some very interesting people in terms of the record world. There were people who recognised very early on that he was something, but it didn't quite happen. It would have happened later; it would have happened eventually.'

Peter Gordon: 'In the fifties, post-World War 2, there was a rightful suspicion of populism in music because it was so misused, especially coming out of the areas of authoritarianism and fascism, tonal music became something to avoid. Arthur was aware of that. We talked about those ideas, he was at the Kitchen at the centre of those conversations. He thought it was a radical idea to have the Modern Lovers there because they were doing songs and tonal music. The fact he could also write the songs that he did – that's a gift. Really on that level the only comparison I could make is Leonard Bernstein, doing his orchestra work and then writing WEST SIDE STORY. I think it was accepted that Arthur was gifted, that he would become the chosen one. You don't know how that works. Mortality plays funny tricks.'

Lucy Sante: 'I'd worked at the Strand Bookstore and it seemed like half my colleagues died right around '89, '90. I was close friends with the film-maker Howard Brookner, who made this documentary on William Burroughs which was pretty well known, and he was making his first fiction film for Hollywood when he was struck down with AIDS-related blindness while he was, I think, still shooting. I lost 40 per cent of my social circle in those years.'

Bill Ruyle: 'For me, a lot of the acquaintances I knew who died as a result of AIDS were theatre people. I'd been making music in the theatre world and a number of colleagues were lost. The earliest AIDS death that was someone that I knew was '85 and then it just seemed like more and more people were dying.'

Steven Hall: 'The East Village, our world, the music world, generally, especially the disco world, where people were hard partiers – I literally lost my best friends. It's kind of blocked out in my memory in a certain way. It's not painful, it's interesting to explore, I'd forgotten about how terrified I was and I felt guilty afterwards about being terrified, but I honestly was.'

Peter Zummo: 'There was a barber I went to during that period, who stopped using a razor on people's necks because he was worried about drawing blood and getting infected.'

Steven Hall: 'It's really hard to remember how freaked out everybody was at that point, because you didn't know, you were scared to touch your boyfriend; you were scared to be breathing near your boyfriend, it was out of ignorance, people just didn't know and it was so frightening. And also, the sublime irony that it was the most beautiful, the most attractive, the most exciting, the most free, the most free-loving people that were dying, among the people that we knew, and the most creative, because the most creative were the ones who got access to the world of drugs and sex. And we were just at the point where that was peaking, so you could say that Arthur was part of the decline of that: if it had been ten or fifteen years later, he might still be alive, because there would have been treatments.'

Peter Gordon: 'The whole collective memory of that culture, people are still trying to make sense out of it, the losses. Not that there is any sense to make out of it.'

Ernie Brooks: 'In 1990 I was living in Paris and Arthur would call me. I was suspicious that he was getting really sick. He would call once a week to try out lyrics. To try out alternate lyrics. I remember hearing twenty different versions of "Losing My Taste for the Nightlife". That song felt like so much a reflection of his life, when he immersed himself in the nightlife at the time when AIDS was emerging. I always thought it was a reference to that, that it was the nightlife that killed him.'

To Steven Hall
March 1991

I'm at the disco now. The Bldg. this song "I'll be your friend" has been on for 15 or more minutes so I decided to try to finally finish a letter to you. I was pleased when I first got here at ten o'clock they were playing more rap beats some hits some not, now by 1:00 AM they've shifted to straight disco. The crowd is pleasantly mixed (mixed) and one really ~~big guy~~ forlorn-good-looking big guy is walking around with a cane. Here he comes again(!) lots of black teen crowd and gay kids dancing the big hit is Gypsy Woman by Chrystal Waters about a homeless woman. Will set me up with the producers but I'm afraid they might not like my voice. One guy was walking around with a big pillow on his chest. Mostly straight one guys in a really bad mood. New York. right after the hit they played the sampled version of Loose Joints, I think they're related.

New York today was spring day and I went to Museum of Modern Art on free night. I don't know why but it all suddenly looked so close to me and I could gasp at it's prescence. A printmaker Otto Dix from the twenties, I'm writing this on Stuart Klipper brochure (photos of Antarctica — they said was held over because "everyone liked it so much". New drawings by Miro'. A wonderful (Really) and small ~~painting~~ by Jason Pollock drawings by Man Ray all in "drawing" room. Just went up, so could still hop up when you Why don't you come back?

A neat video installation by Peter Rose about Benjamin Franklin. A big painting famous by Miro and Picasso in color, of course the obligatory Mike Kelley. Did you tell him me about him? Enormous Richard Serra room sculpture with the ventilators turned up really loud making a nice weird effect (unintentional) making me wanting to do the slide projector noise thing again. I feel stupid about it but I don't care now for the first time in my life I can enjoy my ignorance of painting & printmaking. I just noticed there's Mylar on the wall.

I pitched you to Geoff Travis again this afternoon. I'd like to send him shiny, remix Think Hard did you do it again? My imagination of David Bowie exceeds my ability to find him. Can I get back issues It just switched from an all boy trouble couch to drag queen table. The straight boys seem to take care of eachother. Why don't you come back? It must be wonderful. Did you tell Brad Gooch I was stupid? Do you like Moonroof or Moonwoof as name for label? Black Burst or Black Burst Music or Black Burst CeeDees. You probably think it sounds like

[sideways right margin, top to bottom:] I love it. There's a song called "Today are still young sex" I love slides, chapel waters just came on again I go sideways shooting Maybe Video Technical Term But it's a Black watch

Tom Lee: 'I was so worried about Arthur going out to clubs like that when he was so sick. That felt like pre-dementia to me. I would worry. Did he really meet Will? Would he get home okay? But he was insistent on going out and hearing music. Also around then crack had become an issue. The only time I got mugged living on East Twelfth Street was by a crackhead; they were very aggressive and indiscriminate about who they attacked and why they were attacking that person.'

Bill Ruyle: 'When I first moved to Avenue B between Eleventh and Twelfth heroin had been the drug of choice and you'd see a lot of junkies around the neighbourhood nodding out. And then crack became the thing. And crack was not good, a much more nasty scene. Junkies tended to be a little more passive and crack people were out of control. That whole area around Tompkins Square Park had a communal feeling. There was a lot of tolerance for all kinds of behaviour. I always liked it there. When there was the huge homeless encampment in the park I didn't find it disruptive, more like a wake-up call: this is happening, there are people without homes here, who have nowhere to go. There would be benefits that would take place, where performers would do benefits for the homeless. What was really discouraging was when one night, all these armoured vehicles drove into Tompkins Square Park and drove everyone out. I'd never seen anything like that before. That was Mayor Dinkins.'

Geoff Travis: 'Maybe because I was funding him, he didn't really need to worry about money in that particular period, later. It feels like it was for three or four years. I don't know what was in his mind when he was working on the material. Maybe he was just thinking, I'm going to keep working because this will be my next thing. Or it's a reason to get through the day.'

Ed Friedman
520 E. 14th St. #36
New York, NY 10009
(212) 673-9067

2 May 1991

Dear Arthur,

    I hear from friends that you have AIDS and that you are in what usually turns out to be the last stages of its fatal progression. A miracle cure could suddenly be invented or you could have an amazing remission, and no one hopes for these possibilities more than me, but I didn't want to take the chance that you would die and I couldn't say goodbye to you. Mostly, in recent years, we wave to each other or say hello in passing. I always think of you with walkman headphones on – one of the people I'll be likely run into during spring and summer days when I tend to be out more, walking around the East Village.

    I remember, though, during the mid-through-late '70's, seeing you on a more regular basis: when we'd be part of bands together, when I'd come see your concerts or buy your records (I still have my copy of Dinosaur's "Kiss Me Again"), or when you'd generously lend your time and effort to musical projects of mine. Those were important times in my life. I still remember going to see the Flying Hearts at the Village Gate with the Talking Heads and how great your songs and voice sounded. "Holding Hands with a Heartbreaker" is still one of my favorite songs ever.

    I guess what I'm mostly saying is that I'm glad you were here and are here and it's made my life better to know you and experience your music. Since I don't really know much about what your life is like these days, I don't know if there's any way I can be of help as you battle to get things done in the face of oncoming illness. Let me know if there is anything I can do.

love,
Ed

Ed Friedman: 'Not too long after I sent the letter to Arthur, I passed him on the street in the East Village. He had his Walkman and headphones on. As we passed each other, he smiled broadly and said, "Thanks!"'

Geoff Travis: 'I never really thought, Your career's going up in smoke because you're not doing all these things everybody else does. I guess I was just happy to get some music from him. He was like a writer: "I'm writing my book, he's my editor and when it's done, it's done. I hope when I send it in, they'll like it, and that's it."'

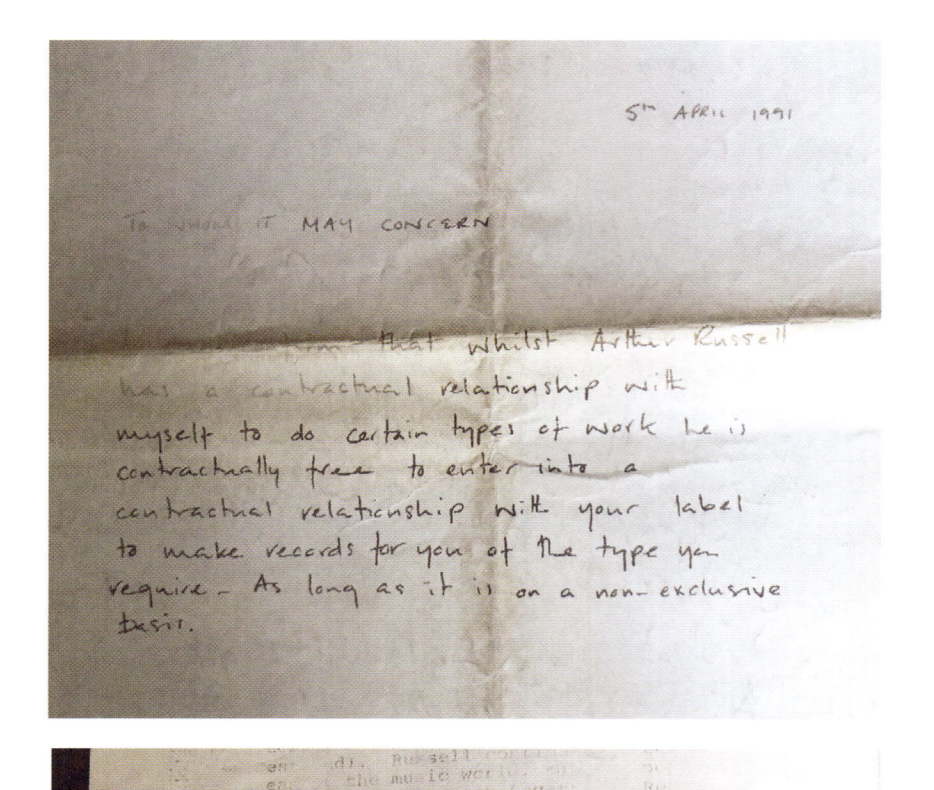

> 5th April 1991
>
> To whom it may concern
>
> [...] that whilst Arthur Russell has a contractual relationship with myself to do certain types of work he is contractually free to enter into a contractual relationship with your label to make records for you of the type you require — As long as it is on a non-exclusive basis.

ARTHUR RUSSELL

Born in Oskaloosa, Iowa, Arthur Russell came to New York in 1973 to join the burgeoning New Music scene after studying Indian music at the Ali Akbar Khan School in San Francisco. A skilled cello player, vocalist and keyboardist, he studied composition at the Manhattan School of Music and within 2 years performed a full-length concert at the old Kitchen in SoHo.

As a cellist, Russell has premiered music by Christian Wolff, Philip Glass, and Peter Zummo and also has two definitive cult jams under his belt (Dinosaur L's Go Bang on Sleeping Bag and Loose Joints' Is It All Over My Face? on West End). Russell continues to work in diverse areas of the music world, turning out a 12" release, Let's Go Swimming, on Logarhythm Records and continuing to explore "serious" music.

Arthur Russell's record World of Echo, recently issued on Upside and Rough Trade Records, uses solo vocal and cello performances with a variety of echo/delay methods; and in concept the maximally widest range of echoes. Other projects exploring the interrelationship of performance and recording events include 24 to 24 Music (Sleeping Bag), Instrumentals (Crepescule), and Indian Ocean (Sleeping Bag). As planning continues, outdoor acoustic performances of World of Echo with no reverb could happen.

In the future, Arthur Russell will be recording for Rough Trade.

Arthur,
 Hi! Here's your license —
Have fun — drive carefully.
See you soon.
 Tom

I motioned (in her direction)
fourteen (people, years, dogs)
show them New York, the way they'd see it
   if they were me

The runway was made in the shape of a
square and airplanes could arrived from four different
directions.

   all around, fields of corn and soybeans were
growing

   The lady wore diamonds and jewels. On the
fingers of her hands, she wore diamonds & jewels
and they shone out to all parts of the world sky
from under the trestle by the river (that night)

   My imagination was limited (I thought of the
things had been thought of already)

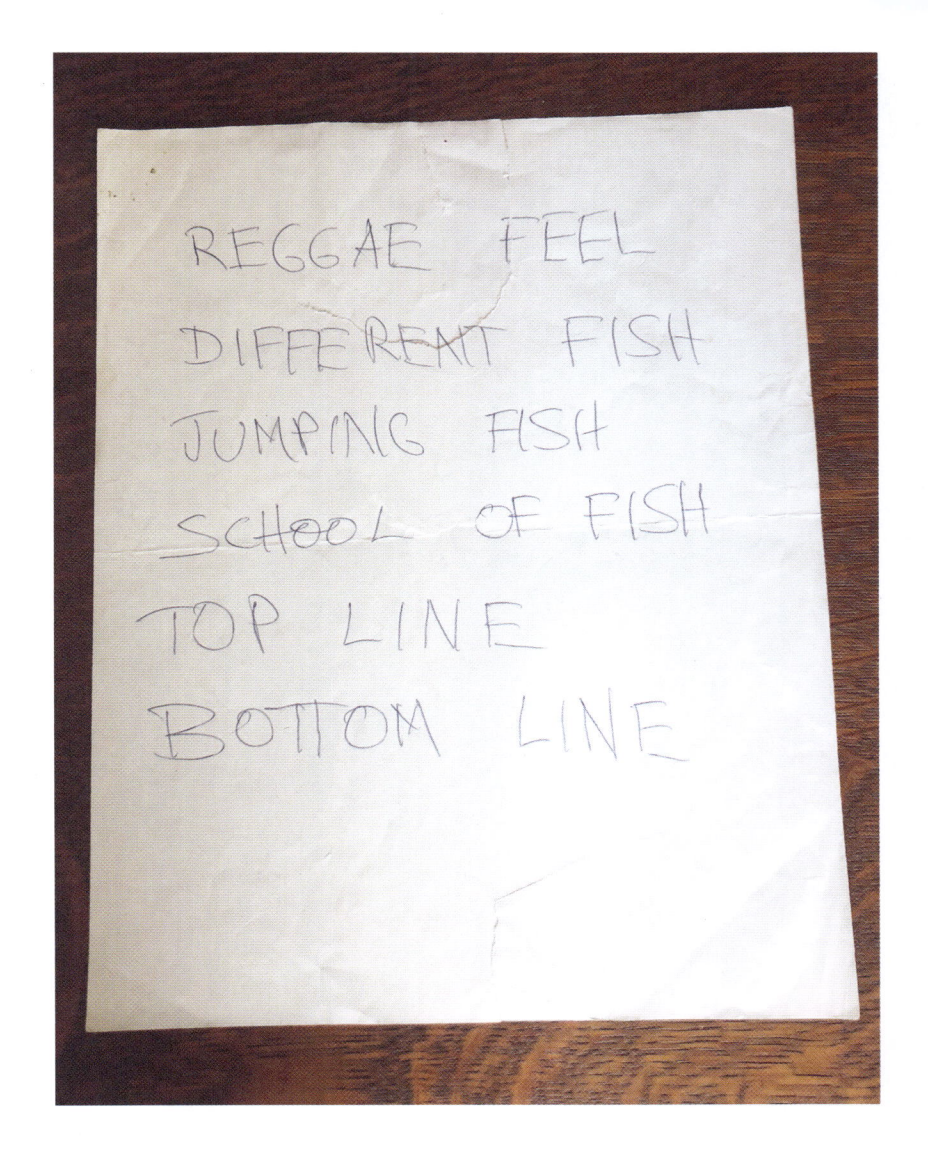

> REGGAE FEEL
> DIFFERENT FISH
> JUMPING FISH
> SCHOOL OF FISH
> TOP LINE
> BOTTOM LINE

Phill Niblock: 'The final show he gave at my place, it was quite late, like '91 or something like that, when he was in quite bad shape by that time. He didn't look very good.'

Bill Ruyle: 'Arthur was invited to perform at this space, which was underneath the Brooklyn Bridge. It was a double header with a group I played in called The Manhattan Marimba Quartet and Tom asked me when Arthur got the gig, and called me up and said Arthur would like to do this show but I would like him to do it only if you are willing to be his chauffeur to and from the gig. So I was really happy to do that. And I remember at that performance, Arthur was really quite weak.'

CODE ONLY FASTER: CROSSING THE LINE FROM VOCAL TO INSTRUMENTAL AND BACK

Fast

ARTHUR RUSSELL

8 PM

FRIDAY MARCH 15 1991

EXPERIMENTAL INTERMEDIA FOUNDATION

Slow

224 CENTRE STREET

NYC NY 10013

— SEPT. 1991 —

HI ARTHUR,
 HERE'S A DRAWING I DID ALONG THE ROAD TO STINSON BEACH AND SOME NICE SMELLS FROM THAT AREA AS WELL. I WISH YOU WERE SHARING THIS TIME WITH ME SINCE WE BOTH LIKE IT HERE SO MUCH.
 SEE YOU SOON
 LOVE
 TOM

Rhys Chatham
110, rue des Cités
93300 Aubervilliers
FRANCE

(tél) 33/1 43 52 00 84

>   Aubervilliers,
>   14 November 1991

Dear Arthur,

On behalf of the Kitchen, its technical team, administrative staff, and board of directors, I'd like to thank you very much for your performance and for helping us to celebrate our Twentieth Anniversary. We appreciated the time and energy you put in, which helped make the evenings a joyous occasion.

It was wonderful to see you again, and even though it was kind of crazy at the concerts, I'm glad we had a chance to talk a bit on the phone. Best of luck in your quest for the "top ten"! I'll be back in New York in March. Hope to see you then.

Warm regards,

Rhys.

Rhys Chatham

Will be sending you a small gift for Xmas separately. Julie got a new car yesterday — a Toyota Tercel — so she has "wheels" to get home for Xmas. She was very disappointed about your not making it home for Xmas. If something happens to your concert — give it some thought. Barbara Jolly Barnhouse asked about you the other night & said she would sure like to see you if you got home.

恭 Happy Holidays
賀 Meilleurs Voeux
新 Felices Fiestas
禧 Поздравляю

Mom & Dad

On Sunday, 15 December 1991, Arthur made his final public appearance, contributing amplified cello and voice as part of Peter Zummo's Zummo Labs II Ensemble.

Peter Zummo: 'I was at his apartment with him working on music with him very late into it all. We did a concert December '91. He was quite weak and I got in trouble for it, because he ended up taking three couch cushions and putting them against a wall and lying down. He did a brilliant vocal lying down.'

Peter Gordon: 'I didn't see him in the last days. I was in Japan. I last saw him in December 1991. He wasn't in hospital yet, but he was clearly very sick.'

Alison Salzinger: 'I was talking to him one day and he mentioned he had a doctor's appointment. I was a little forthright and said, "Oh what's it for?" and he said, "Oh, well it's really embarrassing," that's how he referred to it. I don't know how I found out, and I remember later on wondering how he could say it was "embarrassing" but that was completely in character. It's hard to remember what people went through then. I think he was very self-conscious, particularly about his skin condition on his face. His insecurity was huge, but he knew how talented he was.'

Ernie Brooks: 'One of the things I tried to do was send him an antiparasitic that was available in France and which wasn't available in the US. I got it to New York and Arthur by that time was so mentally out there and confused that he didn't want to take it. If I missed any chance in life, it was to spend more time working with Arthur on music.'

Steven Hall: 'When Arthur was really kind of gone, his mind was kind of gone, but to me, he was like those Buddhist monks that become ... they die but they're still alive. So to me, he sort of went into a state of grace. Now, that may be me projecting; that may be wishful thinking. But also I have bad feelings still about not spending enough time with him, because I was scared. I was terrified. And to Allen's credit, Allen lived downstairs at that time; Allen used to go up I think probably almost every day and just sit with Arthur, and Arthur probably either knew or didn't know at that point that Allen was there, but in terms of Buddhist practice, in terms of being there and being in the moment, Allen definitely came through with that.'

Joyce Bowden: 'I was living in North Carolina then and Tom called me and said, "It's getting close," so I came up to NY. Arthur wasn't speaking much by then. There was a mandala above his bed, because he liked to look at them. I tried playing some music for him. Tom was the warrior. He asked me for recipes and ideas, but there's always that sense for me that you could have done more. Arthur was really, really important, because of who he was. I don't mean to deify him, but he did a good job in his spiritual practices.'

Jill Kroesen: 'A psychic, or somebody I was working with at one point, told me Arthur was one of my guardian angels. I don't know if it's true or not, but I always feel like it is. There was no one as precious as Arthur in that whole world. It was such a loss. I think life was really difficult for him.'

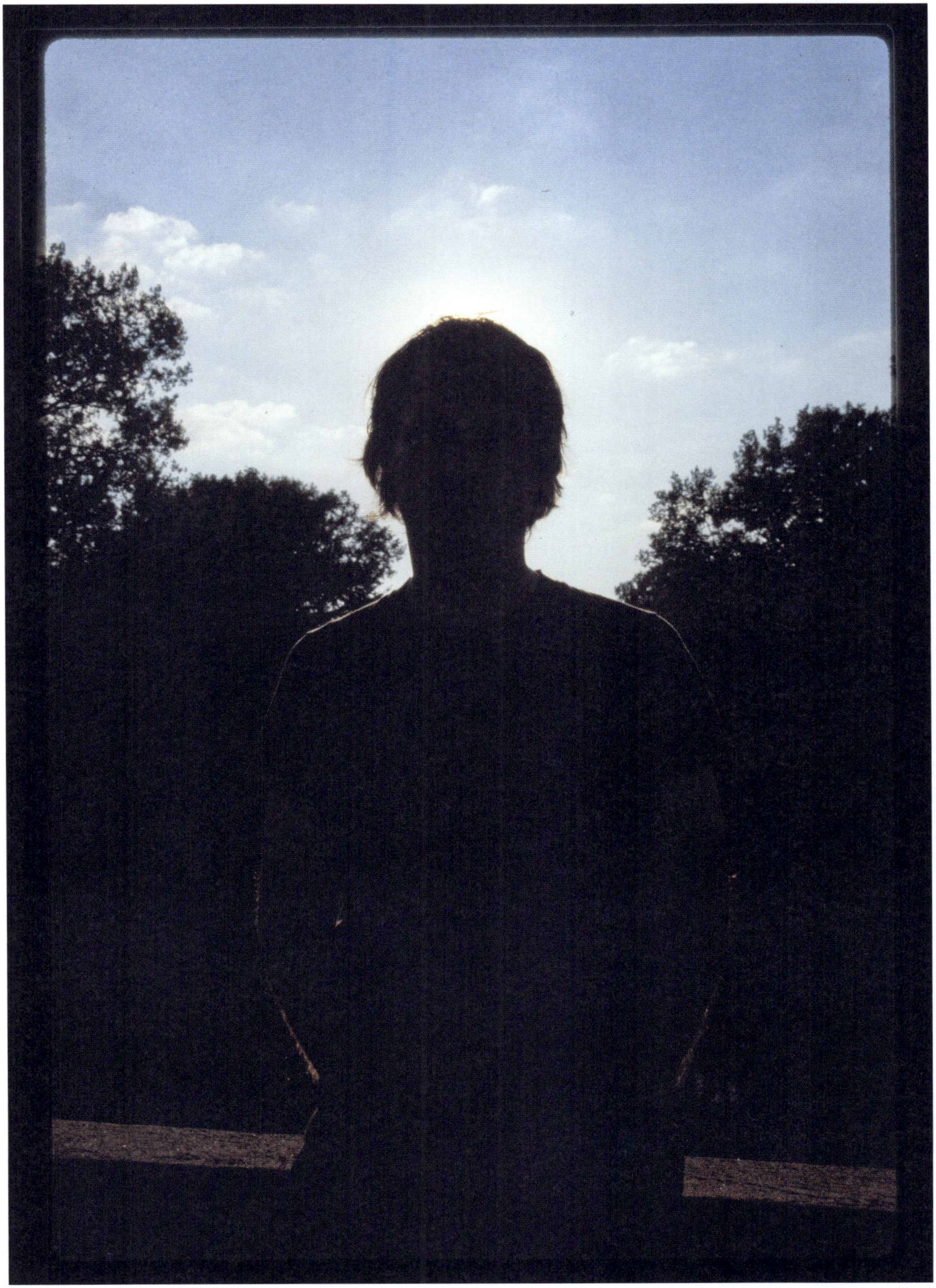

In March 1992 Arthur was moved from his apartment on East Twelfth Street to the nearby Sloan Kettering Memorial Hospital, where he died on 4 April 1992.

Bill Ruyle: 'I visited Arthur in the hospital, probably too many times. It was only on the first time that I visited him that he was still conscious. Arthur died among his family and I like to think that it was very peaceful.'

Tom Lee: 'Arthur's sisters came down a few times and then when he was in the hospital was when everyone including his parents gathered around. They stayed in a place in New Jersey and came and visited with him.'

Phill Niblock: 'I went to see Arthur in the hospital, and it was the night before he died: he died the next day, and I went with my girlfriend at the time, and with Tom, and it was, oh, it was probably the worst experience of my life, I think. It was really horrible. He couldn't talk; you couldn't tell whether he actually knew who you were or not, there was sort of no recognising, any of that stuff; even Tom, I think, didn't have that, had the same feeling. We talked about it, we talked about it all: we couldn't tell whether Arthur understood who we were or was seeing you or some other face.'

Mustafa Khaliq Ahmed: 'I visited with him in the hospital the night before he passed. I had a letter that I had written to Arthur, even though I knew that he was unconscious at the time, the night before Arthur passed away, I was in the hospital room with him, connected. We were that close.'

Peter Zummo: 'I saw him in the hospital and it was awkward. Tom called me the morning he died and said, "He's gone."'

Rome Neal: 'I found out from Tom. Arthur was a beautiful person, he connected with people.'

Tom Lee: 'I rang Jennifer Warnes to tell her that Arthur had passed; she sang "Maybe She" to me, without any prompting, a song from twenty years before and she knew every word and sang it extemporaneously.'

Muriel Fujii: 'After we got out of contact, I didn't hear about Arthur until I heard this interviewee on the public radio talk about Arthur and someone else. This was how I found out he'd died. It was minutes before I was going to teach. I always had public radio on in the background when getting ready for classes, and usually I wasn't paying attention because of doing stuff, but then I heard his name and then I realised the presenter was talking in the past tense, and he mentioned that he had died from AIDS. It wasn't surprising to me to find out that he was gay or bisexual or whatever, because nothing about Arthur would ever surprise me. Oh, my, he was just unique. I've never met anyone like him since. I can't imagine what I would have done or become if I hadn't met him. He was, I think, a genius. He was just so driven and that was just how his life was shaped, around music.'

Peter Gordon: 'It's tragic how Arthur died, but he didn't die alone and impoverished, nor unrecognised. I would say the series of sessions, over years, held during a full moon, that's the work, more than any particular record. The full-moon recordings I think started as soon as Arthur had access to a studio and I'm sure he recorded in East Twelfth Street on his own whenever there was a full moon. The action, the activity, is the work; all we have are the records, but they're residue, they're glimpses, they're a record of a moment.'

Geoff Travis: 'Arthur just seemed to be in touch with something eternal. I think when people started to hear it, that's what they really related to. And also the kind of innocence, as well. The innocence of the word combinations; the kind of childlike-ness, but the childlike-ness spiked with a huge intellectual capacity which you could hear. And a spiritual capacity, as well.'

Mustafa Khaliq Ahmed: 'At his memorial service, I was asked to speak, and I wrote a piece that was based upon the fact that his full name was Charles Arthur Russell, CAR, and my whole theory that I explained to people was that Arthur was a person who took us from one place to another, Charles Arthur Russell, the CAR. I know at the time it was very moving, but, it was the first time I ever was at a funeral for one of my guys at that particular stage in life; I didn't know I'd be talking about it thirty years later.'

Kate Russell: 'After my brother died, my parents had no one in the town, even their closest friends, that they could talk to, and we did not know this – my sister and I did not know this until five or six years afterwards. We were sure that they could talk to their very best friends, but that kind of takes it back, to the world that my brother escaped. When the world around Oskaloosa, Iowa, found out that Arthur died of AIDS and was gay, particularly after he became somewhat noteworthy, people reached out to my parents and said, "Oh, my son is gay and he's a musician." That was the first time that my parents really started to feel part of another community, a community of parents with children that they had lost to AIDS.'

Tom Lee: 'I met Arthur in 1978. Whatever I state, surmise or interpret about him and his music before that moment is speculative. We are fortunate that he diligently saved so many letters, music notes, posters and cards so that something of that time is preserved from his own perspective. He spoke little of his time in California and his boyhood in Oskaloosa, Iowa. Bits of information were revealed as various friends, Allen, Joel, Sydney, and others came to visit and Arthur reminisced over old times, including spending time with his Buddhist mentor, Yuko Nonomura.

'After two years of going back and forth between each other's apartments (mine at least had electricity and a phone), I happily moved in with him. Initially I didn't think I would, due to the general squalor – the roaches, a six-floor walk-up (never fun in the broiling summer heat and frigid winters) – but we settled into a comforting and easy time together. I was at work every day managing a fine art silk-screen workshop, while Arthur was making phone calls, scheduling rehearsals and studio time; always plugging cassettes in and out of ever-evolving styles of portable tape players. At times he would leave a cassette atop a pay telephone kiosk as he paused to trade one for another into the tape machine, and a few blocks later – or even later that day – dashed back to retrieve it ... often long gone. My college experience as an art major close to NYC helped me romanticise the idea of artists struggling in cold water lofts – and in Arthur's commitment to his music I saw that same spirit.

'Money was tight, as I was seemingly the lone contributor towards our expenses, but eventually I managed to get the electricity and telephone service connected, and we either cooked simple vegetarian meals or frequented local bodegas and restaurants. During our meals at home we watched PBS nature shows or the nightly MUPPET SHOW. As I would be tired from my work day, it was usually Arthur who would dash down to the corner store for a pint of Häagen-Dazs ice cream, a late-evening treat! Some evenings we also went to gallery openings or performances at St Mark's Church or PS122.

'As time went on I didn't think anything of leaving Arthur some money as I went off to work, for cassette tapes, soup with Steven Hall or just daily expenses. Neither of us were 'out' to our families in these early years but within the environment of our East Village world, my own work and friends, we were a couple. Sometimes he would drop in at my job, to use the pay phone, check in, even ask for another $10, but I smiled and was pleased that my co-workers got to know him and would call me from the shop floor with an 'Arthur's here.' We made a variety of postcards there advertising Arthur's shows and a few co-workers would even attend his performances.

'Arthur was always busy working on his music, whether splicing quarter-inch tape to create new edits, recording at home or practising at Westbeth, or simply roaming Lower Manhattan considering all those many 'takes' on his Walkman. He would join me for work-related birthday dinners or bowling outings, not participating but quietly sitting to the side. Eventually, he might make a connection with one of my work friends, but more often would quietly ask me when we could head home! I struggled a bit with our partnership due to the financial stresses, but never questioned my commitment to him. As our time together continued I became aware of his parents' financial support but that often was earmarked for studio time and equipment.

'Many people perceived Arthur as a mystery – by virtue of his demeanour, his acne-scarred face, his sometimes playful and often serious responses to others – but to me he was just Arthur, whom I loved. Arthur's humour, intellect and intimacy helped me to accept my insecurities and embrace our life together.

That said, he wasn't without mystery: Arthur followed the full-moon cycle, to which he attributed strength for recording music at home or in the studio; he also saw it as an optimal time to cut his hair.

'Early on in our relationship, I was eager to introduce him to some old school friends in Vermont. They previously knew me as having a girlfriend or two, and I wanted them to meet this new and interesting person in my life. It was so good to be out of the apartment and on the road together.

'Another journey we took together was to drive my mother's possessions to Raleigh, North Carolina, when she moved from suburban New Jersey, towing her car behind a U-Haul truck. Ever quiet, Arthur dutifully helped to wash the windows in my mother's new home. My mother would often comment on how intrigued he was with MTV!

'Thankfully I also had the opportunity to meet his family, when we travelled to Maine to meet his sisters, whom I had only occasionally spoken with on the phone. It was a memorable visit and helped to cement my deep connection with his family, which continues to this day.

'Over time, Arthur began to complain of feeling fatigued, which, as I scrambled out on my bike to work at 6.30 a.m., puzzled me. I pondered, Maybe you just need to have more purpose, like a job; but he only ever briefly entertained that idea – as a messenger. As time went on and people around us were falling ill, we decided he needed to be tested. It was such an arduous process, of worry, time and ultimately the onerous result. The effects of AIDS were readily witnessed, both on the news and within our East Village community.

'Eventually, Arthur also became one of those men: thinner and weaker as he plied the streets, at times even trying to maintain the jogging he had previously taken up. There were many accommodations to be made, even though he tried to maintain a schedule of studio time, buying new equipment, meetings, etc., but he was less able to truly attend to those desires. Much time was taken with meetings at the Community Health Project and procuring public assistance and medical help. But there was very little to do. Experimental treatments were not successful and eventually Arthur was less able to make decisions about his music and his care.

'In retrospect it was a very tender year close to home for us both. He did have a daytime aide for a time and occasionally a friend would sit with him if I were to go out for a meal or visit with a friend. It was at this time that Allen would often gently knock on our door around 8 p.m. or so and ask if it would be okay for him to sit with Arthur. I knew how valuable that time was for both of them. I would go into the next room while they sat, quietly talking.

'During this period, Arthur's parents also generously helped us and after Arthur was admitted to the hospital, his family came to visit. It was heartbreaking for all of us. It was a time of confusion and sadness, but also deepened the bond between us all. My name and our phone number was left on a piece of paper affixed to Arthur's hospital room's wall and when his last day came, the nurse called to tell me to come quickly. He was soon gone after I arrived. I walked home from the hospital, trying to delay all the phone calls I would soon be making.

'A few weeks after Arthur died, I asked Phill Niblock if we could have a memorial service at his loft, the Experimental Intermedia Foundation. Most services are held at churches or halls but Phill's felt the perfect place; in keeping with the spirit of who Arthur was. We showed Yuko's slides and played a great variety of his music while various friends spoke. Both our families attended.

Allen recited a mantra for him. His sister Kate brought a bag full of smooth round rocks from the Maine coast where she lives and they were left at the loft's door for people to take as a memento.

'Later that summer I travelled with Arthur's remains to Maine where his family wished to scatter his ashes at the far side of Baker Island. They had shared a picnic there on a previous visit and together we would now do the same. We boated there, clambered through the brush to the opposite side and tossed his ashes into the Atlantic Ocean. I wondered if they might someday reach the shores of New York, alongside his favoured Staten Island Ferry, or maybe somehow make their way to his boyhood Gull Lake.'

Baker Island, Maine, where Arthur Russell's ashes are scattered.

Down where the trees grow together
And the western path comes to an end,
See the sign, it says clear weather;
I'll meet you tonight, my friend.

'Close My Eyes'

Richard King is the author of HOW SOON IS NOW? (SUNDAY TIMES Music Book of the Year), ORIGINAL ROCKERS (shortlisted for the Gordon Burn Prize, a TIMES and Rough Trade book of the year) THE LARK ASCENDING (shortlisted for the Penderyn Prize, an EVENING STANDARD and Rough Trade book of the year) and, most recently, BRITTLE WITH RELICS, all published by Faber & Faber. He is the current Royal Literary Fund Fellow at Cardiff University School of Journalism, Media & Culture. (Photo: Eva Vermandel)

richardhywelking.com

ask   you   first   I   have